Winter's Dead

~a quick and fascinating read...really was difficult to put down... unexpected twists and turns from the first page to the very last.

~a great mix of characters and the descriptive language suck you into the life of Pennsylvania coal country. A book that's hard to put down.

~Well written and fast moving with a strong message about child abuse and neglect. An ending I didn't see coming.

~If you enjoy murder mysteries, you'll surely enjoy this offering... extremely well written and keeps you "on your toes" throughout... I'll look forward to the next Fletcher Strand novel.

~I read *IRINA*, which I thoroughly enjoyed...I absolutely got hooked by WINTER'S DEAD, finished in 2 days. I hope it becomes a series.

~The characters are interesting and the winter scene is done well.

~An intriguing mystery with twists and turns that kept me wondering "whodunit" until the end. A memorable array of characters.

~I got into this story right away...would rank "Winter's Dead" as top notch, can't wait for the next book in the Strand series.

Irina

~*Irina* is a captivating story of love, hope, pain, and perseverance. I didn't want to put the book down...I found myself thinking of the characters and the stories. I was obsessed with the intertwining story lines...Irina was spellbinding, the character and the novel.

~This book was like listening to myself at the age of 12, starting my own journey, asking all the same questions...Felt good...Amazing research.

~Irina is a wonderful tale of triumph and courage during a difficult time in history...writes beautifully and masterfully weaves several story lines together. Highly recommended.

~A first rate look at life in turbulent Poland in the 14th century...excellent character development and an absorbing story of a woman's reinvention of herself in Medieval France.

~"Irina" took me on an emotional journey both beautiful and lyrical from the first few pages. I could not put it down.

~This is the type of saga that I'd love to see as a mini-series! From beginning to end, it was so well developed and at the same time, emotional. I particularly enjoyed the way Mr. Warren gave detailed information on how to pronounce the names! I have recommended this novel to everyone !

Murder Down Deep

A Fletcher Strand Murder Mystery

MURDER DOWN DEEP

A FLETCHER STRAND
MURDER MYSTERY

Philip Warren

ISBN: 978-1-7367794-8-4 (Amazon Paperback)
ISBN: 978-1-7367794-9-1 (Amazon Kindle)

Cover and Interior Design by Stewart A. Williams
Copyedit by Brooks Becker

Printed in the United States of America

First Printing edition 2023
The PineLands Company, Publisher
New Wilmington, Pennsylvania

www.philipwarrenwriter.com

Also by Philip Warren is the first Fletcher Strand murder mystery, *Winter's Dead,* published in 2022, and the historical fiction novel *Irina,* published in 2021. Under the pen name John P. Warren, the political thriller novels *Turnover* and *TurnAround* were published in 2013 and 2014, respectively.

AUTHOR'S NOTE

Murder Down Deep is a work of fiction, and like many novels, there's a backdrop of historical fact to give it context. Knowledgeable readers may discern traces of truth concerning the privatization of the US Office of Personnel Management's background investigations program in July 1996, but should excuse this writer if in this tale, those changes begin several years earlier, in March 1993.

Because events in this novel also occur in a place and time well before the horrific attacks against the United States on September 11, 2001, I felt comfortable in describing the underground mine in Boyers, PA, where a large part of the government's background investigations program was then centered, and where I worked for nearly twenty years. Inquisitive readers should find a YouTube video about "the mine" several minutes long filmed by Pittsburgh TV station, KDKA, quite a number of years ago.

While I have taken certain liberties with the timing and rationale for the government's decision to privatize that program, it should not be inferred that *Murder Down Deep* is speckled with real persons from that era. Any similarities between them and characters in this novel are coincidental. The only exception is the character of John Lafferty, whose name and title I have incorporated in this story, in large part because he was one of the most decent and honorable people I've ever met. I might add that almost without exception, the government personnel with whom I worked in those years were entirely professional in their demeanor and conduct, and no adverse reflections on any of them may be imputed to this writer.

It is fair to mention that during my tenure at "the mine," no criminal activity imagined for this novel ever occurred, and before anyone asks, I'm not aware of any cave-ins there, either.

The Borough of Foreston is my entirely fictional version of Grove City, PA, and some of the action takes place there. The 1964 bludgeoning murder of an older woman actually occurred, but has never been solved, and the solution in this story has no basis in fact.

Special thanks must go to good friends, Laura and Dennis Kirley, who gave of their time and talent to find *Murder Down Deep*'s raw edges and help me polish them. Without their treasured input, this tale would not be quite right. Once again, professionals like Brooks Becker and Stewart A. Williams worked their magic on the manuscript and gave texture and finesse to the book's cover and interior design. What grammatical, typographical, or plot errors remain are solely my own.

It gives me great pleasure to re-create Pennsylvania State Police Detectives, Fletcher Strand and Joe Bentsen, and all the other characters associated with them and first introduced in 2022's *Winter's Dead*. With that, I hope you enjoy another Fletcher Strand mystery.

Murder Down Deep is an age-old tale about greed, jealousy, and passion.

I

NO SPECIAL TELEPHONE ring announces a murder into a police dispatcher's ear. In the West Central District of the Pennsylvania State Police, Mercer Barracks, calls like this come in a few dozen times a year, yet they're always jarring in their trite sameness. The first Monday in March of 1993 was no different.

"Don't go anywhere, you two," charged Lieutenant Walter Montgomery, longtime head of the district, as he poked his head into the detectives' warren of cluttered desks in tiny cubicles. The subjects of his attention were Fletcher Strand and his partner, Joe Bentsen, who'd made the mistake of lingering a bit too long over their morning coffee.

"Sure thing, Chief," Strand responded, his lanky, six-foot frame draped over a chair while a few feet away, Bentsen groaned, louder than the chair under his mass.

"I heard that, Joe. In my office, men—now."

In Montgomery's dusty nest down the hall, its owner said, "There's a body in the mine at Boyers. It's yours. Great way to begin the month, I'd say."

Strand nodded. "So, what do we know?"

"The caller was an Albert Rieger, Facility Manager for the

government's investigations operation down there. Victim was the Division Director, a guy named Abel Masters, so this is going to be a bit delicate, I'm guessing." Montgomery touched his pencil-thin mustache, thinking.

"How so?" Strand wanted to know.

"It's a federal facility on private property, so naturally, FBI agents are on their way from the Pittsburgh Field Office."

"And we're bothering with this because?" Bentsen wrinkled his face.

"Because it's a murder in our district, Joe, and until we're certain the crime took place within the confines of their operation there, let's see what's what before the feds muscle in. And this Rieger, the guy who called? He didn't call the feds—somebody else called them. He called us. You probably have a thirty-minute head start—if you two have the energy to leave now," Montgomery said with heavy emphasis on his last word.

Strand nodded. "Got it."

"By the way, play your official music to clear the road for you. If you're lucky, Doc McCreary might still be there," he added, referring to the Mercer County Coroner.

"What's he doing in Butler County?" Strand asked.

"Covering for the Butler guy out with cancer." He cleared his throat. "I'm not feeling any air movement with you two leaving my office."

"Yessir," Bentsen said, heaving his huge frame out of the chair and into a parody of a man putting one foot in front of the other. Already, Strand, the younger and lighter of the two, was six feet ahead of him.

~

On their way from Mercer to Boyers, a twenty- mile drive, Bentsen tuned the radio to their favorite, Froggy 95, for news and weather as the skies above shifted from gray to black. State Route 58 to

Foreston was clear and Strand remained quiet as they sped through, siren blaring.

"Bet Georgie Hallon will like that!" guffawed Bentsen, behind the wheel. Hallon—"Hell on Wheels" behind his back—was the Foreston Police Chief, but unlike most department heads, Hallon made sure his men were none too cooperative with Pennsylvania's troopers if they could help it.

"Oh, yeah," responded Strand. "He has a long memory, and how we embarrassed him a few years back with the little murder spree in his backyard will stick with him a long time."

"His own damn fault," Bentsen swore. "If he'd just paid attention to the details around him, we might have resolved it all a lot earlier."

"Try telling him that. All I know is, I don't want to have to deal with him if we can help it."

"But you live there, for cryin' out loud. You have to run into him, right?"

"I fly under the radar, Joe," Strand said.

Several miles deeper into Butler County, amidst the empty, winding lanes around the small collection of buildings loosely called Boyers, an unsuspecting driver might come upon a series of parking lots, chock full of vehicles, seemingly in the middle of nowhere, but otherwise see nothing. No mall, no factory, no nothing. Bentsen had turned into the entrance drive of what everyone called "the mine" only because Strand pointed him in the right direction.

"Wow! I've heard of this place over the years but have never been here. But you seem familiar with it. How's that?"

"Long story. I'll fill you in as we go."

The driveway into which Bentsen had turned went on for some two hundred yards, drifting ever downwards at a twenty-degree angle. At the end, there loomed a gaping portal cut into solid limestone, a mountain spreading out and rising high above it. An awesome sliding steel gate with bars two inches thick guarded the mine entrance, one large enough for tractor-trailers to pass through along with all the other pedestrian vehicles—like theirs.

On a cold day like this one, the temperature-controlled mine air

collided with the near freezing air at the entrance to create billow-
ing clouds of steam enveloping them as they waited for the gate to
shudder open.

Bentsen muttered, "Good God, like the gates of hell."

Strand chuckled.

At the guard desk, Bentsen lowered the driver's side window and
flashed his PSP credentials to the uniformed man standing there.
"You're expected. The Office of Personnel Management operation is
straight ahead, maybe a quarter mile. Park in the cutout," the guard
said.

Bentsen made a right turn and proceeded down the shaft whose
ceiling rose some twenty feet above them. It was wide enough for
vehicles and, on the right, a walking path. The tunnel's darkness was
punctuated only by an occasional light bulb above, each of which
cast a dull gleam on the chiseled limestone painted silver, a mostly unsuccessful attempt to heighten the space's dim illumination.
Deeper into the gloom, he said, "Jesus, what a place! And people
work here underground?"

"A few thousand, I hear. Sorry, Joe, I could have briefed you on
the way over. Keep going straight ahead, and I'll give you a thumb-
nail." The One-Way signs along the asphalt roadway guided them
along.

While Bentsen drove, Strand continued, "This is a unique place
to work for sure, Joe. It's a converted limestone mine, played out
over decades to provide limestone for the steel works in Pittsburgh.
In the sixties, when the government thought a nuclear war was still
possible, it moved a great deal of its records here after it had been
converted to accommodate large record holdings. All of it is owned
by The Underground Storage Company, and there are miles and
miles of paved roads here, some two hundred feet below the surface."

"How do you know so much about it?"

Strand snorted. "When I was a rookie out of the academy in the
mid-seventies one of my first assignments was to liaise with the guy
who had been sent from Washington to establish the government's
background investigations records division."

"I thought the FBI did all that work."

"That's what most people think, but for a hundred years the OPM has been tasked with backgrounding people for sensitive government positions. When it became known OPM has been coming here, that's when I came into the picture. Harrisburg wanted to know what the feds were doing on their turf. Having a connection didn't hurt since Pennsylvania provided information to them, so I worked with the manager, a guy named Lafferty, to make all the right things happen with the state. It was good duty."

"So, what backgrounds does the FBI do?"

"As I recall, they do all the ones you read about in the papers. OPM does all the other stuff."

"Have you ever been back?"

"Not until today, my friend, and it should be interesting."

"Your contact isn't still here, I take it."

"Nope. Still in DC, I'm guessing."

Out of the gloom, the detectives found themselves in a brighter, open area, and on their left, there was the so-called cutout the guard described. It was a large opening carved through the limestone rib, on the other side of which more One-Way signs directed them on what was apparently a parallel road leading to the mine's exit. Bentsen steered the state Crown Victoria into one of the parking spaces the guard had indicated.

When they exited the Vic, they saw what appeared to be the front of a one-story office building set in and surrounded by rough-cut limestone. It could have been a lawyer's office in any small town, but behind the façade, it would prove to be another world entirely.

II

J UST INSIDE THE main entrance of the Investigations Center, they were met by a nervous, bespectacled man in his forties, clipboard in hand, shifting his weight from one foot to the other. He offered his hand. "I'm the guy who called it in, Al Rieger," he said as he scanned Strand's and Bentsen's proffered credentials. "Th-this way, gentlemen."

Strand noticed three things immediately about the man. His glasses had the thickest lenses he'd ever seen and he'd already had too much coffee, but he didn't seem to have the energy to move quickly. They followed him through a series of doors, down a hall or two, and into what appeared to be a small reception area. Flanking the secretary's desk were two executive offices. The space was shared by limestone walls covered with a pastel blue coating, and abutting them were standard plasterboard walls, trim, doors, and furniture as one might find in any office above ground.

Carpet softened their footfall as Rieger stepped into the office on the right, then stepped back and aside to let the detectives view the scene where the coroner knelt over a dead body. McCreary was an old-time doc in his late fifties, topped with reddish hair, albeit somewhat thinner than when Strand and he worked their first case together. Although the air in the room was fresh, kept that way by constant ventilation, McCreary's presence was underlined by the faint whisp of tarry cigar smoke that seemed to linger long after the coroner had one of his El Producto's ablaze.

The office in which they were standing befitted an executive with responsibilities. Of course, the dead man on the floor in front of him no longer had any responsibilities at all, and had no need for a walnut desk the size of an aircraft carrier.

Looking up, McCreary said, "Like two bad pennies. Whadya say, Fletch and Joe? Of all of Montgomery's guys, I'm sure glad it's you."

"And same to you," Strand said. "What have we got?"

McCreary stood up to give them a full view of the body lying in what seemed to be careful repose. "Victim is Abel Masters, late thirties. He's about 5'6", 150 pounds, maybe a little less. He's not been dead for more than twelve hours."

"Cause of death?" Strand saw that the victim was lying on his side, his face in profile, eyes open. He was comfortably dressed, wearing a white shirt but no tie, pressed slacks, and his shoes gleamed with fresh polish, yet they were heavily scuffed at the heels.

"Strange thing, that. Looks like somebody crushed his skull from behind. If you take a good look, he's got a nasty depression back there, and there might have been a lot of blood, but there's none here. Not a drop. No splatter. Nothing."

"Meaning?"

"The obvious. This body might be in his office, but he wasn't killed here."

"Just wanted to hear you say it."

"Another thing. See that?" McCreary said, pointing to Master's eyeglasses askew on his face.

"What about it?" Bentsen wanted to know.

"As hard as he'd been hit—it looks like it had been a surprise to him—those glasses should have flown across the coffee table here— if he'd been killed here. I think they were placed there as we see them—another indicator this setting was staged for us."

"Supporting that notion," Strand said, "is that the shoes suggest he might have been dragged at some point."

"And if he'd been here at work," Bentsen added, "wouldn't he have had a tie on?"

McCreary and Strand nodded.

"If not here, then where?" Bentsen said, knowing there was no immediate answer, as he looked around. "Nice office—but I'm not sure I want to think about all that rock above my head."

"Well, it wasn't the rock above that got him," McCreary snorted.

All three of them stood observing their surroundings, standing as they were in the middle of an irregularly shaped room with painted rock walls and cream-colored drywall. It had a drop-ceiling and upscale government walnut furniture along with an aging leather couch. "The entrance and the office area were obviously built to impress people," Strand said.

Silent until now, Rieger cleared his throat. "If I may say, sir, Mr. Masters had this built so that he could host senior people from Washington, security officers from large agencies and the like. We have a lot of visitors."

~

"You're the one who found him, you said?" Strand asked his first question when they stepped across the reception area into another office, a smaller version of the one in which the body was found.

"Y-yes, that's right." Rieger replied. "I usually get here around 6 a.m. every morning, and take a walk around all of the work units. One of the supervisors actually opens the place up."

"How many employees are here at that hour?" Bentsen asked.

"Oh, maybe two hundred. Most of our female data entry clerks come in about the same time to begin their shift."

"Do they all come in at once?"

"No. We open for business at 6, but they can come in when they want within a two-hour window as long as they work their eight hours."

"That's pretty flexible," Bentsen observed.

"Yeah. It's a system Mr. Masters set up to accommodate these moms—it makes it easier for them when they have a sick kid or something."

"OK, so then what? How did you happen to find Masters?"

"Well," Rieger began slowly, "I usually don't come up here to the front office because neither Mr. Masters nor Mr. Novak nor their secretary, Mrs. Conlon, come in until 8:30 or 9 a.m."

"Novak is who?"

"Mr. Masters's deputy."

"So, again, what brought you up here this morning?"

"After I'd made my rounds this morning, I noticed all the lights on, which is unusual, so naturally, I was curious why that would be. Must have been about 6:45 a.m. or so."

"Why 'naturally'?"

"As Facility Manager, I'm also in charge of physical security for this operation."

"Was everything as it should be, then, Mr. Rieger?

"Y-yes, i-it was, Detective. No alarms went off."

"So, before this place opens in the morning, it's locked tight and alarmed?"

"Yeah, yes," Rieger said, hesitating.

"You're not sure?" Bentsen asked.

"Y-yes, I'm sure."

Strand waited a second. "So, you poked your head in the office and saw Masters, then?"

"Y-yes, yessir."

"You seem nervous, Mr. Rieger," Bentsen said.

"I am nervous, sir. I've never found a dead body before," he said, his eyes doing a dance of some sort, "and I sure didn't expect to find him, I mean, Mr. Masters, dead in his office." With one hand he brushed a lock of dark hair that had draped itself over one lens.

"You didn't touch anything?"

"No. I bent down, called to him, but saw his eyes were opened. He was still," he said, breathing hard, "so, I called you."

"OK, Al—can I call you Al?—so, how many people could have

been up here before you?" Bentsen asked.

"Jeez, in that forty-five minute, almost anyone who was already here."

"And you said that could be around two hundred people?"

Rieger nodded.

"Good God—that's already a long suspect list," Strand said. "Would any of them have any reason at all to be up here that early in the day?"

"No, no one. Ordinarily the lights would have been off—everything up here would have been dark."

"But somebody here killed him, Al. Any ideas who that might have been?"

"I have no clue—r-really."

"A guy like Masters—head of a large operation like this—must have had an enemy or two," Bentsen joined in.

"Mr. Masters did a lot of good things here. Most of the employees thought he walked on water—he made working here a lot nicer than the previous guy."

"Most?"

"Well, there were some who didn't care for him much."

"Enough to kill him?"

III

"**Y**OU WERE SAYING?**" All three men were standing, making it easy for Bentsen to lean forward and peer directly into Rieger's eyes—or, at least, through the thick lenses barricading him from the world.

"W-well, I don't know, sir," he said, not knowing who to address.

"Any personal relationships gone wrong? With any of the female employees, for instance?" Strand asked, leaning in a little closer.

"N-no way," Rieger said. "That wouldn't be like him."

"Was he married? Children?"

"No."

"I hate to ask this, but could there have been something going on here with another man?"

"Oh my God, no! That wouldn't go here."

"Wait a minute," said Bentsen, "isn't this the place the new administration in Washington is trying to put out of business? It's in the *Sharon Herald* every other day, practically."

Rieger seemed to breathe easier. He licked his lips, and did his best impression of looking them in the eye. "Y-yes, that's true."

"What does this new administration have against a backwater agency like the Office of Personnel Management?" Bentsen asked. "They just came into office."

"Some people think it's about the FBI—the outfit that does a good number of White House background investigations."

"What does the FBI have to do with this place?"

At that moment, the office door burst open, and in walked two men in dark suits, each with pressed white shirts and striped ties.

"I'm Agent Flaherty, and this is Agent Kempinski—Pittsburgh Field Office—just what in the world is the Pennsylvania State Police doing here in a federal facility?" It was the taller of the two who spoke.

Strand introduced himself and his partner. "We're here, Agent Flaherty," he began as civilly as he could, "because we were called to the scene by Mr. Rieger here."

"I don't care who called you," Kempinski said, uncivilly. "You guys have no jurisdiction here. Bug off."

Strand looked at Bentsen and said, "Joe, see if Doc McCreary—the Coroner," he emphasized, eyeing the two agents, "—is still here and ask him to step in, will you?"

They stood in silence until the coroner appeared in the doorway. "What's up, gentlemen?"

"Doc, give these two G-Men a quick rundown, will you?"

McCreary proceeded to provide what details he'd had a chance to observe, concluding his remarks with the observation that Abel Masters had not been murdered where he'd been found.

"So, you see, Agent Kempinski," Strand said, casting his gaze at Flaherty as well, "it's not at all clear whose jurisdiction this is. Mr. Masters may be a federal employee, but it appears he was murdered elsewhere and his body placed—or staged—in his office across the way. If he was killed just a foot outside the front door of this facility, it's you two who will need to bug off."

"Hey, Strand, no need to get feisty, here," Kempinski said, his entire head reddening.

"Tell that to your buddy here, Agent Flaherty. We're here because duty called, and until we resolve what's what, maybe we should work together on this."

Flaherty nodded, not unreluctantly. Kempinski rolled his eyes.

"No matter how you slice it, guys," Bentsen chimed in, "you're in our neck of the woods, so let us do some poking around for you, and believe me, if it's your case, we'll be glad to hand it over."

"Our Agent-in-Charge won't like this much, but hey, we've got better things to do, too. We'll make our own report on what we find here now, but your coroner, here, and you guys have to give us everything until we decide who's going to carry the ball. That's the deal."

Strand looked at Bentsen, smiled, and said, "OK. Done. First thing we'll need whatever federal records there are on Masters."

"Not a chance. Off limits," Kempinski was happy to say. "You guys don't need his personnel file to determine jurisdiction."

"Sounds like a one-way deal then. This is what the taxpayers love about us," Bentsen said, sarcasm lacing every word.

"Love us or not, when this is all over, we don't want some court throwing the case out because we screwed up the very first hour of investigation." In unison, the FBI men made their exit.

∼

After a moment or two, a woman who looked not to be trifled with opened the door, introduced herself as Judy Conlon, and said, "You'd better come, gentlemen. One of Mr. Rieger's employees found smears of blood in the warehouse."

"Point the way, please," said Bentsen, and moved with speed unusual for him, with Strand right behind Conlon.

While walking through a labyrinth of hallways—several large, open, and well-lit rooms which Conlon referred to as shafts—they felt the stares of the dozens of employees who stopped to monitor their every step. Into another open space, which appeared to be a shipping and receiving depot, there were a couple of Ford vans, several dozen of what looked like steamer trunks, and industrial-sized microfilm and reproduction equipment. Here, too, a half dozen employees paused what they were doing to catch what glimpses they could. No one talked.

Standing in the middle of a small group of people was Al Rieger, clipboard in hand, speaking to one of his employees. When Strand and Bentsen walked up, Rieger said to one and all, "These two men are from the State Police. We will give them our every cooperation." Peering over their shoulders, he called to the onlookers in a louder voice, "Hey, folks, nothing to see here. Let's get busy, please." A few moved, but most remained where they were.

A short, balding yet unshaven man spoke up. "You sure we're supposed to be talking to these guys, Mr. Rieger? Isn't this FBI stuff?"

"Since when are you an expert in police jurisdiction, McKenna?" Rieger's tone said more than his words. Then, turning to the PSP detectives, he said, "This is Artie McKenna. He has something to show you."

McKenna led them to the far side of one of the Ford vans and pointed to an open trunk. The inside was cream-colored, heavily scuffed, the visual broken only by the two large splotches of what appeared to be dried blood, one on the trunk's bottom, and the other on an upright side panel.

Both detectives stooped low, Strand bending further to sniff the clotted mess. "Smells like it, but we'll need to test it, of course." Looking up, he said, "Hey, Al, please see if Doc McCreary is still here and find out if our lab techs have showed up—they were supposed to be only a few minutes behind us."

"No problem," Rieger replied, and did his version of a trot toward the warehouse door.

Strand let his eye follow him, supposing the steel door opened to where parked cars lined the main underground roadway—and to a shorter path to the main entrance.

"So, Artie, tell us what you know about this."

"I don't know anything—but I didn't see your ID and didn't get your name, sir."

Strand and Bentsen produced their creds, gave their witness their "Now are you happy?" look and waited for the man to go on.

"Like I said," McKenna said, addressing them both, "there's nothing to tell. I came in this morning with the others…"

"Were you the first one here?" Bentsen asked.

"Hell, no. Mr. Rieger is often here before anyone else in this unit."

"So, you saw no one in this area?"

"Y-yessir."

"And then what?"

"I was having coffee and accounting for the number of trunks, when I noticed the open one."

"Is it the same number every day?" asked Strand.

"Yeah, pretty much. We send twelve trunks down to DC and twelve trunks come back. Hardly ever varies."

"What are these trunks used for?"

"Fingerprints to the FBI, case files to our offices downtown on H Street. Coming back are fingerprint results on the same cards, returning case files and all the administrative stuff for the front office."

"How does that work, by the way?" Strand asked.

"A van goes down the Pennsylvania Turnpike loaded with trunks, meets up with a guy from DC at Breezewood who also has a van loaded up. They switch vans, and our guy returns with the new load."

"So, it's a federal driver then?"

"No, sir. It's all done under contract with the people who own this mine, The Underground Storage Company."

"Jeez, that's a boatload of paper," Bentsen observed.

"You bet, and that's what we do five days a week, but that could end soon."

"Why is that?"

"This president wants to put us out of business, but even if we stay, they've been digitizing all this work, and who knows what it'll mean for us," he said, waving his hand to encompass the people in the shaft where they stood.

"Who exactly stands to lose out in all this?" It was Bentsen.

"Well, we all do if the politicians are successful, but at the very least, the bunch of us who do the warehouse work and file transport."

"Any idea how the blood—if that's what it is—could have gotten in this trunk?"

"Hell no. I mean, sorry, I hope that's not Mr. Masters's blood."

"How do you know whose blood it might be?"

"The word came through here like lightning. People are stunned, and the worriers are wringing their hands already. Jesus! Who knows what'll happen to us now!"

Bentsen nodded.

McKenna went on. "People are scared. Not many good jobs like these deep in Butler County, I can tell you."

"Do we know if this trunk is one that came in from DC yesterday or what?"

"I can check the roster, but I'm pretty sure this trunk didn't go down or come back. Actually, it's a spare."

"How do you know for sure?"

McKenna began to reach for the trunk lid.

"Don't touch that!" Bentsen commanded.

"Oh, sorry, but you can see the hinge is loose. The trunk can't be secured for transport. It's waiting for repair or disposal. Never left here, I'd think."

"Hmm! Thanks. So, what did people here think of this Masters guy?" Strand prompted.

"Oh yeah, he's, I mean was, OK, as suits go."

"Suits?"

"Yeah, anybody around here with a tie is management—women, too. If they're wearing a skirt, they're one of the bosses."

"You have any problems with Masters?"

"M-me? You must be kidding. Nah! He didn't bother me, most-ly because he seemed like he was for the workers. He was all about quality work for all the government agencies we work for—stuff like putting the right fingerprint file in the right case folder, you know."

"Yeah, good thing," Bentsen said. "Did Masters know a lot of the employees?"

"Oh, sure. Haven't you heard his story? He helped to build this place with the guy who started it. I wasn't here then, but I heard. Then came back as boss a few years ago."

"Hmm! I guess there's a lot we don't know about Mr. Masters."

A pair of state employees, evidence techs, marched up, and without a word from either Strand or Bentsen, followed Strand's gesture to the open trunk. "One. Is it blood? And two. Is it Masters's?"

"Got it," one responded, and they bent to their work. "We'll get a sample, tag it, and take it in."

"You through with the body?"

"Yeah. Already on its way to McCreary's shop."

"Thanks. Oh, and get whatever prints there are on the trunk and circle back to the office before anyone pollutes it," Bentsen said.

"Already done, Joe."

Strand snorted.

"What?"

"We're testing for prints on a trunk whose only function is to carry thousands of other people's prints to the FBI."

"Yeah, but not too funny," McKenna said.

Rieger reappeared in a moment, winded. Strand said, "Looks like we have a lot to talk about, Al."

IV

STEPPING OFF TO the side, and out of Rieger's earshot, Strand said to his partner, "The blood in the trunk—if it's the victim's—still doesn't solve the jurisdictional problem, does it?"

"Guess not," Bentsen said. "He could have been transported here in the trunk, or it's just supposed to look like that."

"If Masters was brought here in the trunk, was he small enough to fit in it? And if so, from where was he brought? Not from DC in that exchange they do in Breezewood, right?"

"Right. But what the trunk does suggest is that the murder happened elsewhere—likely in our jurisdiction."

Strand nodded, his thoughts elsewhere.

"By the way, Fletch, if Masters was here when the place opened way back when, wouldn't you remember him?"

"I was just thinking about that, but no, I don't. There were several dozen helping Lafferty set the place up as I recall—and there was a contractor with Amish workers, too."

The pair walked back toward Rieger, who'd been off by himself, tapping his thigh with the clipboard.

"Nervous about something, Al?" Bentsen wanted to know.

"N-No. Let's go to my office," he said and turned toward an office half carved into the limestone. It was just big enough for Rieger's government-issue wood desk and a few guest chairs. "What do you want to know?" he asked after they were seated and the door closed.

"When the FBI interrupted us earlier, we were talking about the president's people wanting to abolish this place. Did Masters support that move?" asked Strand, taking the lead.

Rieger's lips moved silently, then formed words. "Abolishing the place may be off the table, the rumors say."

"Which means what, exactly?" Bentsen asked.

"Mr. Masters never really told us directly, but we've heard they might try some privatization scheme," Rieger said, then added, "all of which makes some people pretty nervous."

"Because?" This time it was Strand who asked, taking his attention from the doodads around Rieger's office.

"Who knows how this is all going to turn out?" Rieger began. "Maybe people could lose their jobs, you know. There's a lot of pushback from the federal agencies we serve about abolishing us. The FBI doesn't want the work and would rather we have it. That's why, apparently, the privatization thing has come up."

"You mean this whole operation could become a private corporation?"

"Right."

"And Masters? Where was he on all this?"

"Like I said, he didn't say much about that part of it."

"Either way he leaned on this privatization thing, wouldn't that make him some serious enemies?"

Beads of perspiration appeared on Rieger's brow. He licked his lips. "You just never know about what makes people tick."

"Yeah, we know," Bentsen said. "If you're not nervous, Al, you're doing a damn good imitation of it."

"You keep saying that. It's my nature. All these questions. A-and I don't want you to think I had anything to do with it, just because I found him."

Neither detective said anything. Bentsen just nodded, waiting.

After a moment, Strand asked, "Any timeline on this move?"

"This could take years."

"So, in the meantime, anything else going on?" Bentsen asked, joining in.

"Like what?"

"C'mon, Al! What's all this about digitizing a lot of the paper-work passing through here? Could put a dent in your empire, couldn't it?"

Strand and Bentsen could see Rieger's clipboard begin to bounce on his thigh. "N-not really," he said, beginning to take deep breaths.

"Seriously, Al, you don't expect us to believe that," Strand said, his eyes sweeping around the office. "Your souvenirs seem to suggest you're not from around here."

"N-no. San Francisco, in fact."

"So, if you're not from around here and you lose your job, with no family, you've got a lot riding on all this, right? You don't seem old enough to retire."

"Well, that's right, I suppose, but I married a local girl—from Foreston—and she works at the hospital. If worse comes to worst, we'd get along."

Strand nodded. Bentsen stared, leaning in closer.

"I-I don't know why you would consider me a suspect," Rieger said, "I've always supported Masters, and I can't get over the fact that he's dead. And here!"

"OK, Al," Strand said, "just calm down, but you can see why we need to ask, and you can bet we'll be back to ask more questions."

"I understand," he said, so relieved he appeared to be deflating.

"In the meantime, we'll need a list of your people, besides McKenna, who are involved with the shipping trunks, and now, could you help us find our way back to Mrs. Conlon?"

~

"It's Judy, isn't it?" asked Bentsen in his best voice, despite the fact that all 6'4" of him towered over the reception desk where Judy Conlon ruled, guarding time and access to Abel Masters and Joe

Novak. "Can we step into this office," he said, gesturing to Novak's, "to chat for a few minutes?"

"Sure thing," Conlon said.

"How long have you known or worked for Mr. Masters?" Strand began.

"I was just looking that up, knowing you'd ask," Conlon answered. "So, let's see. This is March 1993. Mr. Masters came here as Assistant Chief right around five years ago, in 1988. He'd been a Supervisory Investigator in the field—in Denver, I think—before that, but really, I know little more about him or his background."

"Married? Dating? Interests?"

"Never married, as far as I know, and no love interests, certainly not here."

"So, he's not from around here?

"Like I said, I really know little about him. With all of us, he's very outgoing, knows the names of nearly everyone who works here, but never lifts the curtain, so to speak, about his personal life. This job was his life." Realizing what she'd just said, she bit her lip, and dropped her eyes.

"I'm guessing some senior people would be more comfortable with a married man in his position—given all the women who work here," Bentsen interjected.

"Perhaps," Conlon said, "but Mr. Masters had a lot of friends among the higher-ups, and I guess they must have decided to overlook that part of it."

"Friends, like who?" Bentsen persisted.

"Like Mr. Lafferty, for instance. I think they've known each other for some years, in fact."

"How so? Any notions about that?"

"No, not a clue. When Mr. Lafferty comes up from DC a few times a year, they go out to dinner, and it's just my sense that they're not new acquaintances."

"So, where did Masters live, then?"

"Oh, in Foreston—I can get you the address."

"Ever been there?"

"Oh, no. I doubt that anyone here has. What else do you want to know?"

"What's his relationship with his deputy—Mr. Novak?"

"Fine. Mr. Novak just transferred here from Pittsburgh."

"Did they know each other before?"

"I'm pretty sure they did not. From what Mr. Masters mentioned one day, he'd been asked by Mr. Lafferty to take him on as deputy."

"Gee," Bentsen jumped in, "so many people come here—to Nowheresville!"

"Excuse me," Conlon said, laughing, "but I'm from here! And for us, Detective, this is not nowhere. It's home."

"Sorry. What am I talking about? I live in Mercer." They both laughed.

"Thanks, Judy," said Strand, "could you get that address for us, and Mr. Lafferty's phone number?"

"Of course."

"And let Mr. Lafferty know that Fletcher Strand will be calling him, will you, please?"

V

N THE MAIN tunnel, walking toward the Vic, Bentsen looked at
his partner and said, mimicking Stan Laurel, "What a fine mess
we have here, Ollie!"

"Tell me about it," Strand said, unable to keep laughing himself.
"We have a body, but we don't know where the crime was committed, we have a million suspects to eliminate, and now we learn the
poor bastard lived in Foreston, which means we'll have to tangle
with 'Hell on Wheels' Georgie Hallon!"

In the dim light, Bentsen replied, "Should I call Montgomery
and give him a heads up?"

"Right," said Strand, "but don't try your cell phone in here. No
signal. If you get the car, I'll step back inside and use their landline."

With Masters's street address in Foreston, they easily made the
eleven-mile trip, hoping all the while they'd have no need to intersect
with the local police chief, a Carroll O'Connor lookalike, beefy middle and all, who'd evidently blustered his way through life and into
his current job. Never warm to outside law enforcement agencies, he
was particularly unwelcoming to PSP sleuths like Strand and Bentsen. Three years earlier, in fact, Hallon made turf his only interest,
it was said by many, when a child killer descended upon Foreston.

That Strand and Bentsen wound up resolving the string of connected murders in Hallon's sacred domain only made worse his fury.

Past the well-reputed college in town and, of course, the local McDonald's, and out Center Street, Bentsen turned the Vic onto a quiet street of well-maintained homes. About half-way up Garden Avenue, the detectives pulled up in front of a neat, white frame house, an unpretentious affair fitting in well with its neighbors. As Strand put his hand on the door handle, he put his left hand on Bentsen's forearm to stop him.

"Joe, in the driveway."

"Yeah, so?" Then, "Oh, right, so I guess he didn't die in the mine after all."

"And shame on us, we didn't ask to see if his car was there, and no one mentioned it. Probably because it wasn't there, duh!"

"Wait, maybe we're getting ahead of ourselves," Bentsen moaned.

"Only if that white Olds Cutlass isn't his car, we aren't."

"Couldn't it be a cleaning lady, or a visitor of some kind?"

Strand looked sideways at his partner. "Good luck with that idea, Joe! Anyway, we'd better be careful here since we don't know what we've got."

Donning gloves, Strand and Bentsen checked the Cutlass's car doors. Locked. They walked up the front steps under the small overhang just as a cold drizzle began.

No one answered Bentsen's knocks, and the door was locked. Without a word, they turned and walked toward the back of the house to see if there was another entrance.

"Holy crap," Bentsen said as they came within a few feet of a screen door askew and hanging by one hinge. The inside door was standing open, a clear invitation to the two detectives to enter. Both men pulled their weapons, chambered a bullet, and quietly stepped through the open door. It was a two-bedroom affair with a small living room, eat-in kitchen, and one bathroom. No second floor.

Back in the kitchen, not far from the back door, the waning light of a cloudy day revealed a possible piece of evidence they didn't expect: a splotch of what appeared to be dried blood.

"My, my! I'll flip you for the pleasure of telling Kempinski."

Bentsen did a long exhale. "Whoever did this didn't want to make it easy! Let me call the evidence techs—we'll have to make this a crime scene."

"How many crime scenes do you think we'll have—for one murder?"

"Freeze!" commanded a voice just outside the kitchen screen door. "Don't move and put your hands where we can see them." Two police officers, service revolvers drawn, drew a bead on them.

"Keep your holsters on, men. We're PSP, Strand and Bentsen."

"Oh, for God's sake, not again!" came another voice, that of Chief of Police Georgie Hallon.

Re-holstering their weapons, the two officers stood aside so that Hallon could enter first. "Just what the hell are you two doing committing a burglary in my jurisdiction?"

"Nothing of the kind, Chief," Strand began. "This house belonged to a man named Abel Masters—now a murder victim, so come no further. This is a crime scene."

"How?"

"Blunt force to the back of the head, McCreary says."

"Right, in my jurisdiction, guessing by the blood on the floor. So, fill me in, guys." There was no request in the man's tone.

Strand gave him the bare minimum, indicating that the murder was thought to have taken place in the mine. The blood on the floor, if it was blood, Strand told the Foreston officers, suggested another possibility.

"If that's true, hotshot," Hallon said, looking directly at Strand, "the murder took place here, and you guys are off base."

Strand just looked at him without agreeing. The more Strand thought about things, the angrier he became as he stared down the porky police chief. "You know, Chief, I can't believe you didn't recognize the unmarked car with state plates out front, and now you come here with your weapons drawn? And why are you here, anyway?"

"Don't get smart with me, pal, or I'll be callin' your boss, Montgomery. He just loves to hear my voice."

"That he does, Chief, so why don't we all just calm down and let us sort this out!" Bentsen spoke up, doing his best at soothing words and phrases. Coming from a giant of a man who could knock down a house with a shoulder, the plea may have been a stretch, but he'd made the effort, and it worked.

In a more collegial tone of voice, Hallon said, "OK, let's do that. By the way, if this guy was a fed, how come the Bureau guys aren't handling it."

"The evidence indicates that the murder didn't occur where the body was found—that's what we're trying to establish. So, the Bureau agreed to let us sort it out. If it's theirs, they can have it. If it's yours, you can have it, but give us a few days to see what this is all about. Montgomery assigned this one to us since the call came in to us."

Hallon nodded. "So, it'll be PSP resources and not on my budget, then?"

"Right," said Bentsen, trying not to roll his eyes at the lawman who disliked spending money solving crimes.

"Alright, then, a few days, but I want you to keep me in the loop. Hear?"

The PSP men nodded.

"And in answer to your question," Hallon said as he and his officers turned to leave, "this is Foreston, and the old ladies on the street pay attention to what's going on—they know everybody's business. Evidently, the one next door," he added, using his head to gesture which house, "looked out for the dead guy."

"Did you know Masters, Chief?" asked Bentsen.

Hallon stopped. "I knew he lived here—my business to know—but we did not cross paths. And one last thing."

The detectives waited, not saying a word.

"Stay the hell out of my way."

VI

WHILE THE TWO Foreston police cruisers disappeared down the street, Strand and Bentsen taped off the Masters home, made sure the techs were on the way, and then marched to the neighbor's house Hallon had indicated. The door snapped open at the first rap of Bentsen's knuckle.

"Why, I've been expecting you!" Ethel Richland greeted them.

All smiles, the pair offered their creds and stepped into her front hall. "You can come further if you take off those dirty shoes, gentlemen," purred the woman who wasn't more than five feet tall and every bit of ninety years.

"This'll be fine, thank you, ma'am," offered Bentsen, "if you don't mind standing a bit."

"So, you called the Foreston police on us, did you, dear?" Strand said with the best smile he could muster.

"Of course, young man! Neighbors have got to look out for one another, and Mr. Masters is a fine young man."

Strand cleared his throat. "Then, I'm terribly sorry to tell you that Mr. Masters is dead."

The woman's eyes clouded over. Without looking at them, she said, "Never mind about the shoes. We'd better sit," and she led the way into her modest, but tasteful living room.

Seated, Strand said, "Mr. Masters was found at the mine this morning, and we're here to help find out exactly what happened."

"I see." She went quiet for a moment, as if to fully process either what she'd just heard, or to consider what she already knew.

"What can you tell us about him, then, ma'am?" asked Bentsen.

"Very little, I'm afraid, gentlemen. You see, I hardly knew him. Indeed, I doubt that anyone in the neighborhood knew him."

"I understand," Bentsen said easily. "But you watched his house for him, is that right?"

"Well, surely, but that's all. Every once in a while, Mr. Masters would bring over a small peach pie for me—I'd told him I like them—and I guess he'd stop at one of the Amish stands near New Wilmington and pick one up for me."

"What business did he have out that way, did he say?"

"Oh, he never said. He got up very early, winter and summer, went to work, and came home in the dark, most often. In the warm weather, he'd be out cutting his grass or puttering a bit, but his is a small piece of property, just right for him."

"Then," joined Strand, "he lived alone? And you saw no visitors?"

"Oh, yes, alone. Occasionally, with the windows open, I could hear classical music on his record player, but that was it."

"No strangers, then?" Strand persisted, but gently.

"Well, none, except you two this morning," she said, then paused. "Well, just a minute, there was that white van so early this morning—before sunup, I'm sure—and I thought maybe someone was picking him up for work."

"White van?"

"Yes, plain white—I saw no markings," she said, her voice rising as she realized she'd known something of interest after all.

"Did you see the driver, then?"

"Oh, no! It was still dark, and with the house all shut up, I could just hear the rumble of the motor, so I looked out the window. The van was waiting. I must have dozed off because when I woke up a bit later, it was gone."

"Do you know how much later, Ethel?" Bentsen smiled at her.

"It was just becoming light, that's all I know. Maybe a half an hour?" She reflected for a moment. "I can't believe that I'll never see Mr. Masters again. What a nice man, but life is fleeting, isn't it, gentlemen?"

Strand's cell phone buzzed. He wasn't entirely used to the new devices the PSP insisted its personnel carry at all times, but acknowledged that in police work, they were like magic—when you could get a signal. He glanced at the little screen and saw the call was from his home number. *Very unlike Aurora to call me at work.*

"Thank you, Ethel," Strand said. "I hope we can call on you if we have anything else to ask about."

"Oh, most certainly, young man, and if you think of it, will you bring me one of those little peach pies?"

~

Stepping outside in the late afternoon cold, Strand returned his wife's call.

"Hon, I just wanted you to know that Paul was taken to the hospital in Sharon this morning. They called me. You should go in, if you can get away, they said."

Strand exhaled. His brother's health was fragile. "I guess we shouldn't be surprised, huh? Did they say what's going on with him?"

"He was complaining about his back, Bob said," Aurora reported, referring to Paul's partner.

"His back? It doesn't sound all that serious."

"But now, he's unconscious—maybe a coma?"

"Strange. Joe can drop me at the house and I'll get the car and head over."

"Fletch."

"Yeah, hon?"

"I'm sorry, but this doesn't sound good."

Strand hung up and thought about it. Bob, Paul's partner,

roommate, or whatever he was supposed to call the other half of two gay men living together, was a sometimes-hysterical dude, and he might be making a lot over nothing, but then again, he trusted Aurora's judgment.

Paulie, as Strand always called him, was the middle son, one year younger than Jonathan, the political mover and shaker in the current president's White House, and never a favorite of theirs. As the youngest by six years, Strand never minded his role in the family as the "baby" of the brood, but Jonathan always seemed to mind the fact that Paulie didn't fit the mold of what he considered "normal." *Truth be told, Jonathan has always been ashamed of him.*

For Strand, in 1993, Paulie's lifestyle sometimes presented awkward moments given the hysteria over AIDS, but he was his best brother, and he loved him.

VII

ON THE WAY across the small Borough of Foreston toward Strand's hundred-year-old brick pile of a house on East Pine Street, Bentsen broke the silence that had enveloped the Vic.

"I sure hope things go well with your brother, pard."

"Thanks, Joe, I hope so, too. I should get a pretty good idea this afternoon. Will you make my excuses to Montgomery for me, then?"

"Sure." After a moment, Bentsen continued, "But before you go, about this body in the mine, Fletch, it's beginning to look like Masters was murdered here in Foreston, which puts the whole thing in Georgie Hallon's jurisdiction. So, what next?"

"It does, Joe, but there's no hurry to pass that information on, is there?"

Bentsen chuckled. "I get it. Let's see what Montgomery has to say. I'll bet he'll go along, but what I don't get is that whole business with the blood in the shipping trunk. You think Doc McCreary can tell us if the killer was able to stuff Masters in that trunk and somehow get him into the mine this morning before everybody else?"

"That seems to be the only explanation, doesn't it? And Al Rieger seems a lot more nervous about things than just another innocent guy, right?"

"Yep. Apparently, he stood to lose his job without Masters's support for their operation, whether the fingerprints are digitized or the place is privatized. Now, he says he was at the mine at his usual, early time, but he could have been there earlier. He has the keys to the place, can get in without anyone thinking anything about it, and has access to the trunks and the vans."

"Sounds like a person of interest to me, Fletch, but probably not enough to turn the screws at this point."

"Right, and if Masters was murdered in Foreston, there's a jurisdictional problem—maybe."

"Well, nobody's going anywhere, so as you said, we can sit tight for a bit."

Bentsen pulled the state Vic into the Strands' back driveway.

"Only one problem, Joe."

"Yeah?"

"Remember back in '90. All the facts in the Foreston murders pointed in only one direction and…"

"And we were dead wrong."

~

It took Strand about twenty-five minutes to reach the hospital's lot off of State Street, and another few to enter via the ER and ask about his brother, Paul Strand. He took the elevator, stepped out past the nurse's station, and found room 328.

Once inside, his eyes first went to Paul, in bed, motionless and attached to several medical monitoring devices. Then he noticed Bob, Paul's roommate, and to his surprise, his oldest brother, Jonathan, standing near the corner, out of the light.

"Johnnie, how did you get here so fast?"

"Sorry, Fletch, I should have called you earlier. You know, Paul's doctor, Nate Robertson, and I were friends all the way through school—he called me early this morning, and luckily, I was able to escape the usual White House madness for an early flight. Again, sorry I didn't think to call you."

Strand ignored his famous brother's lame excuse and turned to Paul's partner. "Bob, can you fill me in on exactly what's happened?"

"Hi, Fletch," he said, keeping his voice at a normal pitch, "well, you know Paulie's been having a lot of issues with his Crohn's disease, and no one here in town has been able to get things under control," he said, glancing at Jonathan. "Then his back started bothering him a few days ago, and so he went in to see Dr. Robertson, who gave him a shot of whatever to relieve the discomfort. We went home and thought everything was fine, but then this morning, when he got up, he was real groggy, and said his back was killing him, so we came in to the ER right away."

"And now what?" Strand asked, eyeing his middle brother who had not moved, even in response to the three familiar voices around him.

"Dr. Robertson came in after they admitted Paul this morning, and they've already run a bunch of tests." Bob inhaled and exhaled, shaking slightly. "Sometime around eleven, Paul just seemed to slip away into what you see now."

"A coma, or what?"

"I don't know, Fletch," he said, then turned to the other brother. "Jonathan, you talked to the Doc just a bit ago, what'd he say?"

The eldest Strand cleared his throat. "Actually, nothing more than you already reported, Bob, and Nate seemed puzzled—that's why all the tests."

"Did he say when we'll get the results?" Strand asked.

"Later today or early tomorrow," Bob said.

"And Paul's going to stay this way?"

Neither Bob nor Johnathan spoke.

Strand edged closer to the bed, leaned down, and kissed his brother on the forehead. "I'll be in later," he said, and turned to the door.

"Wait, Fletch, let me walk out with you." It was Jonathan, his tone solicitous.

〜

In the hallway, Strand said to his brother, acid lacing his voice, "I'm so glad the White House could spare you, brother, but you were just too busy to call?"

"Fletch, again, I'm sorry. Being an ass has always been part of who I am."

"So, what's your grand title again, Poobah shoe shiner?"

"Come on, Fletch, that's beneath you, but you asked. I'm Assistant to the Chief of Staff for the Vice President."

"How nice," Strand said, making a mock bow. "But I didn't realize you and Robertson had remained close—at least that's the impression you gave in the room just now."

"Well, if you must know, we're not that close, but there's a vacancy in the Office of the White House Physician, and I thought Robertson might be good for it."

"You're kidding. I guess the old boy network continues to work its wonders."

"You don't have to put it that way. Nate is undergoing a background investigation right now, and assuming it's clear, he'll likely get the appointment in a month or so."

"Lucky you. Tell you the truth, Johnnie, I've never been much impressed with Nate Robertson, and seeing our brother in there doesn't change my opinion much."

"You're not giving him a chance, Fletch. Let's wait and see what happens here."

"I just hope Paulie has the time to wait," he retorted, then turned and walked away.

Once back in the car, he cursed himself. Jonathan was an ass, to be sure, but that didn't mean he needed to sink to his level. They'd never been close, but an invite to dinner was in order, and he'd blown that. *Ass or not, there'll be another opportunity, I hope.*

∼

On the way home to Aurora and the kids, Strand could think of nothing else but his mother. Their mother. The woman tasked with raising Jonathan, Paul, and him. Irene Kosniewska put up with a lot to marry Fintan Strand, her ultimate surrender being to attend the Presbyterian Church in Foreston, to which the Strand clan belonged.

She never surrendered her faith, however. When the old man went to work in the mornings supervising operations in the coal mines running deep beneath Foreston's streets, she took the three boys to the Beloved Disciple Catholic Church for Father Quinn's 8 a.m. Mass two or three times a week. Her husband very likely knew what she was doing but never let on and even to the boys, never said a word about it.

The boys were a challenge from the start. Jonathan, precocious from birth, was the oldest, possibly the brightest, and then came Paul, not two years later. Always quiet, even as an infant, Paul spent his life listening, observing, possibly because unlike Jonathan, he was but modestly accomplished in his academics. Fletcher Strand knew himself to be an oops baby, but his folks made sure to love him nonetheless.

As boys, they went in three different directions athletically, intellectually, and academically. Self-awareness being one of Fletcher Strand's strong suits, he knew he was not in Jonathan's league, but he was crazy about Paul, the quiet one often tasked with getting him ready for company, and for church.

That he and his brothers had drifted apart seemed only natural. Jonathan, the Ivy League representative of the Strands, had gone off and left, rarely to return, except for their parents' funerals, and Paul's disinclination to go beyond high school left them little in common as adults. To add to their differences, Paul embraced his homosexuality and made a life for himself. They saw each other on occasion, but not as often as brothers living within a short driving distance.

Deep inside, Strand carried a bag of guilt for not having made more of an effort with Paul and Bob, but he also knew that in the 1980s and 90s, were his fellow law enforcement to know of Paul's lifestyle choices, his own career might have been more difficult than it needed to be.

Growing up and being thought of as an everyday Protestant in western Pennsylvania did one no harm, and to maintain that status he disabused no one of their assumptions. Never would he have ever mentioned his mother's faith or going to Mass to the guys in the squad room. He had experienced enough sideways glances when he married the beautiful Aurora Tomaselli, a through and through Italian Catholic, and the comments became more audible for a year or two after he converted to Catholicism. For him, it was merely a return to his true religious home. For so many others, it was a betrayal.

Glad he was that his mother had not lived to see how far apart her sons had grown, but his soul ached wishing she was still with them, especially now, when Paulie needed her most.

VIII

MARCH 2ND PROVED the adage about the lion when Strand rolled out of bed that Tuesday, and he hoped the weather's lamb would make an early appearance. Having worked criminal cases all over west central Pennsylvania forever and a day, March was always the greatest challenge in terms of freak ice storms spurred on by frigid temperatures. Snow was falling.

Aurora was still asleep, breathing deeply, and so he rose and padded around as softly as he could, knowing that the slightest click or clack would stir her or the two younger Strands across the hall. Now eleven, Anna was a treasure while Aaron, nearly fourteen, was beginning to feel all the usual testosterone jolts. Their mom was the real force in their lives given Strand's long and often irregular hours, but every free hour he had was with them and not at the golf course, poker games, or bar nights with the guys. Not that he was the best dad in the world, he knew, but giving them his best was the least he could offer for the tranquility of the Strand household.

Despite his efforts at complete silence, the one living thing in the Strand household he could not deceive with his morning movements was the newest addition: Mac. Bo, his beloved pal and companion, went to wherever dogs go the October before, but Aurora, ever the resourceful woman that she was, vowed the kids would have another dog. Somewhere, somehow, she linked up with a family who bred beagles, and she claimed one when it was born in early November.

The owners kept the pup for six weeks to wean him and start on house training, and on the previous Christmas morning, Strand brought him home, to the great delight of Anna and Aarie. Mac, a strong name for a dog, fit in immediately. Though Aurora and the kids spent the most time with their little puppy, the dog seemed to have identified Strand himself as the real master of his time and fate.

"C'mon, Mac," he whispered, "let's get you outside." The little guy's wagging tail practically knocked him over with early morning enthusiasm and some attention from the big guy. *Hah. Little does he know what'll face him when he steps outside!*

Strand waited for him as he did his duty in the deepening snow. Surprisingly, Mac decided to frolic a bit, having earlier discovered how much he enjoyed rolling around in the powdery stuff. Strand gave him a short whistle, and at once, Mac scampered back, shaking himself off, once inside.

Hurriedly, Strand made himself some coffee, showered, and shaved, with Mac on his haunches watching his every move. Outside, as the wind brushed the triple track storm windows they proved less than perfect in keeping out wisps of arctic air. Once ready, he kissed Aurora on the cheek, gave Mac a good neck scratch, and skittered down the stairs to jump in the waiting Vic that Joe Bentsen was keeping warm in the driveway.

"Hey, Joe," Strand said controlling his shiver as he climbed in the passenger seat.

"Hey, yourself. Strap in because the county is a little slow this morning salting the roads."

"Sorry it worked out this way. Otherwise, I would have driven the State beast home and picked you up in Mercer since we're going there anyway."

"No problem, Fletch. Anything more on your brother?"

"Nah! Not a word from the hospital or Robertson. Tell you what, though, I really don't like that guy."

"What's the problem with him?"

"Aside from the fact that he and Jonathan are unlikely buddies, I've never thought much about him as a physician."

"What do you mean?"

"I don't know, but he has the bedside manner of a dead fish wrapped in old newspaper."

Bentsen chuckled. "Now there's an opinion founded in fact." And he chuckled again, his 6'4" mass shaking behind the wheel.

"Hey, Bigfoot, keep it on the road, will ya? The next time I see Doc McCreary, I want to be walking in."

"In fifteen minutes, you'll get your wish, Fletcher my boy, so keep your shirt on."

∼

Coroner McCreary's digs in the basement of the Mercer County Courthouse were exactly what one might expect for a place populated by the dead. Strand never knew if the overpowering formaldehyde smell was there to cover the cadaverine odors or to preserve the evidence, as it were. Either way, he and Bentsen kept their basement visits to a minimum.

"We're meeting you here instead of your office upstairs because?" Bentsen started.

"Because, I like to occasionally remind people like you why you need to do your damnedest to catch the bastards who do rotten things to other human beings."

"OK," Bentsen groaned.

"Listen, Doc," Strand said, "we've earned our degree in dead body smells, so could we make this morning less miserable by getting to it?"

"Take it easy, guys. So, which do you want first, the 1980 corpse, or the 1993 corpse?"

Strand made a face. "Is this a gag—no pun intended in this place—or what?"

"I asked Montgomery to assign you guys to the 1980 case because if anybody can spot something everybody else missed, it's the two of you bloodhounds."

"Gee," Bentsen said, "it would have been nice if the boss had mentioned it."

"Yeah, surprise, surprise. So, what's the story, then?" Strand prompted.

"In November 1980, an old guy on Daugherty Road, just off of SR173, a few miles north of Foreston, is walking his dog just after dusk, around 6 p.m. I think the file says, and he both sees and smells something that shouldn't have been there. As he got closer, the stench was too much for him. He thinks it's a burning animal of some kind, but whatever it is, it shakes him up enough to hustle home and call you guys."

"But Doc," Strand interjected, "that was thirteen years ago. Everything's changed."

"Not on that corner—diagonally across from the Palmer Smith shop that's there. Sure, there'll be overgrowth, but all we want you two to do is go out there when the ground is clearer, take a good look—you'll be able to fix the spot where the body was found from the photos—and then review the files and the evidence box. That's it."

Strand and Bentsen exchanged looks.

"So, are we done with that one?" Strand asked, seemingly preoccupied.

"Yep, so now, we get to Masters," the coroner responded, pulling out one of his famous cigars and lighting up. In a moment, the dingy little office was full of the gray-blue smoke his stogies produced. While he puffed a red-hot end to his El Producto, he grabbed the next file on his desk and opened it wide.

"I don't know which is worse, the smell of your work space, or the old rags they used to make that thing," Bentsen said.

McCreary laughed out loud. "It's my coping mechanism, Joe, so get over it." He turned some pages. "Ah, here it is. Pretty much what I'd told you yesterday. A blow to the back of the head appears to have been the killing stroke, but you'll note there wasn't that much blood in Masters's office, the trunk, or his kitchen floor. Given the wound, there should have been more, I would think. Did the techs find anything else in the house?"

"No report yet," Strand said. "Why?"

"Nothing about this adds up," McCreary insisted. "I've ordered a few more blood tests, a bit more sophisticated than we ordinarily perform," he said, scratching his head with his free hand.

"And?" Bentsen pursued.

"And," McCreary said, "we might be in for a bit of a surprise."

∽

"And what was that look for?" Bentsen asked, out in the hallway.

"The I-80 case. The guy's been dead for thirteen years. Not high on my hit list."

Bentsen chuckled. "When Montgomery finally gets around to mentioning it, we'll have to come up with something."

"Yeah. 'We're giving it all the attention we can right now.'"

IX

THE PSP'S MERCER Barracks was a dispatching operation, an office space for troopers to do their paperwork, and it had over-night accommodations when necessary. And then there were the holding cells, not regularly used, but there and available.

First of all, it was a command post for the West Central District ruled over by one Lieutenant Walter Montgomery, a wisp of a man no more than 5'7" tall, but all muscle. About him, drive and dedication were the first words to come to mind in 1993, but they were not the same words used to describe him when he came out of the US Marines, a decorated combat veteran, and joined the PSP as a trooper in the late 1960s. A lot of veterans did that, but he was the only one who was Black.

Montgomery had evidently made up his mind he would be the best of the best and proved it year over year. A few tried to claim his promotions came because of his race, but over time no trooper anywhere in western Pennsylvania would put up with such nonsense in their presence. They became his loyal troopers to a man—and the one woman as well.

District Commander for the past decade or so, Montgomery stood as one of Strand's heroes, in part because they had a few things in common. Military service was one, being on the receiving end of bigotry was another. Strand never doubted Montgomery's row to hoe was in much rougher soil than his own, and that was just one more reason he looked up to a man a half a foot shorter than he was.

Strand was reminded of that imagery as he and Bentsen stood in front of Montgomery's desk later that Tuesday morning.

"Sorry to hear about your brother, Fletch. Take what time you need with that." He eyed Strand directly giving no doubt that he meant it.

"Thanks, Chief. Joe just caught me up on what's going on with the tech stuff from this morning, and of course, Doc McCreary will be giving us more when he gets it."

"Joe said you guys were starting to eyeball this Rieger guy for it, but you're not ready to bring him in, I take it?"

"Right, boss," Bentsen said. "Nothing hard yet, and we don't want to run afoul of Georgie Hallon if he concludes the Masters killing was actually done on his terrain. He's fussy about that."

"Speaking of fussy," Montgomery said, "I've gotten two calls from your new FBI pals wanting to know if you're ready to turn the case over to them."

"You know, Chief," Strand said, "it would be fun to do that just to see ol' Georgie crumple like an empty beer can when the Bureau walks all over him." He and Bentsen chuckled. "But the fact is, it probably did happen on Georgie's turf."

Montgomery laughed too, but said, "OK, enough of that, just decide what you're going to do in the next day or two—no later—so we can move on to other stuff. Oh, and did I mention the other one I've got waiting for you."

"You mean the thirteen-year-old burning body in Wolf Creek Township that Doc McCreary just told us about?" Bentsen asked.

Montgomery smiled. "Did I forget to mention that one? Well, McCreary is having the devil's own time coming up with an identification on that one, but cases like that are what you two are good at. Now, beat it, and keep me posted on Masters before anything else happens. Close the deal on this Rieger if that's what it's going to be."

~

Checking in with the dispatcher of all things, Gloria Moses, Strand and Bentsen picked up the file already being built on the case and learned the Garden Avenue house was pretty clean, according to the techs. No fingerprints were there other than the victim's, and aside from the blood on the kitchen floor, nothing else was amiss except the notation that a few drops of what appeared to be blood were found.

"It says the blood spatter, very little, was found at the top of the chairback, about where someone might rest their head if they were taking a nap," Bentsen said reading from the two-page report as Strand's cell phone gave off its familiar buzz.

Strand answered the call and turning, he spoke into the device for a moment before clicking off.

"Or, if McCreary is on to something," Bentsen went on as if there hadn't been an interruption at all, "where a head might rest if the victim was deceased—assuming this was the victim's blood and it got there at the time of death. There's other stuff here, including all the usual photographs."

"Right. Did the doc say when his additional tests might tell us anything?"

"We should have asked, but Harrisburg isn't known for its speed."

They left the building and jumped back in the Vic before Montgomery could tag them.

As they drove out of the lot, Strand said, "Hey, Joe, want to do me a favor?" And without waiting for Bentsen's answer, he said, "Let's head to Sharon for an early lunch, the Wendy's on State?—and then if you wouldn't mind dropping me at the hospital up the street, I'm hoping to catch up with Dr. Robertson about my brother. That's what the call was about."

"Sure thing, Fletch." Cutting over to SR58, they headed west to Sharon and one of their favorite lunch stops—the seemingly eternal Wendy's on State Street. "You know, the tech report pretty much cinches McCreary's notion that Masters was killed away from the mine, right? And now, possibly, right there in his easy chair."

"So, our killer shows up at dawn, goes in the back door—a weapon of some kind already in hand—finds his victim in the chair asleep, pops him a good one, then drags him out through the kitchen and tosses him in the trunk they showed us."

"Wouldn't Masters have heard the guy come in?" Bentsen asked.

"True—unless he was a helluva sleeper. As for the trunk, Masters didn't have to fit completely inside because the killer needn't have closed it. It was just a convenient way to move the body. Maybe he took the trunk in the kitchen, shoved the body in it, realized it wouldn't close, then dragged it out, smashing the screen door while he was at it."

"That floor was old and pretty scuffed up, but I didn't notice any marks there. By the way," Bentsen said, "robbery wasn't a motive, apparently. There wasn't a thing missing from Masters's house from what the techs could tell. His wallet was still in the house on the bed-side table, along with his watch."

"Right. Let's get the techs back there to check both the kitchen floor, the wooden stoop just outside, and the step off the driveway to see if anything shows up there, you know, fresh scratching from one of the brass corners on the trunk."

"Then, if the trunk has some traces of the same lime and sand composition as the Masters driveway, we can confirm an answer to the big question."

Strand scratched his chin. "So, if a white van from the mine was there, along with the trunk we saw, doesn't that confirm another answer?"

"What's that?"

"Our killer is someone from the mine."

"And muscular enough to handle one of those trunks with a body in it."

"Not a woman."

"Then, Rieger or somebody else there?"

≈

At Wendy's, the longtime manager, Don Stemple, recognized the two police detectives and gave them his grandest smile. A few months earlier, Bentsen had foiled an attempted armed robbery at the store, and the manager never forgot it.

Strand and Bentsen had just sat down at the front of the dining area with their sacks of burgers and fries with Pepsi chasers, when a wiry, tatted-up specimen walked in brandishing a Glock. In his early twenties and full of himself, he ordered the manager and all the patrons in the order line to surrender their cash. Apparently, he'd failed to check out the rest of the store before pulling his gun, and didn't notice Bentsen calmly walk up behind him and cold cock him with the butt of his service pistol. The would be bandit dropped to the floor like an anchor in the ocean and within seconds it was all over with no injury to anyone except the ill-starred perp.

Bentsen had said at the time, "This guy won't make the finalists for the Darwin award, but I hope he deserves an honorable mention." Everyone in the restaurant cheered the towering Bentsen for his casual bravery, and the store gave them fresh food when the Sharon Police arrived and took over.

Ever since, the manager told them they could always enjoy lunch on the house, as some with a badge expected, but Strand and Bentsen never did, and today was no exception. After a few pleasantries with Stemple, the pair sat down and happily inhaled their hot food in the middle of a cold day.

X

THE HOSPITAL PRESENTED itself as a stone-cold block of brick and limestone barring unwanted intrusion from the outside world, and miserable weather did nothing to warm a visitor's welcome. Bentsen agreed to sit in the lobby making a few calls and tidying up his notes—of the pair, he was the notetaker of record—while Strand tended to family business three floors above.

When he walked into Paul's room, Jonathan and Dr. Nathaniel Robertson were already there, somber and silent. In the bed, Paul's chest went up and down rhythmically, but otherwise, there was no sign of his presence. He was pale, almost blue. Bob was not there.

"Have I missed something? Where's Bob?"

"Nate and I arrived just a minute ago, Fletch, and where Bob is, I have no idea."

"Should we wait for him?"

Jonathan shook his head. "He's not family and this is family business." He turned to the doctor. "Nate?"

"Hi, Fletcher," he said extending his hand, "you may not remember me, but I was your mother's physician before Paul."

"I remember," Strand said, shaking the proffered hand. "But I don't like the idea of proceeding without Paul's partner," Strand continued, turning back to his eldest brother.

Jonathan shrugged. "Well, he's not here so that settles the question in any event. Let's get on with this."

"Fletch, I was just going to tell you that Paul has MRSA—that's Methicillin-resistant Staphylococcus Aureus—an infection frequently found in immune-suppressed patients like your brother."

"Where did he pick up something like that? Did he have it before he came in here?" Strand's words were polite but not the tone in his voice.

The doctor shrugged his shoulders and looked at the bed. "I can't honestly say where Paul picked this up. It could have been in any medical facility in the last few weeks, or it could have gotten into his system right here in the ER."

"Wasn't he in your office not that long ago getting an injection for his back pain?" Fletcher asked.

"W-well yes, that's right, but that's no reason to assume my office is compromised."

"How do you know, Doctor?" Strand was not on "Nate" terms with the man and refused to inject any indication of friendliness toward someone for whom his reaction was mostly visceral.

Robertson cleared his throat. "That's unfair, Fletch. I run a clean shop, and I'd prefer no suggestion to the contrary." He looked directly at Jonathan, as if in appeal.

On cue, Jonathan jumped in. "Jesus, Fletch. The guy picked up MRSA. With his lifestyle, what's the surprise? We're lucky he doesn't have AIDS."

"Oh, God, don't even mention the possibility," Robertson said. "In today's climate, this hospital would wheel him out into the parking lot if he did."

"Then he's been tested?" Fletch wanted to know.

"Most definitely," Robertson answered. "Gay men and their issues are not exactly welcome in any hospital right now, mostly because so little is known about the contagion factor in AIDS and there are no treatment protocols established."

Strand nodded. His brother stood stone-faced.

"What's more, social mores are not exactly sympathetic to men who do with men, spreading the disease like wildfire in that population."

"You can knock that off, Doctor," Strand said, his voice graced with disgust and sarcasm. "My brother and his partner have been together for over ten years now and as far as I know, they're monogamous. Was Bob tested as well?"

Robertson seemed to take a step back as if he might pick something up from a man, even a state policeman, who defended someone like Paul Strand. "Yes, we asked him and he complied. He's clean."

"Clean?! Is that the best word to use?"

"Alright. Enough, you two," Jonathan intervened. "Where do we go from here, Nate?"

"It's wait and see. We're treating Paul aggressively with antibiotics known to be effective with MRSA, but with his Crohn's disease—and there's an indication of Hepatitis non-A non-B—the outlook is questionable."

"Questionable? What does that mean?" Strand's voice dripped a lack of patience.

Again, Robertson stared at his motionless patient. "It means there's little promise of a good outcome," he said, and added, "I'm sorry, but I have others to see," and left the room.

When they were alone, Jonathan stepped close to his youngest brother and said in a shouted whisper, "What the hell are you doing? That's his doctor, for Christ's sake!"

"And now you sound like his malpractice lawyer, brother. What about Paulie?"

"Paulie is Paulie's problem. My problem is that this doctor for whom you show no respect is up for a top job in the White House and I don't want you screwing it up by shooting off your mouth about him or his office."

"Listen up, big shot, I get the real issue here. You're not the least bit concerned about your flesh and blood and you sure as hell don't give a shit about this quack. It's about you, isn't it, Johnnie? If his background investigation has a smell about it, the stink might stick to you. Isn't that the real issue?"

Jonathan's face purpled. "You oh-so-noble bastard, Fletch, I've got the chance to be something big in this family and you could care less."

"You'd have been big in this family, Johnnie, if you'd ever put this family ahead of your ambition."

"Don't call me Johnnie. The President of the United States calls me Jonathan and you can, too."

"Sure, Johnnie, and now, what about Bob? You like to play head of the family. Who's going to give him the news?"

Jonathon looked at him, the definition of "smug" etched on his face, "You do it—you love these people."

XI

"WHERE'RE WE GOING?" Strand asked after he'd found Bentsen in the hospital lobby. Together, they walked out to the car, pulling their coats close as the wind sliced through them.

Bentsen didn't respond until they were in the Vic, the engine started, and he was driving them in an easterly direction. Strand wasn't talking, lost in thought for a few minutes. Finally, Bentsen said, "I'm sticking to our plan. It'll take almost an hour to get there, but we're heading to Boyers and the mine. It's time we leaned on Al Rieger and milk that cow for whatever information he's got and hasn't been telling. Agree?"

Still silent for a moment, Strand just nodded, pleased yet a bit surprised Bentsen was taking the lead. It was an unusual place for Bentsen to be, Strand thought, but he was glad to see it. In this particular case, clouded as he was by Paul's medical situation, he was content to follow in the big man's footsteps for a change.

Turning on the radio, Bentsen tuned it to Froggy 95, "for the weather," as he always said. Of course, his fingers played tunes on the steering wheel as one country singer after another moaned about a lost girlfriend, their dog, or the truck they truly loved. Strand teased him unmercifully, but over time, he came to enjoy the music. It allowed him to think.

Through Mercer and Foreston they went, turning south on SR8 at Harrisville until they found the Branchton Road. At the mine, they were waved through the clouds of steamed air and drove down to the Investigations Center. Once inside, they asked for Rieger, and in a few minutes, he appeared, clipboard in hand down at his side tapping his thigh.

"Gentlemen, good afternoon," he said. "Let's step into the conference room, shall we?"

Strand was surprised that Rieger was not surprised, but in fact seemed to be expecting them. Once seated, a young woman came in and offered them coffee, which all three accepted. Rieger seemed settled, but once the coffee came in, which was almost immediate, his hand trembled slightly as he took the cup to his lips.

"You don't seem surprised we're here, Al. Why is that?" Bentsen, never one for subtlety, went right for it.

"W-well. W-well, Detective, the last time I saw you, you wanted some lists and I've prepared them for you," he said, tapping his clipboard.

The door opened and in walked a suit. Strand supposed him to be the Deputy Division Director. Another man of short stature. *What's that all about?* Novak couldn't register more than 5'5" but with his stocky frame he somehow made a presence, his prison haircut notwithstanding. He stood with his hands on the back of a conference chair, using it as a fulcrum as he leaned forward and back.

"Gentlemen," he said, "I'm Joe Novak, and sorry we didn't connect when you were here last. And sorry, too, our meeting has to be under such circumstances," he finished, waiting.

"Good to meet you, Joe," Strand said, offering his hand. "Detective Bentsen and I need more time with Al to fill in some gaps, if you don't mind."

"Not to be officious, Detective Strand, but Mr. Lafferty, the head of the program in Washington, has placed me in charge here temporarily, and he wants me to make certain that all proper steps are taken in resolving this horrible crime."

A bit of a martinet? "Right, Joe, that's what we're doing—taking one of the proper steps in this investigation."

"Just a moment, Detective, because I'm in charge of this federal facility at the moment, I do not want you strolling in here unannounced taking my employees' time. I hope that's clear. I want to be apprised of every step of your investigation in this facility."

A lot of 'I's' there? Unblinking, Strand faced the would be giant. "Since we're making things clear, Joe, right now this is a murder investigation under the jurisdiction of the Commonwealth of Pennsylvania, and Joe Bentsen and I, as its representatives, will conduct whatever investigation we think appropriate without asking anyone's permission. And if that's a problem, we can chat with Mr. Lafferty, if you really wish to do so. I need to talk with him anyway, if you want to set up a call."

Novak raised his hand, palms forward, in surrender. "Sorry if I overstepped, gentlemen, but I'm just trying to do my duty here. After all, Mr. Rieger has a lot of responsibility in this operation and we don't want too much time lost, do we?" he asked, with a nervous little laugh.

"No, we don't," Bentsen chimed in, "and so if you'll excuse us, we'd like to continue here with Al, and of course, we'll want to speak with you, so don't get too busy this afternoon.

"A-as you say, Detective," he said with the slightest bow. "I'll be in my office," he said, and backed out of the room, as if in the presence of royalty.

Bentsen rolled his eyes at Novak's exit and said, "Now, where were we, Al?"

The tension in the room, thick to begin with, now seemed opaque. "Listen, Al, just relax," Strand lied, "we just want some information, and you're the guy in the spotlight right now, that's all."

Rieger exhaled even as the damp spots on his shirt betrayed the fact that his anti-perspirant wasn't doing its job. He swallowed hard. "So, what do you want from me?"

Strand said, "First, would you mind handing over your lists? I think we were interested in all those who might have been inside this operation at or around 6 a.m. or earlier. Then we need a list of your employees who would have had access to the vans you use as well as the trunks. Last, since you've had more time to think about it, we need the names of anyone here who might have had a reason to eliminate Abel Masters."

"Phew!" Releasing the paper captives from his clipboard, he handed them over. "The first three pages list the names of the employees who timed themselves in between 6 and 6:30 a.m.—all 168 of them. Then this one-pager is the list of my guys, all men, who handle the trunks and drive the vans—the five of them."

"Good job, Al, thanks," Bentsen said. "Now, let's get down to it."

∼

"OK," Strand said, "let's start with the first name on your list of warehousemen—Lindy Johnston. What's his story?"

"Lindy's been with us ten years or more, good guy, about fifty-six, I think, has a family and lives in Harrisville. He was working on Monday, but didn't check in until about 10 a.m.—had a dentist appointment, I believe, but I can verify that."

"That's alright," Bentsen said, "that's our job. Now, about Manzini."

"Angelo Manzini is a family man in his forties, lives in Butler, but has been on vacation—I heard he took his wife and kids to Italy."

"Fine, we'll need the addresses for all these guys. Next is this guy Meister. What about him?" Bentsen asked.

"Elgin Meister is a bit of a loner. He's been here a few years only. He's single. Sticks to himself. A good worker."

"OK," Strand joined in while Bentsen caught up with his notes, "Artie McKenna is next—he's the wise guy we met already, right?"

"Yessir," Rieger said. "As you could see, he's about the same age as Johnston, maybe a few years younger. Always has something to say, but a good worker, and not a problem. He lives in Harrisville as well, and sometimes, he and Lindy carpool together."

"Was he here early on Monday?"

"Yes. He came in a few minutes after I did."

"Then Frank Sharpe?"

"Frank is also in his forties, lives in Barkeyville with his family. He's the only Black on my crew, and never a problem. Here every day, and yes, he was here Monday morning. He and Artie walked in together."

"Any of your guys have a grudge against anyone, especially Masters?"

"Not that I know of," Rieger answered. "These guys are always grumbling about something, but I would have noticed if somebody was out of line."

Strand leaned back in his chair and eyed Rieger carefully. Bentsen scribbled. Rieger drummed his fingers on the clipboard. It was making a small racket as the clipboard itself vibrated against the top of the conference table. Rieger stopped when he noticed it.

"Now, Al, is there anyone else here who had a grudge against Masters, somebody who had a lot to lose?"

"Well, yes," he answered, his fingers now still, "there is somebody."

XII

ENTSEN LOOKED UP from his notepad, fixing his eyes on Rieger. "C'mon, Al, spit it out."

Strand kept still, fully concentrating on the exchange.

Rieger took a deep breath, drummed his fingers for a moment, then said, "If there's anybody here who had it in for Abel Masters, it would be David Stoddard." He paused, looked down at his fingers, drumming again, willing them to stop, and continued. "Hey look, guys, I really hate to do this, but you asked."

"That's OK, Al," Bentsen said in his most soothing voice. "We'll check everything out, and if Stoddard is in the clear, then no harm, no foul, right?"

"Yeah, I mean, yessir, I guess so."

"So, what's his story?"

Rieger was choosing his words. "Stoddard is a Branch Manager. He came here from Washington a couple years ago to take charge of the Case Review Branch."

"Hold it right there, Al," Bentsen said, holding up his pencil. "Could you tell us what all this stuff means as we go, so I can get it down correctly?"

"Sure. This Center is the beginning and end of all background investigations conducted by OPM each year, probably about 100,000 or so."

At this, Strand leaned forward, whistling, as his government-issued chair creaked, "Did you say 100,000?"

"That's about right, but not every investigation has the same level of scrutiny. If some Senator wants a constituent to go to Cape Kennedy to observe a space launch, we do a name check in various databases. That's a low-level background check, and it goes up from there, all the way, say, to a full field background investigation on an astronaut candidate for NASA. We also do similar investigations for the Atomic Energy Agency, the Bureau of Prisons, the Immigration and Naturalization Agency, and the like."

"Then, if I'm hearing you right," Strand said, "Stoddard was in charge of reviewing these cases?"

"Yes, he has case examiners who check the lower-level cases for issues relating to suitability or security, and he also has reviewers who handle the full field cases—they constitute about 30,000 of the 100,000 I mentioned."

"Got it. And so what happened?"

"As I said, Stoddard came from DC, which is the actual headquarters of this program, and he seemed to think he was pretty hot stuff, knew everything, because that function used to be done there. God's gift, if you know what I mean," Rieger said.

"I'm not sure where this is going," Bentsen said.

"So, Stoddard shows up and begins insisting that Masters do everything the way they did it in DC, and what Masters always said was, 'If we did it the way you guys did it, that function would still be there.' His point was that we proved we could do all the same things here with first class college grads faster and cheaper than DC ever could."

"'Faster and cheaper' because Masters took short-cuts?"

"Just the opposite," Rieger said. "Masters was a stickler for accuracy and integrity, but we don't have to pay the same top salaries as they do in DC, and because the review function is done here where the rest of the case file is assembled, those thick files don't have to go back and forth unnecessarily. That part alone saves three days a case."

"I still don't get it," Strand said. "What was Stoddard's problem? And how do you know all of this, by the way?"

"Once a week, we have a division meeting with all the branch heads, and everybody's underwear went on the table, so to speak, so Stoddard, on the same level as me, had to bare his operational problems just like the rest of us."

"And?" Bentsen was writing furiously, but impatiently.

"And one of the problems that kept coming up was the repeated complaints from agency security officers."

"Say that in plain English, for cryin' out loud," Bentsen insisted.

"When the entire case file is assembled and reviewed for completeness and accuracy, it's sent on to the agency that requested the background investigation in the first place. They're the ones who actually grant the person a security clearance, not us."

"Oh! So, the spotlight was on Stoddard?"

"Riiiight! And naturally, that's a black eye for the entire division, and Masters, who was a big believer in quality, was having none of Stoddard's bullshit reasons for the problem. It's just a guess on my part, but John Lafferty probably got a few calls about it and you know what rolls downhill."

"I still don't see why Stoddard would kill Masters, if that's what you're trying to tell us."

"It had gotten to the point where, rumor had it, Stoddard was on the bubble. He rubbed everybody the wrong way with his holier than thou stuff and then didn't do the job. A bunch of us thought Masters was about to fire him."

"But killing Masters wouldn't save Stoddard's job, would it?"

"Here's the other part. Stoddard thought he was in tight with Lafferty because he'd worked right down the hall from him when he was in DC. Stoddard probably considered himself a successor to Masters—what a laugh! He probably had no idea Lafferty might have put some pressure on Masters. Get it?"

"I'm beginning to," Strand said, "but there has to be more."

"Well, here's another piece, then," Rieger said, his fingers veritably pounding out a concerto. "There was bad blood between the two even earlier, according to the rumor mill. About a year before Stoddard showed up here, Masters broke his arm into a pretzel falling off a ladder at home one day, and because his arm was so messed up, they didn't put it into a cast but did what they called an external fixation—kinda like an erector set drilled into your arm. Masters had to wear that thing for about eight weeks. It was pretty grotesque."

"So? Jesus, Al, you sure drag things out," Bentsen mumbled, his pen resting on his notepad.

"Masters traveled to DC a lot, to headquarters, and to pay calls on our customers—all these agency security officers. He also held briefings for Lafferty's people in central office, including Stoddard. Well, Stoddard was so grossed out by that thing on Masters's arm, he began complaining loudly to anyone who would listen that Masters shouldn't be out in public. Looking back on it, it was as if Stoddard was trying to get Masters shoved out of the way so he could come here as the Division Chief, not the Case Review Branch Manager."

"Sounds a bit far-fetched, Al," Strand said. "Really petty."

"Well, you asked."

Strand nodded, then said, "Joe, you got everything?" When Bentsen nodded, Strand turned back to Rieger and said, "Speaking of Lafferty, I need to have a chat with him. Mind if we use your office?"

Rieger stopped his fingers from their rattling, and seemed surprised. "Shouldn't you check with Joe Novak?"

"No."

∽

"What do you think, Joe?" Strand asked when Rieger stepped outside and closed the door.

"Hard to say, Fletch. Mr. Fingerdrum worked very hard to shine the light on this guy, Stoddard, and although there's clearly something amiss there, did Stoddard hate his boss enough to kill him?"

"Gimme the list with the other names." Going down the pages of names with his index finger, Strand said, "Here it is. Dave Stoddard was here at 6:02 a.m. Monday morning."

"Well, OK then, we'll have to have a chat with Stoddard. But Fletch, what do you think about Al Rieger?"

"He still could be our guy. He was here, he has the keys to everything, and maybe, he had a motive. We need to hear more from Al, but while I'm talking to Lafferty, how about checking with the guard staff at Underground Storage and find out exactly who came in with a vehicle Monday morning."

"Got it."

Strand dialed Lafferty's number and schmoozed his secretary for a bit. Soon, he heard the man's voice on the line.

"Is this the same Fletcher Strand I knew a hundred years ago?"

"Yes, sir, it is. And how are you, Mr. Lafferty? It sure has been a while?"

"Older, grayer, Fletch. And you? Detective grade with the PSP, I hear."

"Yes, again, sir. And sorry we have to re-connect on a matter like this."

"Same here, my friend. My wife and I take this loss very personally. How do you want to proceed?"

"Well, sir, we're just at the beginning of this, and so we're trying to get a handle on who and why someone might want to murder Abel Masters."

"Am I assuming correctly, Fletch, that the jurisdictional question has been settled? I've had three calls from the Bureau's Pittsburgh Field Office."

"We think it's settled, but we still need to sort out some details, if you don't mind."

"I understand. How can I help?"

"This privatization thing seems to be a gorilla in the room. Can you tell me more?"

"Indeed. Everybody is either running for cover or trying to figure out which side to be on."

"What about Abel Masters? What can you tell me about him, sir, and where he fits into this whole privatization thing?"

"I'll make this as concise as possible," Lafferty said, care for words a trademark of his from long ago. "I've known Abel for a long time. When we were setting up the mine for the investigations program way back then, we used local labor, one of them being a young Amish boy named Abel Masters. You would have had no reason to know him then, Fletch."

"Amish, did you say?" Strand asked, searching his memory.

"Yes. He'd made his decision to leave the Amish community a year or two before, and was finishing high school somewhere in the area. I took a liking to him, saw some promise, and when he had his diploma, I helped get him into a small Catholic college near Pittsburgh. He shined. When he had his degree, he came on with us as an Investigator, GS-7, stationed here in Washington."

"Good thing he knew you, sir."

"I got him in, Fletch, but didn't need to help him a bit. He was a star. In less than ten years, he was a GM-13, a very successful Supervising Investigator out West. Then he took the Assistant Division Chief's job—with no competition because no one else wanted to go to Boyers—and within four years, became the Chief of Investigations for that Division. I stayed out of the selection process, of course, but had no trouble signing the promotion papers."

"Thanks. That's good background. Now, what did Abel Masters stand to gain or lose with privatization?"

"For one thing, he would have been fine either way. The government would have wanted him to oversee the program since I'll be retiring soon, and the private people couldn't find a better man to run it."

"And the employees?"

"The employees want to remain federal, of course, because with privatization, it's an uncertain future, right? Truth be told, Abel would have preferred that privatization never came up, but he was a smart guy and saw there was no point in lying down in front of an unstoppable steam roller."

"And did a lot of people know about the connection between you two?"

"I doubt it. I made a point, and he did, too, I'm quite certain, not to let our acquaintanceship be known."

"What about David Stoddard?" Before the second syllable of the man's name crossed his lips, he heard a long intake of breath on the other end of the line.

"I'm not surprised you brought him up. Mr. Stoddard was a problem child here, and a problem child for Abel. Federal rules meant he had to be offered the job in Boyers even though neither Abel nor I thought it a good move. I think we both thought it would sort itself out."

"I guess not." There was no response. "Do you think, sir, Stoddard could have hated Masters enough to kill him?"

"I don't know about hate, but Stoddard has always been jealous of Abel's success—a guy coming out of nowhere. Stoddard himself comes from a somewhat prominent Maryland family, but he couldn't hack it elsewhere, so lucky us."

Strand remained silent, thinking there was more to come. There was.

"But in answer to your question, Fletch, jealousy is a dangerous thing, isn't it?"

XIII

WHEN STRAND NEXT saw Bentsen, he had just come back from his long walk out to the portal and back for his chats with the guard staff. Bentsen never walked at a quick pace. He lumbered, much like a locomotive at the slowest speed possible. "So, what'd you get?"

"I don't get it, Fletch. I quizzed those guys six ways from Sunday, went over the schedules, and nobody remembers any of the Investigations Center's vans coming in on Monday morning."

"So, then, how did the body get here? According to Doc McCreary, he was probably killed the night before, somewhere else, and brought to his office."

"Right. And now we know he was likely killed at home."

"So, if we can piece this together, he was taken from his house in the wee hours—when Ethel Richland noticed the van there—and somehow made it to his office before 7 a.m. How the hell could that have happened?"

"Wait—if Rieger is lying, then it would have been easy peasy for him to have done the job and gotten him in here in his SUV, right?"

"Well, well, once again, the spotlight shines on Al."

~

"Will we ever see daylight again?" Bentsen moaned.

The two detectives caught Rieger in his office and casually mentioned they'd like to meet him away from the mine. Could he come to the Mercer Barracks the next morning around 9 a.m.? Rieger, seeming surprised, stammered a "yes."

"Let's see if we can find this Stoddard before everybody goes home."

Rieger fumbled with his phone as he called the front desk to have Stoddard paged.

They waited for several minutes until Rieger's phone rang and he was informed Stoddard had left early. Strand and Bentsen exchanged glances.

"Thanks, Al," Bentsen said. "See you in the morning."

Rieger only nodded, staring straight ahead.

~

As the Vic eased toward the mine's portal, Bentsen craned forward as if doing so would allow him to see the last rays of the sun.

"Forget it, Joe, it's dark. This is March, not August."

"You know, I don't know how these people work down here, hardly ever seeing the daytime sun."

"Maybe we could suggest they install tanning beds for them to use on their breaks."

"Yeah, you do that."

Strand pulled his cell phone out of his jacket pocket to see if he had a signal. Not yet. Maybe in a mile or two. As they roared along the Branchton Road, they reviewed their crazy day, especially the business about a body's move from place to place with no one except the killer taking any notice.

His phone buzzing, Strand could see there were two messages, one from Lieutenant Montgomery and one from his wife. "Aurora," he said when she answered, "we just left the mine. Sorry, no signal down there. I'm on the way home now."

"Hon, I've got something for you to eat—on the run—the hospital called and you should go. They said Father Pallison was on his way to give Paul Last Rites."

Strand closed his eyes tight. He didn't want Bentsen to see his tears if they came.

"Fletch, are you there?"

Strand blew out his air. "Yes, sorry. I heard you. Do you want to go with me?"

"I think I should—and the kids are old enough. I'll get them ready."

"I'll be there in about twenty minutes. Love you."

Strand remained silent after ending the call, deep into images of his brother when they were younger. Working on their American Flyer train layout at Christmas with Paulie showing him how to wire the transformer, learning the ropes of the paper route as Paul handed it over, and all those other snippets of memory siblings tend to share.

"Sorry, Fletch. Doesn't sound good. Anything you want me to do?"

"Nothing, Joe," he said after a moment. "I'll call you tonight if I have to change the plan for tomorrow with Rieger. I had another call from Montgomery. Will you get back to him for me?"

"No problem at all, and I'll just hold Al off, let him stew some more, if that's what it comes to. Whatever you need to do.

"One dead guy this week is enough, Joe. I don't want to see another, especially my brother."

XIV

A T THE HOSPITAL that evening, as the wind blasts shivered the glass and aluminum entry doors to the ER lobby, Strand and his family made their way to the third floor, then to Paul's room.

When they walked in, Bob was sitting quietly off to the side, while Father Mike Pallison performed the Last Rites of the Church for the sick and dying. Paulie lay motionless. Seeing that the priest was midway through the rite, the Strands stood off to the side with Bob. Aarie and Anna Strand huddled close to their parents.

With specially blessed oils, Fr. Pallison anointed Paul, then leaned over to give him Holy Communion. That part Strand could not see as the priest evidently touched the communion wafer to Paul's lips, but he wasn't sure exactly what transpired. Going to Mass with his mother early on did not make him Catholic, so he'd never witnessed the rite in person and actually knew little about it, except that Confession would not have been possible given Paul's comatose state.

Aside from the small movements Father Mike made walking around the bed and from the mechanicals keeping Paul alive, the room was still. Strand could see his children were especially affected by the sight. Aaron, or Aarie, was Paul's godson, and as such, he and his uncle had a special bond, one which Strand could see moistened his son's eyes. He put one arm around each of his children while Aurora leaned on him from behind Anna, their youngest. To Aurora, a cradle Catholic, it wouldn't feel "right" without these final blessings.

At last, Father Mike placed the communion wafer in its case, sprinkled Paul and everyone in the room with Holy Water, and removed from his shoulders the silk stole, kissing the cross stitched at the mid-point. Strand could see the priest, his friend, praying silently.

When he was finished, Father Pallison walked over to Bob, bent down and said a few quiet words of comfort, then came over to the Strands.

"Fletch, Aurora, hey kids, sorry it has to be this way. I don't know if Paul could hear me, but honestly, I thought his breathing seemed less labored, that he was more at peace as I concluded the ceremony. If he had any mental discomfort, he seems at ease now—whatever happens."

"Thanks, Father, I know your being here means a lot to him— and Bob—and he'd say so if he could."

"What's the outlook then?"

"As you suspect, probably grim, Father. I notice that he's not been moved to ICU—he has MRSA and with his other health issues, the antibiotics may be doing little good."

"I'm sorry, yet I've seen so many situations like this where in a day or so, they're ready to jump out of bed."

"Thanks for saying so, Father," Aurora said. "That means so much to all of us."

Anna stood still, staring at her uncle. Aarie's head was down, eyes probably still damp.

Father Mike spoke to Aarie. "I remember the day you were baptized, and Paul was so happy, thrilled to be your godfather—you're lucky to have had him for so long, Aarie. You'll pray for him, won't you?"

Aarie nodded, then cried without caring who saw.

After a moment or two, while everyone tried to let Aaron shed his tears without embarrassment, Strand said, "Father, could I see you out in the hall for a minute?"

~

"What can I do for you and your family, Fletch?" the priest asked when they'd stepped out of Paul's room and walked a few paces to where it seemed quieter.

"Nothing at the moment, Mike, thanks for coming." Strand always used the proper title in front of others, but when the two of them were together, it was always "Mike."

"I didn't see your other brother. Did he come?"

"Oh, Jonathan's somewhere around. He flew in from DC, and you're right, I'm surprised not to see him here."

"Is something else on your mind, Fletch?"

"Yeah. Abel Masters."

The priest nodded again, then waited.

"You know about him being murdered, right? He wasn't your run-of-the-mill Catholic, Mike, and I'd like to talk to you about him tomorrow sometime.

"Sure. I happen to know him pretty well. It's not every day we get an Amish refugee who becomes Catholic—we're practically at opposite ends of the Christian spectrum," he said, and chuckled quietly.

"Good, thanks. Tomorrow then, late morning? I'll stop by the church if you have any decent coffee."

"For you, the best, Fletch. See you then—it should be an interesting conversation."

XVI

THE NEXT MORNING, Strand and Bentsen waited at the Mercer Barracks for Al Rieger to show up for his appointment. Nine o'clock came and went, and no Al.

"Do we have his number?"

Bentsen checked his notebook. "No, but I have his home address. Let me call the mine and see if he checked in, and I'll get his contact numbers." Using the PSP landlines, he dialed some numbers, had short conversations, and hung up. "Hmmm!"

"What?"

"No Al at the mine. That's odd."

"You think he might have forgotten?"

"No way. Mr. Clipboard, the Man of Lists? No, something's not right, Fletch, what do you want to do?"

"Well, I promised Father Pallison I'd stop in to chat with him later this morning about Masters. Why don't I do that now and if you don't mind, scoot past Rieger's house—he lives in Foreston, right? —and if he's not there, go to the mine and see what's what. Then call me and we'll meet for lunch."

"Yeah, that's a good plan. Not being Catholic, lightning might strike if I walk in there with you, and besides, you two can talk your language without this good old Lutheran spying on you."

Strand laughed. "Some sense of humor, Bigfoot. See you later."

"I'm betting it's sooner than later," Bentsen said and trundled toward the coat rack, then out the door.

Strand stood and was draining the last dregs of barracks coffee when Walter Montgomery's shadow shaded his desk.

"Let's talk," he said, and turned toward his office.

"What's up, Chief?"

"Did you call our fed friends?"

"Sorry, I haven't checked that box yet." When Montgomery's pencil thin mustache began to quiver, Strand hastened to add, "I've been dawdling on that, I know, Chief, but if I tell the Feds it's not their show, then I'll have to tell your cousin Georgie Hallon it's his."

"Don't be a wise guy, Strand. Georgie's not my cousin, but I get your point. Give me one good reason why we shouldn't just turn this over to that idiot and be done with it."

"Why? Well, we have a reputation to uphold for one thing, and second, Georgie couldn't solve this kind of crime if Sherlock Holmes came down and planted a deerstalker cap on him."

Montgomery chuckled. "Nice image, and you're right, but what's our reasoning for holding on to this one?"

"Well, I can practically assure you that the head of that program in Washington, John Lafferty, would much prefer the PSP handle this carefully and discreetly rather than hand it over to Mayberry RFD, if you know what I mean."

"You know this guy, Lafferty?"

Strand explained their connection and recent phone conversation, then said, "In fact, I need to call him back, so I'll ask him to write something official for you to use. How's that?"

"First good news I've had all week. Now, get out of here."

～

Strand made the twenty-minute drive from Mercer to Foreston's North Broad Street, where he found Father Mike Pallison in his rectory office across the alley from the parish church. Built with the nickels and dimes of several hundred Italian families, its English cottage architecture dominated the skyline of that edge of town.

The priest was doing some paperwork while nudging a Danish toward the end of its useful life. Strand knocked on the doorjamb and went in.

"Thanks for seeing me a bit early, Mike. I appreciate it."

"No problem, but just so you know, if Masters said anything to me in the confessional, it's off limits, right?"

"Got it," he said, eyeing Pallison's steaming cup of coffee at the same time.

"Mary," Pallison called out to his secretary, "would you mind getting this parishioner a cup of our finest?"

"Thanks, Mike. It's cold out there, and I need something to warm up a bit."

"So, what do you want to know?"

Mindful of Pallison's comment in the hospital, Strand asked, "So, what's a good Amish boy doing in a place like this?"

They both chuckled at the unlikelihood of such an occurrence.

"Well, it's like this," he began. "When your friend Lafferty took him under his wing some twenty years ago, according to Abel, he did nothing to try to convert him, but over time, he liked the example John and his wife set. Unofficially, they sort of adopted him when Abel decided to leave the Amish community, because as you know, Fletch, once they leave, the community wants little to do with them."

"What a piece of luck for Masters."

"Or the hand of God, Fletch. Were it not for the Lafferty's, he might have become a common day laborer, or God only knows what else. When they took him in and saw that he finished high school, he was ready to convert to Catholicism then, but they sent him to St. Vincent's for his college degree, and at his graduation, he insisted."

"But the Lafferty's didn't live here, did they?"

"No—only for a few years when he established the Investigations Center."

"So, when Masters was at St. Vincent's, he would go to DC summers and holidays, I guess."

"That would be about right."

Strand paused. "Since you've known him, Mike, how has he struck you—I mean as a person?"

"I can say without mental reservation, Abel Masters was one of the most decent human beings I've ever run across. His Amish upbringing did a lot to instill in him a respect for others, while not trying to shine a light on himself."

"That didn't stop him from being ambitious, from what I've picked up about him."

"It's been my experience that his kind of talent takes him to the top like a high tide—like you, Fletch, a force of nature."

"Hah! Thanks, but I don't think I've been playing in Masters's league. Can you say anything about his personal life? How come he's never married, for example? His Amish heritage would have pushed him that way, I would have thought."

The priest nodded, thoughtful. "You're right about that last bit, but Masters was a pretty intense introvert, you know. He could make himself be 'on' all day long, if need be, but the real Abel Masters coveted his privacy and didn't get much out of being with others."

"He had no friends around here or in the parish that you knew of, then?"

"None, actually—except, perhaps, me. We had dinner about once a week. Once or twice a month, he'd sneak out of town and spend some time with the Lafferty's, and several times a year they'd come up and the four of us would have dinner." He laughed. "We even took up Mahjong and played at the rectory when they visited."

"So, no hobbies, interest in sports, or any activities in the parish? The Knights of Columbus or anything else?"

"Nope. I'm afraid not. Our loss, but that was just not him. It was work and relax at home for a bit. Period. Well, wait a sec. I didn't know everything about him, Fletch, but I had the feeling he maintained some sort of contact with family members in New Wilmington, but I can't swear to it. That was one subject he never discussed."

"Hmm! That might explain the peach pies."

"What?"

Strand's cell phone buzzed. It was the mine at Boyers, and Bentsen came on the line. "What's up, Joe."

"Better get on your horse and head over here, Fletch," he said pausing for effect. "Our prime suspect is dead."

"Rieger?"

"None other."

XVII

ON THE DRIVE over to the mine, Strand called the hospital to see how Paul was doing. No change, the charge nurse said, but yes, his older brother and the doctor had been in to see him. Strand was relieved, but at the same time wondered what his brother was up to. Against his better judgment, he called Jonathan on his cell, and he picked up right away.

"What's up, little brother?" Jonathan said sweetly.

Strand blanched. Sweetness from Jonathan was an unknown. "Just the usual, Johnnie, one dead body after another. Just like your world—isn't politics a blood sport, like they say?"

Jonathan snorted. "You got that that right, Fletch. So, you called just to jab me about my career choice, then?"

"Not at all. Isn't this normal conversation between brothers? Passive aggressive stuff? Hey, seriously, Jonathan, I am calling about a sensitive matter and I don't know if you can help me."

"How sensitive? And why wouldn't I help you?"

"Well, this is part of an official inquiry, but definitely off the record."

"I'm not sure how I fit in here."

"You're aware, I'm sure, we found the body of one of OPM's

senior people down in the Boyers mine, and I'm wondering if this privatization initiative your boss, the Vice President, is pushing has anything to do with it." Strand could hear his brother blast out the air from his lungs.

"Wow, now there's a helluva question, Detective Strand. I'm not sure I know how to answer it. First, this is high on the President's wish list. My boss is the spear carrier."

"How 'bout we skip the political answer and just give me some straight stuff?"

"You said 'off the record,' right?"

"Sure."

"There are some key members of this administration who do not like background investigations—at the highest level, if you know what I mean—and they'd be happy if they just went away."

"Aren't there laws and executive orders in the way of that dream?"

"You bet. A lot of them, but you can read the papers yourself. They call it Filegate."

"Right, but doesn't that have to do with the FBI, not OPM?"

"Uh-huh, but that doesn't matter to some of these people—free spirits all of them. They think any of their friends, and emphasis on the 'any,' should have whatever job they appoint them to, no matter what."

"So, heavy drinking, drugs, mental illness, child abuse—no big deal?"

"That's about it, Fletch. On the other hand, if they have a big donor, say a New York gazillionaire who wants to be Secretary of Fartonomics, Ambassador to Nowhere, and they don't want to be embarrassed to find out the guy likes young girls, for example."

"Yeah, I hear you, Jon, but for cryin' out loud, there've got to be some standards, some limits to the creepos representing the United States, right?"

"You'd think, but they don't think. They're my party, but nobody is turned away if they have cash."

"So, is this going to happen, then?"

"Let me tell you something, the Vice President has been tasked with getting this done, and dealing with him is like beating your head against the wall—the head of OPM has experienced that little headache, I can tell you—so it's going to happen, no matter what Congress says or does."

"So much for democracy, I suppose."

"You suppose correct."

"Hey, this is a longshot, but have you run into a wealthy family from Maryland, name of Stoddard?"

"Jesus, Fletch, that's no longshot. How do you know about them?"

"They have a son named David who works for OPM."

"Christ! The father made millions in cardboard, of all things. A bit on the outer edge, if you take my meaning, and the kids have a big entitlement problem. Even so, they know his name well at party headquarters."

"No problem. I can verify what you just told me independently if I even need to."

"But why are you asking? And please don't tell me the son has a light shining on him."

"Bingo, but remember, Johnnie, you agreed it was off the record, too."

"I did, Fletch, but for Christ's sake, don't step into a bear trap there."

"I won't."

"Do I need to give anyone a heads up?"

"Better not. You don't want anyone accusing you of interfering in a murder investigation, do you?"

"Never mind. We never had this conversation."

≈

Strand lost the signal when he drove out of cell tower range deeper into Butler County. *Just as well.* He knew the next words out of his brother's mouth would be ones they'd both regret. On Branchton Road, he turned his focus to what Bentsen had told him, and he wasn't prepared for what he was about to see.

It was true that he and Bentsen had determined to their satisfaction that Abel Masters was murdered outside the mine, and his body was transported, somehow, to the mine, and somehow, smuggled in. *Why? Why didn't the killer leave Masters's corpse right where the crime was committed? Moving him made no sense and moving him to the mine made even less sense.*

Now, their prime suspect was dead. Joe didn't say if Rieger was on federal property, but he was willing to bet not.

The killer was lighting a smoke fire to confuse their investigation, but one fact seemed clear: whoever killed Masters—and, apparently, Rieger—was the same person, someone who worked in a highly sensitive position for the federal government, someone who held a security clearance.

As he steered his car down the ramp toward what his mind perceived as the gates of hell, he wondered just what kind of hell existed there down under.

XVIII

LREADY, THERE WERE several state cars lined up just outside the Investigations Center, their blue lights gyrating strange patterns on the silvery limestone walls. *Good thing none of the drivers thought it cute to play the official music underground.* While it might not have caused a cave-in, Strand mused, the noise bouncing off the stone walls would have caused any number of people to go screaming into the darkness.

The noise, lights, and action were coming from the cut-through where he and Bentsen had parked the day before. There were several people standing around one vehicle in particular, a black Chevy Blazer with the front doors open. Bentsen, giant of a man that he was, easily appeared amongst the small throng of official and other onlookers.

When Strand walked up, other staties parted for him. He looked around and asked Bentsen, "Any reason we need to have all these good folks here?"

"None, Fletch. You're right, I should have noticed," Bentsen replied with some deference even though neither detective held seniority over the other. He turned and nodded at one of the uniformed staties, "Get these people away from here unless they have some business or have identified themselves as a witness."

Strand eyed the twenty or thirty souls looking for any familiar face. Nearly all were women, probably part of the data entry cadre, and only a few were men. He thought a man resembling David Stoddard's description was one of them. He stood apart, staring.

Then he turned to Doc McCreary's form bent over and leaning into the driver's seat. Strand cleared his throat, loud enough to startle the coroner, who took a step back and stood straight up and turning at the same time.

"I might have known," groaned McCreary, his sandy brown hair somewhat disheveled. "What is it with you two? It's never just one body. If there's one and you two show up, there's soon another."

~

"And good day to you, Doctor," Strand said with mock gravity. "And every time there's a dead body, you show up. Imagine that!"

"Are you through, Detective Obvious?"

"Sure. Can you give us a rundown?"

"The deceased has been identified as Albert Rieger, and to the best of my ability, I'm thinking he's been here since sometime early last evening, let's say 7 p.m."

"You seem to be hedging your bet a bit."

"Notice the ambient temperature here, Fletch? It's a steady fifty-five degrees outside of the office spaces, and that skewers body temp timetables a bit, if you know what I mean."

"Right," Bentsen said, "but not as much as if we'd found him outside in the parking lot, where the temp last night went down to about 28."

"Exactly, Joe. Now as to manner of death," McCreary continued as if on auto-play, "it seems to me that Rieger had gotten into his car, closed the door, and was preparing to depart. You see," he said, pointing, "he already had his seatbelt on."

"Got it," Strand said. "So you're telling us this body was not moved. He was murdered where he sat?"

"I believe so. I'll know more when we get him to the lab. As far as I know, no one has touched anything, so you'll want to check his keys in the ignition. I cannot tell if he'd started his vehicle and the killer turned it off, or never started it at all."

"And?"

"And here's what I'm supposing, based on what I see here: As I said, Rieger gets in, shuts the door, puts on his seatbelt, and someone comes up and knocks on the window to get his attention. Rieger lowers the window. Remember, it's not well-lit here, but it's likely he knew the killer."

"Right. He'd have known everyone who worked here. No strangers."

"Exactly," said McCreary. He exhaled. "When he lowered the window, the killer shoved the end of a heavy, round steel bar into the side of Rieger's head, just above and behind his left eye, probably killing him instantly. The skull was fractured and there was blood loss," he said, and pointed to several drying puddles on the vehicle's upholstery.

"Anything more?" Bentsen asked.

"Not right now, gents, but I can tell you that if whatever bashed in Rieger's head was what did in the back of Masters's head, it was used differently."

"Can you translate that?" Bentsen asked.

"Sure. Imagine, say, a steel bar a bit over a foot long. Masters's killer used the bar like a blackjack and smashed in his head with the long end of it, while here," he said, gesturing to Rieger's corpse, "the killer rammed the end of the bar into the side of his head." He held his finger up. "I imagine such a weapon, men, because a bar of that kind would have the heft to do the damage we've seen on two different bodies."

"Thanks, Doc," Strand said, then turned to look at Bentsen and the two of them stepped off to the side.

"What do you think, Fletch?"

"This ties the knot, doesn't it?" Strand was grim. "The killer is right here. It shouldn't be a problem to get the list of all those who last left from this facility last night, and from there we can begin narrowing it down."

"Right. What I still don't get, though, is why the killer went through all that business with Masters and moving his body, but he left Rieger's body right here."

"What's puzzling me even more right now, Joe, is what did Rieger know that got him killed?"

XIX

STRAND AND BENTSEN walked together to the front gate, where a guard eyeballed every person as they entered or left. "Do they have a system for checking employees in and out, Joe?"

"Not that anyone mentioned, but I'm pretty sure not. There're about twenty different facilities down here, Fletch, both federal and private, and I'd bet they'd never get everyone to agree on a process."

"Yeah, I can see that, but does that mean anyone can walk in here?"

"No way. Did you notice everyone has a picture badge on them somewhere—green must be the color for the Investigations crowd. And when I was talking to these guys yesterday, I noticed that as people walked through the man-gate from their break outside, each person lifted their badge for the guard to see."

"OK, but that area isn't particularly well-lit, so I'm wondering if someone who didn't belong here, but had a badge in their possession, could fake it."

"A possibility," Bentsen said. "The pedestrian walkway is a good twenty or more feet from where the guards stand, so they couldn't with any certainty match the face on the badge to the person."

"Crap," Strand said. "That opens up a whole new kettle of stinking fish."

"Maybe, maybe not," Bentsen countered. "Thinking about the odds of that, as opposed to the much greater likelihood that the killer works here is where we should put our energies, I think."

Strand eyed his partner with appreciation. "OK, so let's see what they tell us."

Crunching their way to the portal, or front gate as everyone called it, they saw the mine's general manager there, as if waiting for them. He stepped forward and introduced himself as Roger Davis.

Strand and Bentsen showed their credentials and re-pocketed them. "I'm glad you're here, Mr. Davis. We need to speak to the guard on duty last night from, say, 6 p.m. and afterward."

"The Underground Storage Company is happy to cooperate with this investigation, gentlemen, but I hope whatever is said publicly about this second death—Al Rieger was a friend of mine, by the way—does nothing to lessen confidence in the safety and security of this facility."

"I can't help what people think or conclude, Mr. Davis, but I think the message that gets out will be one more likely to focus on someone working in the Investigations Center, so the people who'll have a PR problem are in Washington, DC, not here."

"Sorry for them, but I'm glad you appreciate what something like this could do to our small business," Davis said, then gestured to one of the guards at the podium. "This is Daryl Richardson, Sergeant of the Guard, if you will, and he can make sure you're helped."

Richardson, a beefy man of better than six feet, nodded, his chins nodding with him, and asked what was needed. Strand could not picture Richardson chasing anyone. Bentsen repeated Strand's earlier request to speak with the guard on duty the evening before. Once more Richardson nodded rather than speaking, as if he was saving up his words for a better occasion. "Actually, that would be me. What do you want to know?"

"As the supervisor, would you normally be at the guard station? Bentsen asked.

"Not normally, no."

"And?"

"One of the guys was off sick, so I covered for him."

"Can you tell us, since I'm guessing Al Rieger was a well-known figure to USC, what time he normally left the mine in the evening?"

He thought for a second. "Al—Mr. Rieger usually left here no later than 5:30 p.m. You know, he was always here at 6 a.m. every morning so he put in long days."

"No family?"

Richardson chuckled. "He told me he and his wife preferred cats. No lifetime commitments, he said."

"Interesting," Strand said. "Obviously, he never left last night. Wouldn't that have been noted?"

"No sir. You see, he could have left much earlier in the day, so the night man, me, wouldn't have known his schedule. There are nearly 2,500 people who work underground here."

"Wow, I didn't think that many," Bentsen said, "so it must be hard to keep track of all of them."

"Not our job to do so, sir. Their employer is responsible for keeping track. We give them their badge when they come in in the morning, and they hand it back as they leave. We don't take a count, usually."

"So, no one had reason to notice that Rieger had not turned in his badge?"

"No again, sir," Richardson said, pointing to the badge boards off to his right.

"Doesn't that get to be a problem?"

"The only time we ever do a serious count is when we have evacuation drills—then we have to account for every soul in here."

"Got it," Bentsen agreed, then described for Richardson the possibility he and Strand imagined, that someone posing as another could enter with their badge.

Richardson rolled his eyes, his chins moving in rhythm, "Nah! We have a lot of people here but we know who the strangers are."

"But you never count the number of people coming in and the number of people leaving."

"Heck, no! Some of these facilities work more than one shift. It would be a nightmare."

"So, then, Mr. Richardson," Strand said, starting again, "would you have any idea who would have left the Investigations Center after Al Rieger would normally have left?"

"Holy cow!" he said, then went on, "Well, wait a minute. That's not so hard when I think about it. Most of the rank and file are gone well before 5 p.m. unless they're working overtime, and that's not been the case lately. Only the managers and a few of the warehousemen would have left around then."

Richardson proceeded to name seven or eight people, but only a few sounded familiar. Bentsen copied them in his notepad.

"Was David Stoddard one of them?" Strand asked.

"Oh, yeah. We all know him," he said with little respect.

"When did Stoddard leave, then?

"Well, like I said, we don't keep track, but I'm pretty sure it was around 6:30 p.m. I was just starting my sandwich and up he comes with that stupid grin on his face."

"A grin?" Bentsen asked, lifting his pen.

"Yeah—a wise-guy grin, always the same with him. I don't think he likes living or working up here in the woods. Not as cool as the big city," Richardson opined with judicial aplomb.

"Thanks, Mr. Richardson, you've been helpful. There wasn't anyone else, sometime later, was there?"

He shook his head. "Definitely not. After 7p only the bats were moving around down the shaft."

"Got all those names, Joe?" he asked, but knew he didn't have to. Bentsen nodded.

As they turned away, he said, "Nice final image there, Rieger and the bats."

"Yeah," Bentsen chuckled, "but don't forget."

"What?"

"Along with the bats, there was Rieger and his killer."

XX

OUT ON THE Branchton Road, Strand waited a mile or two before punching in John Lafferty's number into his cellphone, and was amazed that after four rings, it was Lafferty himself who answered, not his secretary.

"I knew I'd be hearing from you again, Fletch," he said after exchanging hellos. "What's up? And how is the investigation going, if I'm allowed to ask?"

"I think, sir, my questions to you will answer yours to a degree. First, however, you should be aware that another of your employees, Albert Rieger, was found murdered in the mine, but outside your facility, a few hours ago."

There was a moment of silence before Lafferty said, "Good God, man, just what the devil is going on down there?"

"I wish I knew, sir, but I need your help. Yesterday, I meant to ask you for all the official records for Abel Masters—there's a lot we don't know and need to. And now, with Rieger's murder, I'm certain something connects both men in a way that's not obvious to us yet. We're certain the murderer works at your facility, and several people have come up on our radar. That's why I need to ask you for access to the Official Personnel Folders of about eight people, and if it's not too much trouble, to their background investigations as well."

"Whoa!" Lafferty exhaled. "That's a big order, even for a murder investigation, Fletch."

"Two murders, sir, and I'm guessing that what's going on here is not over."

"Do you have any sense of why this is happening?"

"Sir, it's been my experience that when a series of clearly connected homicides occurs, something said or done triggers the killer into action. Someone here is afraid of something, and he has to kill to protect himself."

"You just said 'here' and used male pronouns. Are you telling me something?"

"Take it as you wish, sir. Detective Bentsen and I are convinced the murderer works in the mine, nowhere else, and is male, but I could be wrong about gender, I'll admit."

"But why do you need to see their background investigations? I understand about their OPFs," he said using the common abbreviation used amongst Feds, "but why the other?"

"I'm convinced, sir, that buried in those files is the identity of our killer."

"Let me think about this for a moment," Lafferty said, obviously considering options. "Alright, Fletch, if this is an official request, give me the list of names. I'll need a day or two to retrieve the files from OPM's security officer, but then what?"

"Here's my suggestion, sir. I'll meet your designee at Breezewood, and take possession of the files."

"Hmmm! You know, I haven't had lunch at the Bob Evans there for some time now. I'll get back to you with a date, but of course, there'll be strings attached, for your protection and mine."

"Such as?"

"I'll need a written request from someone higher up in your chain of command, you'll have to sign a custody slip for each file, a confidentiality statement, and a guarantee they'll secure with the State of Pennsylvania."

Strand chuckled. "I wouldn't have expected it any other way. Thank you, sir."

"No thanks necessary, Fletch. If you can solve these murders, and soon, the media storm will blow over, and worse…"

"Worse?" Strand interrupted.

"Oh, yes, worse. The worst thing to happen to career executives, like me, in the federal establishment is to have a blankety-blank po-litical appointee breathing down my neck."

"May I ask at what level, sir?"

"Given that the administration is attempting to do this privatiza-tion thing, this kind of attention is high in the morning briefing book of the Vice President, none other."

"Hmm!" Strand said, unwilling to breach his brother's confidence.

"I'll say no more, but I'm sure you're aware, he is no one to cross."

～

No sooner had Strand closed his conversation with Director Lafferty than his phone buzzed and he saw a familiar number. "Hey, Doc, didn't we just talk?"

"We did. I'm probably on the same road as you heading back to Mercer County," McCreary said.

"So, what's up?"

"As soon as I left the mine, my office called, and the special drug tests I ordered on Abel Masters have come through. I didn't get the full report over the phone, but my assistant was clearly shocked by what the report contained. Any chance you and Bentsen can spend an hour with me tomorrow morning?"

"Joe's not with me right now, Doc, but let's plan on seeing you at the courthouse at 9 a.m. Sound good?"

"Not upstairs. Come down to the basement."

"Not the best place for a cozy cup of coffee and a little chit-chat."

"It's chilly there, I'll give you that, but not as chilling as what I think this report is going to tell us. But before you ask any more, I need to get back there, read it myself, and consider the implications."

"Can't you say more?"

"Hmmm! Just that Abel Masters didn't die the way we think he did."

XXI

THURSDAY MORNING, STRAND and Bentsen were in the office by 8 a.m. as agreed, the first order of business being to make certain Lieutenant Montgomery knew what he needed to know.

"Good morning, gents," Montgomery said when Strand knocked and they walked in. It seemed clear their boss had been in quite early as usual, yet his desk was clean and tidy with a large, steaming mug of coffee in the middle of his blotter. Even as he leaned back in his state-issued desk chair, endangering the battered venetian blinds at his back, he waved his men in and then leaned forward, clearly with anticipation.

"It's about time you two showed up," he said with mock despair.

"Whatever you need, boss," Bentsen said.

"Yeah, sure. Always the last to know. I understand you finally brushed off the Bureau boys, and I'm only guessing that because they've stopped calling. Not because you told me."

"Sorry, Chief," Strand said. "We've been busy having all the fun you assign for us."

"So I hear. Now you've got two murders, and I'll bet little to show for it."

"Not so fast, Lieutenant. We've got this pretty well narrowed down. Neither murder was committed on federal property, so that let the feds out. One was committed on our turf, the first on Georgie Hallon's, so I need to ask you to make a call to him and give him the brush as well, so we don't have to run the obstacle course every time we're in Foreston."

Montgomery laughed. "Yeah, I heard you two nearly got arrested." He clearly enjoyed the image.

"OK, enjoy yourself. Now, we also need you to make an official request to Uncle Sam to release to us several employee personnel files and their associated background investigations."

"Hold it! That's no small deal. You know damn well, Strand, that puts the state in a box if anything amiss occurs, and I have no interest in attracting the attention of a US District Attorney for a security breach."

"Believe us, boss," Bentsen joined in, "we'll be careful, but Fletch is right, we're down to seven or eight suspects and those files will likely get us closer to the finish line."

"Not that I don't have a lot of confidence in you two, but didn't I hear you say your prime suspect was Al Rieger, and now he's left the building with Elvis?"

Sheepish, Strand replied, "OK, OK, that's ours, but we didn't know there's a lot more going on here, reaching into the political stratosphere, maybe."

"Please don't tell me that. I'm not that many years from retirement and I don't want to get there sooner than I plan to."

"I hear you," Strand said, "but you didn't get all those medals and commendations for being a shrinking violet, so I'm sure you're up to the task."

Montgomery stared at them. "Get the hell out of here and don't come back until you've got something to tell me over a good lunch. I'll get going with Hallon and a letter, and you might get going on that burning body case—the snow's melted, so you have no reason not to get out there."

"Shouldn't we have told him about what McCreary hinted to us?" Bentsen said as soon as they left Montgomery's office and were out of his earshot.

"Nah! We gave him enough to chew on. Dealing with Georgie and working that request through his boss in Harrisburg will give him indigestion as it is."

The pair boarded the Vic for the short ride from the Mercer Barracks to the courthouse, an eye-catching square structure of brick and limestone topped by a gleaming, gilded dome seen for miles around. They hustled out of the cold into a side entrance and clomped down the stairs to the chilly dungeon where McCreary worked his magic.

In his office, they found him at his desk wrapped in a tan wool sweater, well-worn with several food stains.

"Can't you get the county to get this office above sixty degrees?" Bentsen whined after their greetings.

"It's warmer than that, Joe, so make yourself comfortable. At least you guys are dressed for the winter weather down here." All three laughed.

"OK, so what's with all the drama?" Strand asked. "Just how did Masters die?"

McCreary cleared his throat, reached for his El Producto, tapped the ash, and put the stogie to his lips for a moment. "So, here's what we've got, men," he said, finally, always one to enjoy the drama.

"Can we get to the chase, Doc?" Bentsen said, coughing out a bit of smoke. "By the way, I thought no one was allowed to smoke here."

"Nobody has the balls to come in here and remind me of that," McCreary said, and put his cigar down. "Let's get to it, then. You'll remember that when we found the body, I said that something didn't add up about the scene. These findings confirm that suspicion," he said, tapping the paper in his hand.

"Get to it, will you?" Now it was Strand who was impatient.

"Masters was already dead when someone bashed his head in."

"What?" both detectives said at the same time.

"Yep. That's why there was so little blood. I'm speculating, of course, but it seems like the 'killer,' and I say that carefully, approached Masters from behind, thought he was asleep in his chair, and bashed him in the head without thinking about it."

"So," Bentsen said, while Strand nodded, thinking, "the man who hit him in the head didn't kill him at all. Then, how did Masters die? Heart attack or what?

"Oh, it was a heart attack, all right, Joe, but not one caused by nature. Masters was in perfect physical health. The autopsy proved that."

"Then what?" Strand said, gritting his teeth.

"When I did the original autopsy, the one anomaly was low blood sugar. What the more sophisticated test results show is that he'd been overdosed with insulin—that's putting it mildly—and that's what induced a heart attack, but right now, I can't give you a good time he died the first time."

"Holy crap!" said Strand. "So, when the would be killer dragged the body out, to him it was still warm enough in a warm house to have fooled him, is that right?"

"Yep," he said, nodding. "But I'm assuming the killer may have been wearing winter gloves, perhaps, and he wouldn't have noticed much cooling at all."

"Then who the hell killed Masters?" Bentsen said, throwing up his hands. "We're back at square one."

"Not really, Joe, because now we know the real cause of death, and the circle of suspects may get a little smaller."

"Not on our list, Doc," Strand said. "I don't think there's anyone on our list with any kind of medical background."

"Could be someone with medical knowledge or not," McCreary opined. "You see, a diabetic would know what an overdose would be, so it didn't have to be a doctor or nurse."

"Gee thanks, now the circle expands."

"Again, Joe, it depends upon your viewpoint. You're now looking for someone with knowledge of diabetes and access to insulin or a medical person of some sort."

"OK," Bentsen said, "but wait a minute. The real killer didn't just walk up to Masters and stick him with insulin, so how did that happen?"

"Joe, give me the Masters file," Strand said, gesturing to the folder Bentsen had thought to bring along. "Give me a minute."

Bentsen and McCreary waited, the latter taking a long puff from his El Producto, the former doing his best not to cover a cough.

"Here it is, maybe. When the forensics guys did their usual inspection of the house, they found two glasses that had been washed and put on the dish drain in the kitchen to dry. Is it possible, Doc, the real killer came in for a visit, drugged whatever Masters was drinking, and when he was unconscious, stuck him with the insulin?"

"Bingo. That's why you're still not giving tickets on I-80, Fletch. That's as likely a scenario as I could imagine."

"Can those glasses be tested, even if washed with soap?" Bentsen asked.

"We can, although getting a good result now would be chancy."

"But now we know," Strand said, "this was no simple murder.

XXII

A S THEIR MEETING with Coroner McCreary came to a close, Strand asked if he might have a private moment. "Joe, I'll just be a minute." Surprised, Bentsen shrugged his shoulders and stepped out into the hall.

"Doc, we've known each other a long time professionally, right?"

McCreary stopped tapping the ash from his cigar to look up, cocking his head as if to catch any nuance there. He smiled. "Sure, we have. What's on your mind, Fletch?"

"This is also a professional question I'm hoping you'll answer just between us."

McCreary lifted his cigar, took a puff, and waited.

"My brother, Paul, is in the hospital. He went in with a little back problem after getting a shot at his doctor's office to ease the pain and now, he's comatose with MRSA."

"And you're asking?" he prompted gently.

"I'm just a layman, of course, but I'm not sure how you get from A to B."

"An interesting question. Who's his doctor?"

"Nate Robertson," Strand answered, keeping his eye on McCreary for any reaction. There was.

McCreary looked down at his cigar, then to the side at something on his desk, not at Strand. "That's interesting as well."

"Your reaction suggests it's an answer, Doc. What're you telling me?"

McCreary nodded. "Robertson would not be my choice of medicos in this area—there are many better."

"What about my brother?" Strand asked and filled his friend in a bit about Paul, his medical history, and lifestyle.

"Oh, God, Fletch," McCreary said, weariness shading his voice, "even the best doc would have a handful there, but with Robertson, well…"

"You've got to say more to me, Doc. This is my brother. What should I do? Is it too late to get someone else in the picture?"

"I wish this were 2023 but this is 1993, and there's not much they can do if he's not responding to whatever mega doses of antibiotics Robertson is pumping into him, I'm sorry to say. And Fletch, to be clear here, I'm not a practicing physician for live people—I get 'em when all of that fails."

"Are you telling me you've seen too much of Robertson's handiwork—say, compared to others?"

"Truth be told, they all wind up here, but I do seem to see more of his patients."

"Dammit! I knew it all along when I heard Paul was seeing him."

"Listen, Fletch, I'm sorry about your brother. Again, even if he'd had the best guy in the area, we might have ended up in the same place. How long has Paul been unconscious?"

"Less than a week. We had the priest in already. Robertson seemed to imply it's a matter of time now."

McCreary lowered his eyes. "In that, at least, he's probably right. I'm sorry, Fletch, I wish there was more that I could do for you."

"Thanks, Doc. You've been a help," Strand said, and went to find his partner.

In the hall, huddling in his overcoat, Bentsen was doing fatal damage to a donut from the blind stand a floor above.

"Sorry, Joe, I just wanted to ask him about Paul."

"No problem, partner, I get it. I'm guessing your conversation with McCreary had as much to do with who his doctor is rather than what's going on with him."

Strand appraised his partner with growing appreciation for the accurate observation.

"Hey, not that it's any of my business, Fletch. I'm sorry I said anything."

"No apologies necessary, but since you brought it up, what's your opinion of Nate Robertson?"

Bentsen swallowed hard. "Hey, it was never for me to say, but when you said Paul was in the hospital and under Robertson's care, I only wished he'd be treated by someone else, but you know, there's no way to say anything at a time like that, is there?"

"No, I guess not. And your opinion of him isn't so good, then?

"My opinion isn't worth much on stuff like this. I know mostly what Sylvie tells me—the women are always comparing notes, and Robertson is not high on their list of the best and brightest. As far as medical stuff is concerned, he's a mile wide and an inch deep, they say."

At that moment, Strand's cell phone buzzed. "It's the barracks, for cryin' out loud. Are they lonely or what?" Strand answered, holding the phone so Bentsen could hear.

"Did you guys tell me McCreary had ordered more tests on Masters? Did you get the results yet?"

"Jesus, Chief, do you have microphones in the coroner's office? We just came from there."

"And?" Montgomery's voice was laden with sarcasm, as if to wonder why he had to ask the question.

"And it sure looks like someone with medical knowledge got to Masters before the guy who came in later and bashed his head in."

"Someone from the mine, then, or not?"

"Looks that way, Chief. That's what we're trying to find out."

"What's on tap for today, then?"

Strand looked at Bentsen and rolled his eyes. "Just what the citizens of the Commonwealth of Pennsylvania pay us for: detecting."

"OK, wise guy, just keep me in the loop. Calling Hallon is on my list, just doing your dirty work."

Strand laughed. Bentsen smiled. "Better you than us, Chief. Enjoy yourself," he said and clicked off before Montgomery could add to their burden.

"You know, Joe," Strand said, looking at the device in his hand, "I'm not sure if these things are going to help us or drive us crazy."

Bentsen chuckled. "Oh, you're right. It used to be if we wanted to check in, we'd get on the car radio, and even then, there'd be signal problems, or we'd find a landline to call in. But that communication was mostly one way—we were calling in, not the boss calling us every two minutes."

"That's the core of it. Now, we're reachable almost anytime, anyplace. We don't even have a minute to ourselves to think about what we're going to say when we do call in."

"Right again, but we do have to admit, these damn phones come in handy when we're chasing someone or something down, a report or whatever, which makes detective work a bit easier, don't you think?"

"Oh, don't get me wrong, Joe. You're right about that, but the downside of people calling us is all about their expectations. Everybody wants an immediate response. It's like this email thing they want us to use. Some people think we have nothing better to do than sit in front of that silly screen waiting for their stupid messages."

"You know one thing I like about this thing? It's about the same size and weighs as much as a piece of Sylvie's cheesecake."

"Is it all about food with you?" Strand asked laughing. "But you know what scares me most?"

"What?"

"I'm already getting used to having it in my pocket, and feel like I'm not all together without it. What's worse is that I'm worried that my kids will begin to think one of these devices is their best friend. Maybe we should just have a bad signal most of the time," he added, and winked.

"Hah! Don't let 'em hear you talk like that, Fletchy boy, they'll put you out to pasture with the dinosaurs, and you're not even close to retirement."

"One of the things we always loved about this job, Joe, besides doing the job and bringing bad guys to justice, is the freedom of our workday. Now, Montgomery, or whoever, can push a few buttons and have us by the scruff of the neck within a few seconds."

"Makes me want to run my state car into one of those new cell phone towers some days."

"Shhh! They might hear us."

XXIII

"JOE, WHY DON'T we get lunch and head over to Foreston and see what there is to see with that John Doe burning body case Montgomery's been bugging us about?"

After a stop at Arby's, next to the Walmart store in Foreston, the pair threaded the Vic through the borough until they found the left turn next to the old Carnegie Library, and headed north toward I-80.

No matter what was going on in the world around it, the Borough of Foreston always seemed to go on. Aside from several thriving smaller industries, the town boasted a top-notch college of about 2,400 students that consistently found itself on the best small college lists across the country. Strand and his family lived on a street that led to one of the school entrances, and the annual Homecoming parades added to the town's *Leave It to Beaver* ambience.

A town of about 8,000 people and 1,000 dogs, there wasn't much crime, except for the killing spree three years earlier. To say that cooperation between the borough's chief of police, Georgie Hallon, was at a low ebb back then was putting it mildly. The fact that Strand lived on the very block where the first murder occurred and that his own son was endangered, did nothing to change Hallon's attitude toward the Pennsylvania State Police.

It was all the more reason that surprise joined their day when a Foreston Police cruiser flashed its lights at them as they passed the Broad and Pine Streets junction. Bentsen steered the Vic to a spot near the jewelry store as the cruiser pulled alongside. Bentsen lowered his window as the passenger-side window went down on the cruiser. Inside was none other than Chief Georgie Hallon himself.

"Hey, Joe. Hey, Fletch. Just heard from Montgomery, and I just wanted to say thanks for the heads up, and if there's any support you need, just let me know." Hallon said all of this without a smile or a grimace, without a snarky word or a sarcastic snort.

For a moment, Bentsen and Strand were struck speechless, as Hallon stopped speaking and stared at them.

Strand broke the silence and said, unbelieving what he'd just heard, "Thanks, Chief. We'll keep you posted." It was as if the iceberg that sank the Titanic had just melted on North Broad Street.

Bentsen could force only a nod.

The cruiser's window went up, and Hallon drove off, leaving the troopers dumbfounded.

"Christ, Joe, what was that all about?"

"He's off the hook, Fletch! His budget is safe," he added, then laughed out loud. "That guy is unbelievable."

"Other words have crossed my lips over the years, but I guess he's turned a page, whatever the reason. We'll have to go with that."

Bentsen pulled back into traffic, and as he did so, the largest snowflakes either man had ever seen began to pelt the Vic's windshield. By the time they'd reached the Chestnut Street light, every horizontal surface boasted a new, glistening white coat.

"Think we can drive out of this?" Strand asked.

"Let's see what a few more miles gives us."

When they reached Crestview Cemetery, two more inches of snow had fallen, and visibility was near zero. Without asking for Strand's opinion, Bentsen turned the Vic into the cemetery's main entrance and made a quick U-turn. "I've never seen the lake effect this far south, Fletch, and I think we'll do well to make it safely home this afternoon."

"I can salute that, Joe. Even if we could go the next few miles to the crime scene, there wouldn't be anything to see there today."

"Hey, you know what's bothering me?" he asked, continuing without a pause. "It's the insulin business. That's one tricky deal from what McCreary said."

"Not a crime of passion. The killer went there with a purpose."

"And if the doc is right about the glasses in the kitchen, they had to have known each other," Bentsen said.

"But Masters had no relatives or friends around. Just who the hell would that have been?"

XXIV

I T WAS THE beginning of the weekend, and Friday night was usually movie night on TV at the Strand house, but if there was something good at the Guthrie, it was an easy ten-minute walk to the venerable theater on Broad Street. *Groundhog Day* was playing and it was one of the few Fletcher and Aurora Strand thought the kids could safely see and appreciate. Mac the beagle was not keen on missing out on movie night, but it couldn't be helped.

At fourteen, Aarie enjoyed movies with a sense of humor. Anna was just turning eleven and ready for what she must have thought was adult fare. What they especially enjoyed about the film was that it took place not that many miles from where they lived, and its subject was something everyone talked about and awaited with some amusement every year. That the real Groundhog Day had occurred just a month earlier, and that Bill Murray had them all confused before it was all over made it even funnier.

Strand laughed with his family, held hands with Aurora, and scarfed down the warm, buttered popcorn, but his mind was on Paulie. A call to the hospital told him there'd been no change in his condition. He was stable, but comatose, they said, yet his body continued to process fluids and his vital signs were acceptable.

Had they not already invited Jonathan over for dinner the following evening, it would have been a good time to take the kids back in to see their uncle, but given commitments hemming them in, a visit earlier in the day was not going to happen.

On their walk home, Aurora said, "Fletch, I know you were with us tonight, but were you really with us?"

Holding hands, he squeezed hers through her mittens, and gave her a weak smile. "I wasn't thinking about work, if that's what you're asking, hon. Paulie won't leave my mind, and quite frankly, I'm not looking forward to Jonathan tomorrow evening."

"What's he been doing all this time?"

"I think he jetted back to DC for a couple of days, but came back for the weekend. For whatever reason, he likes to hang out with Dr. Robertson, who's been putting him up."

"You don't feel guilty about that, do you, Fletch?"

He looked at her, made a face, and said, "Heck, no! He's hard to take over a dinner table, and if he stayed here, it'd be like he was using us as a focus group."

"He wouldn't like our opinions, would he?" she asked and laughed.

"So, Sunday, hon, let's go to Mass and head right over to the hospital with the kids. I just don't know how much longer Paulie can go."

Aurora squeezed her husband's hand. She had known the feeling of great loss herself and made it her life's goal to get her family through whatever faced them.

∾

Promptly at five o'clock, Jonathan Strand rattled the tarnished brass knocker on the front door of the old white brick house on Pine Street, and just as promptly, Anna pulled the door open and welcomed her godfather into the front hall.

Someone used to Washington courtesies, Jonathan came laden with flowers for Aurora, a bottle of wine for Fletch, and a thoughtful gift for the kids to share: a five-hundred-piece jigsaw puzzle, something he knew they always enjoyed together.

The chatter was pleasant as the adults stood around the island in the kitchen, munching crackers and cheese and sipping a room-temperature Merlot.

"So, what are we having, dear sister-in-law?" he asked sweetly.

"You're at the home of an Italian girl through and through, Jon, so you know it's not going to be pork bellies!" she responded and everyone laughed. "Seriously, this is just Saturday night supper here in Foreston—nothing like in our Capital City—so you'll have to be satisfied with seven-layer lasagna, a salad, and the best garlic bread you'll ever have."

"Sounds good, Aurora, but can that bread match the garlic bread they used to serve at Anthony's Restaurant—swimming in oil?"

"Better not be! I told Fletch the second time he took me there, the food was great, but I'd have to have my clothes dry-cleaned after each visit. The garlic!"

"Ah, but you'll have to admit, it kept the vampires away, right?"

They all laughed at that, too, a shared memory they could all enjoy. Then Jonathan changed the subject.

"Perhaps we shouldn't talk about work, Fletch, but you knew I'd ask about the Masters case—how's that going?"

"I won't talk details, of course, but you're aware there's been a second murder?"

"I heard—I have someone on my staff keeping tabs on it—from a distance."

Strand nodded, annoyed. "It appears one or both may have been committed by someone working in the mine, someone trusted, with a security clearance."

"No chance of tamping down the media frenzy, is there?" It really wasn't a question so much as a wish.

"The public need not get themselves worked up, I agree, but there's always leaks—you know about those, don't you, Johnnie?—and what gets out won't be coming from me, my boss, or my partner. That I can guarantee you."

"So, what else?"

"Nothing else I'm at liberty to say right now, but there've been a few developments we'll pursue this coming week. This won't take too long, I don't think."

"Hope not," Jonathan said. "You know how politicians like bad news to disappear."

Strand chuckled. "Gee, it must be nice to snap their fingers at people like you, Johnnie, but we're not going to arrest someone who just looks good."

"All right, all right, no pressure. What about Stoddard? The one you asked about?"

Strand looked at his brother squarely. "He'd better not be getting a warning call from your staffer. I hope that's understood. Interfering with a criminal investigation would not look good on anyone's federal resume."

"N-no, Fletch, don't worry about it."

"Now, there's something I want to talk to you about," Strand began and gestured to his brother to follow him into another room, "and it's about the medical care our brother is getting."

"Don't start that again, please, Fletch. It is what it is."

"No, it's not, brother. I realize you and Nate Robertson are asshole buddies and you're trying to boost him into the White House inner circle, and I don't give a rat's ass about that. This is about our brother, the one nobody ever paid much attention to, the one you never cared for because of his personal life."

"Whoa there, Fletch. He's my brother, too."

"Then acknowledge that fact. For your information, I've asked around a bit," he said, not being exactly truthful, "and your pal is not the respected physician you seem to think he is."

Jonathan's eyes grew wide.

"What's more, if Paulie dies on his watch, I'm going to be asking a lot of questions, some of them officially."

"Jesus, Fletch, don't make a mess here—this could be embarrassing."

"For you and your pal, maybe, but that'll be your problem."

"What the hell are you talking about! Look at his credentials. He's the best."

"You may be one of the few who thinks so. I wonder what the docs around here will say about him professionally when an OPM Investigator comes knocking. You do want a really good doctor attending to the White House bigshots, don't you?"

XXV

S UNDAY MORNING WAS like most others except that a new cold front was blowing in from the west to top the freezing conditions already in residence. Nonetheless, Strand and Aurora got the kids up for breakfast and readied themselves for Mass, wrapped in the warmest things they had for the walk from the parking lot to their parish church on North Broad Street. Lest he get himself into puppy trouble, Mac was crated, unhappily, while the family tended to a matter more eternal in nature.

Like most of their fellow congregants, the Strands thoroughly enjoyed the frescoed half dome over the altar and the striking stained-glass windows that caught the light on Sunday mornings. Steam-heated and barely air-conditioned, the old building was showing its wear, but nothing stopped Mike Pallison from making certain his congregants were warm and duly inspired in their house of God.

Strand thought about his brother during the first minutes of the Mass, and felt himself on auto-pilot during the Old Testament first reading, the chanting of a Psalm, and even the second reading from Mark. From their usual pew near the left front of the church, which placed them in the priest's direct line of sight when he spoke from the pulpit, Strand heard Father Pallison read the gospel of Matthew.

"But about that day and hour no one knows, not even the angels of heaven, nor the Son, but the Father alone..."

Is this God's message to me this morning?

"Therefore, be on the alert, for you do not know which day your Lord is coming. But be sure of this, that if the head of the house had known at what time of the night the thief was coming, he would have been on the alert and would not have allowed his house to be broken into. For this reason, you must be ready as well; for the Son of Man is coming at an hour when you do not think He will."

The closing hymn seemed to foretell the day's events. As the congregants sang "Lord of all Hopefulness," Strand shivered, hearing only the song's last words: "...Be there at our sleeping, and give us we pray, Your peace in our hearts, Lord, at the end of the day."

As they filed out of church, he was physically present, but otherwise, elsewhere. Jarred out of his reverie only because the device in his pocket began buzzing, he answered when they reached the vestibule. He and Father Pallison exchanged glances.

Once out the side door and down the steps, Aurora said, "Fletch, what is it?"

Strand glanced at his wife with a look that simply said "something has happened." Calling the number on the screen, he listened and then clicked off.

"The hospital. We need to hurry." He didn't need to say more.

～

On that particular Sunday, the entrance doors to the hospital were sheeted in ice as if warning the Strands the Reaper was present, searching. They hustled up to Paul's room, where the silence was complete except for the low hum of the electronics guarding the man under their care.

Bob was sitting by the bed, whispering into Paul's ear. "It's OK, Paulie, you can go if you need to. We're here with you." Then, "Fletch is here with his whole family. Aarie wants to hold your hand."

Aaron Strand went to the other side of the bed and put his hand into the one attached to his godfather. "Dad, Uncle Paul's hand is cold, really cold," he whispered, frightened, then leaned down and said, "I love you, Uncle Paulie, I'll love you forever."

Strand, Aurora, and Anna stood close, each with a hand on one of Paul's legs. There was no movement, not a flicker of an eyelash. Reaching in past Bob, Strand grabbed hold of his brother's right hand and whispered, "You were the best of us, Paulie! Love you."

Paul's hand rose up, then fell to the bed. The monitors went flat, their only sound a buzz, then a loud chirping to alert the nursing staff.

A young nurse raced into the room, checked Paul and then the equipment, then said, "I'll have to get the doctor, but I think he's gone."

Strand's eyes filled with tears and he turned to hold Aurora tight. Aarie came over to them and held on, too, but Anna went to Bob and put her arm around his shoulders while he sobbed quietly.

In a few minutes, Dr. Robertson entered the room, followed by Jonathan Strand. At first, the doctor did not seem aware of what had happened. It was apparent that when the nurse went for a doctor, it was to find whoever was on the floor, not Robertson.

Robertson went to the right side of the bed and tried to find a heartbeat or a pulse, to no avail. He didn't seem to know what to do next.

The doctor's behavior surprised Strand because if McCreary was correct, Robertson had had plenty of experience declaring someone dead, but Strand himself was too busy with his own grief to take the thought further. He glanced to his right to see Jonathan standing still, emotionless, cold, staring straight ahead. It was as if he didn't know the man who had just died.

XXVI

W HEN STRAND REGAINED his composure some minutes later, he led his wife and children into the hall while he called Father Pallison to give him the news and talk about a date for a Funeral Mass. Bob came out and joined them.

"Bob, before we go any further, what are your feelings about Paulie's burial rites?" He could barely get out the words speaking about his favorite brother in the past tense.

"We were partners, Fletch, but you know I have no legal rights here. I do know Paulie intended for you to manage things if he died first. I'm executor of his estate, but I defer to you and your family as to what's best, and I know Paulie would have wanted a Catholic service." He began to sob again, covering his face in his hands.

Strand put his hand on Bob's shoulder. "We'll get this done the way he would have wanted, Bob, and don't worry, nobody from our side will make any fuss about your role here."

"Speak for yourself, Fletch," Jonathan said—almost hissed—when he walked up to them. "I don't want this, this person handling Paul's affairs."

"You have nothing to say about it, Johnnie, and if you don't want to be embarrassed any further by Paulie's life, you best be as quiet as possible, and play the mourning brother if you have any warm blood in you."

~

Bob accepted the Strands' invitation to come to Foreston for the rest of the day, where they could meet with Cunningham's Funeral Home and deal with the myriad details attendant to a person's death. Strand and Bob spent the late afternoon with the funeral director—confirming some things with Father Pallison on speaker phone—and making sure everything would go well.

It was awkward, but Bob couldn't help himself. "Father," he asked while the priest was still on the line, "will the church object to me being present as Paul's partner? Will his lifestyle receive the blessing of the church?"

Without hesitation, Pallison's words came through the ether as if he were sitting there, comforting them all. "Bob, Fletch, I want you to know that Paulie will leave the church just as he entered it as an infant at the sacrament of Baptism, wrapped in the white garb of innocence before Almighty God. And Bob, you're welcome to be amongst us anytime."

"Th-thank you, Father," Bob said, his words halting in both surprise and relief, "but I have another question. Paulie wanted to be cremated—is that permitted by the church?"

"The Catholic Church's rule on this is pretty simple. Paul can be cremated, but you may not sprinkle his ashes or store them at home with you. They must be interred just as if they were his whole body."

"I understand, and I agree, if it's OK with the Strands."

"No one in my family will object, Bob."

"And Jonathan?" he asked, looking back at Strand.

"What about him?"

XXVII

WHEN MONDAY MORNING came, reluctance was the best descriptor for Strand's willingness to leave Aurora's warmth under their down quilt. Even as the alarm jangled and he slid one arm out into the cold air of the drafty old house, he tried to catalogue all the reasons why he needed to stay in bed. Mac sat waiting. He knew the routine.

"Fletch!" Aurora knew how to shout in a whisper. "Turn that darn thing off before you wake the kids."

"Ummm!"

"'Ummm' nothing," she said, "get up and get going. Joe's picking you up. Remember?"

"Unfortunately, I do." He threw back the quilt and did his best impression of bounding out of the sack, and heard Aurora laughing into her pillow.

One cup of coffee and thirty minutes later, he was donning his winter jacket and with his Christmas scarf from Anna, he was ready to face the world and David Stoddard. Turning back as he left, Strand reached down and gave his new best friend a good neck scratch, and Mac nearly knocked himself over with his wildly wagging tail.

~

Bentsen was sitting behind the wheel of the Vic sipping a steaming cup of coffee from Sheetz and listening to Froggy 95, apparently waiting until Strand was seat belted before saying anything.

"Sylvie and I are really sorry about your brother, Fletch. I'm bringing a meal with me when I get you tomorrow. Sylvie's working on it now."

"Oh man, thanks, Joe. That's really nice of you two—and Sylvie's a great cook."

"Brisket. You know, her favorite funeral meal."

Strand tried to laugh.

"Sorry. I shouldn't joke right now."

"Don't think about it, Joe. After yesterday at the hospital saying goodbye to Paulie and dealing with my jackass brother, Jonathan, I need the smiles."

"Well, for what it's worth, you won't have Jonathan hanging around to annoy you. He'll be gone soon."

"Not soon enough, my friend."

They drove toward the mine, but not at high speed. Between the school busses and skittish drivers, the going was slow on sleeted roads, yet untreated by the county boys. Their talk centered on Stoddard and what else was on the schedule between now and Paul's funeral on Wednesday.

"And if there's stuff you have to do for the service, let's just work all that in."

"Thanks, Joe. Between Father Pallison and Cunningham's, everything's been pretty well worked out. Paul couldn't be in better hands."

"Paul's partner, Bob. Is he OK with everything?"

"Oh, yeah. He'll be fine, but you know, Paulie's personal life was never an open book, so just you wait. When Wednesday morning comes, the tiny wheels turning in every old lady's head might make noise louder than the organ and the singing."

Bentsen laughed. In two more minutes, they were gliding, carefully, down the long ramp and through the wafting air at the mine's portal, but not before passing a gaggle of TV trucks and reporters. They shouted at the state Vic, to no avail.

"Lafferty made a comment about the media piranhas being all over this—good thing we have him and Montgomery to block and tackle for us. That's one complication we can do without."

Bentsen nodded. "You got that right." At the gate, they had to wait a moment until the guard on duty distributed badges to the foot traffic.

"Is there more to know about how the badge thing works?"

"Well, look over to the left," Bentsen said. "You saw the big stand with the series of doors on hinges yesterday. Each person who works here has a badge with their picture and a number, and each is color coded by facility."

"So, no one walks in or out of here without getting their badge or turning one in, is that what they said?"

"Yep, except when they don't notice."

"Then a blank hook on any of the doors would mean someone never left, right?"

"Yep." Bentsen sighed.

"But when we saw Masters's body with McCreary that day, there was no badge as I recall, right?"

"Yeah, come to think of it, and there was none listed with his effects. Hmmm!"

"If their system is as tight as they think it is, that's one more confirmation that Masters was not murdered here, but came in as a dead man," Strand said.

"But Rieger had his on him, didn't he?"

"Of course, he was still in the mine, but on his way out."

"Yeah, on his way out," Bentsen said.

Strand rolled his eyes. "You sound like that cop on *Law & Order*."

Once inside, Joe Novak, the Center's Acting Director, came in the conference room to see them. "And what are we accomplishing today, gentlemen?"

"We," Strand said, with emphasis on 'we,' "need to interview David Stoddard."

"I'll see that he's brought up, and of course, I'd like to join you."

"And of course, that isn't how we work, Mr. Novak. Once we're finished with Stoddard, we'd like to chat with you. We think what observations you might have will add to our knowledge here," Strand added, the butter dripping from several syllables.

Novak nodded, smiled, and said, "I'll get him for you, and when you're ready, I'll make myself available."

It took several minutes, but finally, the David Stoddard they'd heard so much about strode in with an air of ownership about him. That his belt buckle entered the room a full second before him did nothing to dispel the image of bureaucratic caricatures from time immemorial. Not a very tall man to begin with, his height seemed diminished by his width, ill-fitting clothing, and his generally less than kempt appearance. Strand did not wonder why John Lafferty and the likes of David Stoddard were a mismatch, and despite the man's title of Branch Manager, his appearance did not marry up to the office. *Shame on me! Judging someone by their appearance.* As Stoddard shambled in and forced himself between the chair's two arms, Strand avoided looking at Bentsen, but simply wore the best smile the circumstances allowed.

"What do you need from me?" Stoddard demanded without preamble. He sported wispy brown hair, not recently washed, over a face that his mother would love but that would not catch the eye of many passing women. The image screamed couch potato, someone who had never lifted anything heavier than a carton of ice cream, yet Strand wondered if there wasn't more to the specimen in front of him. A lot more.

"We'd like to get your thoughts on a few matters, Mr. Stoddard," Strand began.

As he sat facing the two detectives, he said nothing, but checked to see if his hands were properly clasped on the table in front of him. Pierced by a pair of sunken brown eyes flickering between his hands and the detectives, Stoddard's sallow skin appeared wax like under the fluorescent lights. He licked his lips constantly.

"How would you describe your relationship with Abel Masters?"

"I don't know what difference that makes."

"Let us wonder about that, sir," Bentsen said.

"I didn't like him, and I don't like working here. These people are idiots and he was the head idiot."

Strand: "Why did you come here?"

"Because I needed the job. Mr. Lafferty said this might prove a nice opportunity for me to build a good reputation."

"Nice way to put that," Bentsen said, "but what did he mean by that? Was there something wrong with your reputation in Washington?"

"N-no, there wasn't. Maybe he just thought it would be good experience for me before I returned to take his job. I'm sure I'd be in line for it."

"Wouldn't you have to have Masters's job first?" Strand asked, eyeing him intently.

"Why would I want to be the farmer in charge of this henhouse?"

"You don't like the people here?" Bentsen asked.

"Are you kidding? The big things for them are the foodfests Masters let them have, getting off for hunting season, and weddings at the firehall. You know, stupid stuff like that."

"Some of these folks use that deer meat to feed their families," Strand said through closed teeth.

"If that's what they prefer. That's not my life choice."

"Maybe that's not a choice for them either," Strand went on, "and what's so special about your life choices."

"Listen, Detective whatever your name is, I come from an important Maryland family—people in my family do big things, not tractor pulls."

Strand chuckled out loud. "Wow, you do see yourself high up on a cloud, don't you, Stoddard? Is that how Abel Masters saw you?"

"I could care less how he saw me, and now he's dead. Good riddance. He was a fool just like the rest of them here."

"You're incredibly smart," tacked Bentsen. "I'll bet you've got his murder all figured out."

"I have no idea how or where somebody got him. Same with

Rieger, if you want to know. And neither do I care, just so we're clear."

"But you do care, Dave," Strand stayed in, "because if you can't explain yourself well enough, we just might have to invite you over to our house for a more structured interview."

"It's David, and hey, what the hell is going on here. I didn't kill anybody."

"Now, David," Strand continued, "get a civil tongue in your mouth, and keep in mind this is a criminal investigation involving two separate murders, and we need to know your whereabouts for four time periods. Are you listening?"

Stoddard stared back unbelievingly, but found a nod to offer.

"First, where were you last Sunday evening, after 5 p.m.?"

"God, that was a week ago." Perspiration beads glistened on his forehead. "Let me think. I'm pretty sure I went to County Market to stock up for the week, then to a movie at the Guthrie, then home."

"What time was that?"

"Around 10, I think."

"What was playing at the Guthrie?"

"Jeez, it, it was *Groundhog Day.*"

"Alone?" Bentsen asked.

Stoddard nodded.

"Anybody see you there?" Strand asked.

"In fact, I know the woman who makes the popcorn. She'd remember me. I bought two large with extra butter and salt."

"What's so special about that? A lot of people buy more than one popcorn," Bentsen said.

"Yeah, but I went out in the middle to buy the second one. She was annoyed. She should remember me."

"You'd better hope so," Strand said, "and by the way, where is home?"

"I live in Harrisville," Stoddard said and gave an address on Black Road.

"So, you bought groceries, drove them back to Harrisville, then drove back to Foreston to see a movie?" Strand asked, incredulous.

"Really?"

"That's not how it went. It was so cold out, Detective," Stoddard responded with sarcasm, "I didn't have to worry about food spoiling. The opposite was true. My half gallon of milk was partly frozen when I came out of the theater."

"Where'd you park?" Bentsen asked, his pen poised above his notepad.

"In front of Tower Church. Almost nobody was there, so I got a spot close in."

"That's one, and believe me, Stoddard, we'll check that out. Now, two, what about first thing Monday morning?"

Stoddard exhaled, looked down at his watch, and licked his lips. "That Monday, I was here earlier than usual because we've been behind on our caseload and I wanted to get a jump on the week."

"What time was that?"

"Around 5:45 a.m.," Stoddard said, "no later."

"And the Center was open?"

Stoddard thought about it. "Yes, I'm certain of it. I don't have a key so I couldn't have gotten in if it'd been locked."

"Al Rieger told us the doors aren't opened until 6," Bentsen said.

"I don't care what he told you. I walked right in. There were lights on in the warehouse, so I had no trouble finding my way to the office."

Strand: "And you came in which door?"

"The one nearest the warehouse garage doors."

"Who went in with you?"

"Nobody came in with me, but there were people in here. I could hear voices. Some people get here early every morning—God only knows why—and they queue up at the warehouse door—where all the rank-and-file employees enter."

"Who opened up then? Rieger?"

"I have no idea, but now that I think about it, one of the garage doors was open, and that was unusual."

"Why didn't you walk in through the garage door, then? That would have been the closest entry point on your path."

"Force of habit. The main door was propped open with a wooden wedge, same as always in the mornings."

Bentsen nodded. "You walked in or drove? Can anyone account for your movements after you entered?"

"Walked." He thought for a moment, "I think one or two Case Reviewers were in and getting their first coffee when I turned the light on in my office and went in." He gave their names.

"See any vehicles parked in the cutout?"

"I can't remember whether I did or not. There had to have been at least one—whoever opened up drove in, besides Rieger, of course, but I didn't see him until later.

"OK," Bentsen said, "now three: where were you the afternoon and evening before Al Rieger's body was found?"

"I know I was one of the last people to leave the night before. The fat guard gave me a look. That's something else I could do without."

Without commenting on the irony of Stoddard's description of Sergeant Richardson, he went on: "One of the last?"

"Well, Rieger's car was still there and I think some people from his branch were still there—I could hear someone rattling around."

"No idea who?" Strand eyed him carefully.

"No, of course not. It wasn't my job to be checking everything."

"Was Rieger in his car?"

"How would I know? I paid no attention."

"The next morning?"

"Nothing unusual. I walked in around 6 a.m. with a dozen people on the pathway, there were several cars in the cutout area, including Rieger's. There was only one odd thing."

Bentsen: "What's that?"

"Well, only about six people are allowed to park in the cutout area, but people rarely pull their cars in the same spot. It's kinda first in, first out. But Rieger's black SUV was in the same spot as the evening before."

"Interesting," Strand said. "Who gets to park there?"

"Rieger, naturally, he's the facility manager. Then the opening supervisor—that day it was the supervisor for the Data Entry

Branch—that's where all the women work who come in at 6. I don't know any of them. Then, there's one or two employee vehicles for the disabled, and a visitor's spot or two."

"Who else remained the evening before?"

"Didn't you ask that? No one, except Rieger."

"When Rieger's body was found, I saw you in the crowd," Strand said. "Any particular reason you were out there?"

"N-no. I sometimes walk out of the Center for the cooler air."

"You do see why we have a problem with you, Stoddard?"

"Why is that? What did I do?"

"For one thing," Strand continued, "you had it in for Masters, didn't you, and you made no secret about it. You wanted his job, and made a stink when he walked around with the erector set on his broken arm. You thought you might be out of a job if privatization went forward because then Masters could fire you."

With each phrase Strand spoke, Stoddard shifted in his chair, clasped and unclasped his hands, and looked everywhere but at his interrogators. His shirt collar was wet. "Look, guys," he finally said, "I don't care how it looks, but I didn't kill either of those two, and I'm sure I would have gotten Masters's job eventually."

Strand snorted. "Don't you see, pal, you've got motive and opportunity. We're just not sure of the means yet?"

"So, what would be my motive for killing Rieger? I hardly knew the guy."

"Maybe," Bentsen said softly from the side, "maybe he saw something the morning Masters's body was found, and he made the mistake of letting you know that."

"You're crazy!"

"Nothing crazy about it," Strand said, "and with a few more pieces of evidence, we could arrest you with a smile."

Bentsen looked at his partner, then at Stoddard. "You're free to go for now, David," he said, with a dab of sarcasm attached to the suspect's name, "but don't leave the area. I think we'll have more to talk about—soon."

XXVIII

A S THEY TOOK the few steps up the hall to Joe Novak's office, Strand elbowed his partner and asked, "Why haven't we interviewed this guy earlier?"

"Who? Novak? I guess neither of us saw him as a suspect or even a witness. Jeez! Hope we didn't screw this up."

The next half hour with Masters's deputy underlined the impression of Novak as an unabashedly ambitious bureaucrat who had something to gain by Masters's demise. The interview took place in his office, though they had no doubt who would control the interview.

"We noted that you did not arrive at the mine until well after Masters's body was discovered, Joe," Bentsen began, one "Joe" to another. "Is that the usual time you arrive?"

"That's right, about 9 a.m. usually. I live a few miles south of Butler and so, my arrangement with Abel was to come in about that time. It's not a short drive."

That didn't make a lot of sense to Strand. Where he lived shouldn't affect when he came in, and if Masters stayed late to take west coast calls, wouldn't it make sense for Novak to be the early bird? He decided to let it go because it probably was irrelevant to the matter at hand. Instead, he said, "It just seems odd for the two of you to work later."

"W-well," he said trying to clear his throat and chuckle at the same time, "you know how it is. I'm a married guy with three kids and life's a little more complicated for me than for Masters, who, who had nobody." At once, Novak seemed to realize how asinine he sounded.

Strand just nodded, not in agreement, but just in acknowledgement that a sound was heard. "Yeah—it was probably tough for you working for a dedicated program guy like Masters."

"T-true enough," Novak said, and began to click his ballpoint pen, looking like he wished he was someplace else. "Honestly, for me, this is a job. For Abel, it was his life."

"And death, apparently," Strand said.

"So, both of you worked late, then?" Bentsen asked.

"Well, not always. I like to have my evenings with my kids."

"Then, for certain, you didn't arrive in the mine until your usual time last Monday?"

"Definitely, and before you ask, I had already left the mine—you can check at the front gate—when A-Al apparently was murdered, poor Al, and so I wish you'd quit giving me the third degree."

"Oh, this isn't the third degree, Joe. We save that for our little torture chamber back at the barracks," Strand said with a slimy smile.

"That's not funny, guys," he said looking at both detectives. "Why are you spending so much time with me, anyway?"

"Can't you guess, Joe?" It was Bentsen. "You're the second banana here, and in our experience, second bananas always want to be top banana, so you can imagine why we'd be curious about you and your whereabouts."

"I see, I guess, but what would that have to do with Al Rieger?"

"We think that 'poor Al,' as you call him, must have known or seen something about Abel Masters that got him killed. It's that simple."

Novak nodded.

"You see," Strand said, "it's sometimes like dominoes. Once one falls, well, the killer panics and wants to cover it up. It never works, but killers always think they're the smarter ones."

Novak swallowed hard. "Look, men, it's this way. I know I'm never gonna be the number one here or anywhere. It's just not me." He shrugged. "I guess I've always been pegged as the number two, the guy who does the scut work the top guy doesn't want to do."

"Is that how it was with you and Masters?" Strand asked.

"That's what John Lafferty told me would be a successful combination for me with Abel Masters, yes. That's not to say I wouldn't want and enjoy his job, but except in this circumstance, I..." Novak stopped in mid-thought when he realized the implication of his words.

"Thanks, Joe—that's probably one of the more honest answers we've heard this week."

"Joe," Bentsen continued, "just how many people have keys to this place, anyway?"

Novak cleared his throat. That's an excellent question, one of the first I asked when I arrived here. Seems no one actually knows."

"What?" Strand jumped in. "This is a secure facility and no one knows how many keys there are?"

Novak chuckled, embarrassed. "I'm afraid so, guys. Naturally, Masters and Rieger had one each, I have one, the opening supervisor has one, and the people at Underground Storage have one or more. Perhaps some of Rieger's people."

"So, excluding Masters, there are any number of people who could have come in here early for whatever purpose?"

"In theory, yes, but you know, guys, we've never had the slightest problem with security here. We all have too much to lose."

"When you said 'opening supervisor,' what did that mean?"

"The first line supervisors take turns opening up in the morning, one week at a time, with about eleven people in the pool."

"Holy crap!" Bentsen said. "And they all have keys?"

"Oh, no, guys," Novak said, as if to reassure them. "There's one key fastened to a foot-long wooden handle—actually a piece of cut-off broom handle, I think—and they pass it around."

"But anyone could make a copy if they wanted."

"Of course, but like I said, guys, we've never had a problem with someone misusing it."

"Until now."

"If the key was misused."

"By you, perhaps?" Bentsen asked, smiling.

"No, not by me."

"One last question, Joe," Strand said. "Would you have survived if this place privatized?"

Novak's face reddened. "H-how would I know that?"

"Just wondering, Joe. Just wondering."

~

"What do you think?" Bentsen asked, as they climbed into the Vic parked in the cutout.

"Well, not Mr. 'guys' in there. Whoever killed Masters had to have been taller and more muscular than Joe Novak, who probably has trouble lifting the lifts he wears in his shoes, and what's more, he was probably being honest about how Lafferty saw him. But Stoddard? He's another matter altogether."

"Yeah, him. His puzzle pieces don't fit together, do they?" asked Bentsen, guiding the Vic through the portal and up the ramp. "But a guy his size doesn't strike me as Charles Atlas either."

"That's a point, but," Strand said, "but often, guys like him have more strength than you might think."

"Right."

"We don't have nearly enough to pin anything on him, but yet? You heard me warn him not to leave the area. Something's going on with that guy, but we're just not seeing it yet. A couple of murders, or what?"

Strand's cell phone buzzed a few minutes after exiting the mine. "Marty, what's up?" He spoke into the device for a minute or two and hung up. "Marty Cunningham—just some stuff about Paul's funeral on Wednesday."

"What time will that be? Sylvie and I want to be there."

"Thanks, Joe. It will be appreciated. Paul was well liked, but I don't know how many people will turn out."

They drove through the large snowflakes drifting down, just enough to make the wipers swish and break the silence.

"Well, that was a long morning! I think we earned our lunch. You know what let's do, Joe? Let's stop in Harrisville at The Spot for some lunch, and as long as we're close by, why not drive by Stoddard's residence on Black Road?"

"And tomorrow?"

"Didn't I mention it? John Lafferty and I spoke this weekend. He and his wife are coming for Masters's funeral, whenever that is, but that's too long to wait for the files he's gathered, so I thought I'd scoot down to Breezewood tomorrow morning and pick those up."

"Hey, no problem. While you're doing that, why don't I check out Stoddard's claims as best I can, and see where we're at?"

"A plan. And after we check out Stoddard's place, why not head to New Wilmington and see how the Amish live?"

~

The Spot built its reputation in the 1940s when it was, indeed, the widest spot on Route 8 between Franklin and Butler. A favorite for farmers and truckers and local folks looking for a cooked meal out, Strand always told Bentsen it was a place he had to check out.

"Remember, don't order the coffee here," Strand warned.

Bentsen laughed out loud. "Right, I've heard those stories about the old lady who runs the place. Do you think they're true?"

"We'll see. Let's grab a booth in the room where the counter seats are and just watch."

That they did. As they polished off their cheeseburgers and fries and sipped their Cokes, they eyed the steely old woman working the counter where several truckers and business people were inhaling the hot plate specials. Nearly all had a steaming mug of coffee occupying the standard tan crockery that out-of-the-way places like The Spot put out on the table.

"Watch her, Fletch. Any minute now," Strand whispered.

Bentsen looked up from his notepad. The half dozen men who'd occupied the stools were clearing out, their lunch hour over, and Hattie Reynolds began grabbing plates and silverware, but not the coffee mugs.

For a woman who looked every bit of ninety years of age, she was agile and quick. The detectives were careful not to stare, but soon, she began collecting some tan mugs, but not others. They heard the clatter of dishes going into the tubs behind the counter, and only when she felt certain none of the remaining patrons would notice, she picked up the rest of the mugs—each of which must have had some black coffee left in them—and dumped their contents into the giant urn she'd later top off for the dinner trade.

"Talk about a blend," Bentsen said. The men waited a minute or two, then took their checks from the table and walked up to the register at the end of the counter where Hattie had a comfortable perch from which to survey her empire.

"Coffee smells awfully strong, Hattie," Bentsen said as he paid his check and left her the change.

"Fresh as can be, young man! Best George Howe makes. Want a cup for the road? Awfully cold out there."

"No thanks," Bentsen said and turned his head, while Strand, paying his own check, struggled with his composure.

Out in the Vic, they both guffawed at her public chutzpah. In a stream of debris left to them by the Grim Reaper, Hattie Reynolds's Spot was a welcome island of decent food and comic relief.

～

At first, the detectives had trouble identifying the Stoddard address. Snow covering roadside mailboxes, or a lack of markings elsewhere on the properties along the sparsely populated Black Road, made a bit of work for them. Finally, they narrowed it down to a place most people would never call a home, but an improved shack.

It was a box no more than twenty feet square covered with deteriorating asbestos brick siding along one end of which was a gravel patch serving as a driveway. "The snow actually gives the place a better look than we'd otherwise find it," Bentsen said as he slowly guided the Vic past what appeared to be an empty building. "Stoddard has no family?"

"Right on both counts. You'd think there'd be some smoke coming out of that metal chimney. It does make me curious, though. As a Branch Manager, he makes enough to afford something ten notches above what we're looking at."

"Well, OK, curiosity satisfied, but another piece that doesn't fit. Let's get out of here."

XXIX

I T WAS SLOW going to New Wilmington, some fifteen miles west
of Foreston and the same distance south of Mercer, territory more
familiar to Bentsen than to Strand. For the most part, they listened to the radio as the big flakes of snow they'd earlier encountered
piled up several inches.

"Sure you want to do this today, Fletch?"

"What else? Besides, I didn't see anywhere in the files that anyone
had told Masters's family about his death, and it's been a week now."

"Christ," Bentsen swore. "Who dropped that ball? This won't be
fun."

Before reaching New Wilmington, according to directions from
Lafferty, they made a broad left turn at the Amish Schoolhouse, a
landmark for all who traveled SR208, and skidded up the sloping
road beside the tall pines, up and down several hills, the asphalt
plowed but not salted, and finally made the village of Fayette and
turned left, deeper into a part of the world still thriving in the nine-
teenth century.

A few more turns, and at last they were going up a long gravel
road toward a large farming complex of neat wooden structures all
shut up on a snowy day like today. They'd noticed no buggy tracks

or signs of horse hockey. All was quiet as the snow drifted down.

None of the buildings needed paint, and they gleamed in their white cladding, even in the surrounding snow. There was no fancy trim, just plain boards made in their own sawmills. Even the clapboards on the main house had been made by them or by a neighbor, and the glass in the wooden windows seemed like it had been handed down through several generations. Nothing was wasted. The only color confronting them was the bright blue door suggesting, some said, that a marriageable daughter lived there.

"See the smoke coming out the chimney?" Bentsen asked as he pointed upward. "They cook with wood, heat with with coal, so what that means is one of the women is preparing dinner."

Before they shoved themselves out of the car into the lazy snow, Bentsen said, "I don't know what your experience has been with these folks, Fletch, but they're careful, cautious, yet very polite people of old values and a strict code of behavior."

"I'd heard that, Joe, but I can't recall ever having contact with them on a criminal matter."

"Me neither. I have no idea how this is going to go."

"Since you're Mr. Big & Gentle, you want to go first?"

Bentsen looked at him, as if handed the nasty end of the stick, and nodded.

Up the stairs they went onto the covered porch, swept spotless. Stamping their feet, the men shivered as Bentsen put a gloved hand to the blue wooden door. In an instant, a girl in her late teens or early twenties pulled it open and beckoned them to step in.

"May we please speak to Mr. Eli Mast?"

They could hear a creak of wood against wood, and out of the corner of his eye, Strand could see a bearded man push himself up from the rocker and look their way with some hesitation. He was clad in worn jeans, a light-blue work shirt, open at the collar, and a heavy black wool sweater. He gingerly made his way toward them in several short steps.

"What can we do for you, sirs?" His voice raspy, he planted the corncob pipe in a corner of his lips and waited. He appeared to be about sixty.

"We're detectives with the Pennsylvania State Police, Mr. Mast," Bentsen began as agreed, "and we'd like to speak with you and Mrs. Mast, if she's available."

As if on cue, out from the kitchen strode a powerhouse of a woman about the same age as her husband, but not shy of heft under her heavy wool skirt, purple blouse, and white apron crocheted with small blue flowers. She was drying her hands on the apron as she walked into the room. Present but saying nothing, she appeared to wait for her husband.

"Come this way," said Mr. Mast and the three followed him into what might pass for a living room and dining room with a large cast iron stove in the corner. The old man took his rocker while Mrs. Mast found a chair to the side but slightly behind him.

Strand and Bentsen found other chairs and positioned them three to four feet from their hosts. Bentsen took off his jacket and put it to the side as Strand did the same. The room was warm.

"It's nice and toasty in here," Bentsen said, struggling to begin the one conversation he hated to have more than any in the world. His embarrassed chuckle only added to the awkwardness of the moment. The Amish said nothing.

Strand noticed that four children—all girls, the youngest being in mid-teens—hovered near the opening to another room, not quite out of sight from their elders. What caught his eye was a girl of about seven who was being held by the oldest. The young one had a leg missing below the knee. She was smiling, snug in the arms of her sister.

"Are these four yours, Mr. and Mrs. Mast?" Strand asked, attempting to rescue an awkward beginning.

"Y-yes, they're..." began Mrs. Mast but silenced herself.

"These are our youngest, Mr. Strand," the old man said, "and there's an older son out in the barn."

Strand smiled, taking in the parents who appeared much older than their age. He expected them to have been the children's grandparents. "Detective Bentsen and I are deeply sorry to come with bad news, I'm afraid, Mr. and Mrs. Mast. You see, your son, Abel Masters, was found dead last week, and I'm terribly sorry no one has been here to tell you before now."

Strand could see Mrs. Mast stir, her hands unable to stay in her lap, but with some invisible strength, gripped the side bars of her seat and remained still.

Mr. Mast took his pipe from his mouth and said, "We have no son like that, sir."

"Pardon, me, Mr. Mast, you and Mrs. Mast are listed as his father and mother, next of kin, at this address. Is there some mistake?" Bentsen inquired politely.

"No mistake, Detective. Abel Mast died to us many years ago and to us, his passing is of no matter."

Mrs. Mast could hardly help herself. "Eli?" When there was no response, she repeated herself. "Eli?" It was a plaintive call. The old man turned and looked at her but said nothing.

"You see, Detective Strand, Abel left us at Rumspringa," she answered.

"How old was he when you last saw him, then?" Bentsen asked.

This time, the old man turned to his wife. She said, "As they all do, he left to taste the world at sixteen. Nearly all come back. He came back to tell us he was not returning." She said all this with the slight accent of one for whom English was a second language learned only when she went to school.

Looking at his wife in surprise, and apparently discerning she had kept something from him, he nodded wearily and said, "Yes, to us, he died then."

Tears rolled down his wife's cheeks, and she sniffled, but he ignored the mourning sounds.

"We understand the coroner will release his body sometime next week for burial," Strand said. "Do you want us to keep you informed, and would you want to attend the funeral service?"

"Coroner? What happened to him?" Mr. Mast asked.

"I'm sorry to tell you someone killed your son, Mr. Mast, and Detective Bentsen and I are investigating his murder."

His listeners' eyes went wide. "Murdered!" Mr. Mast said. "A son of mine? How can that be?" Almost immediately, realizing what he had just said, he followed up with, "That's what happens out in the world."

Not holding back, Mrs. Mast let loose her tears. "We knew this would happen if he went out there," she whispered softly.

Bentsen then asked, "But how did you know this would happen?"

"Abel was such a bright boy—we knew he would never stay—but we couldn't stop him. We Amish are not for your English world, Mr. Detective," she said and stopped when her husband put his hand out, as if to steady a mare.

"We'll attend no funeral service, Detective, not one of us," Mr. Mast vowed.

Strand noticed the children, almost adults actually, and wondered if there was any way to speak to them.

"May we ask," Bentsen went on, "where would you like his body to rest?"

Surprised to be faced with that question, he merely shook his head. "He should not lie here with family," he asserted.

"Eli, my husband, but our eldest son has finally come home. Can we not take him?"

XXX

COFFEE AT THE Mercer Diner could be an adventure, but not like what Hattie Reynolds served up at The Spot. To say it had no flavor was to attach a word to it was the kindest way to describe it. Like water with a drop of coloring in it, no one needed to use cream, or so it was said.

"Well, let's see what this fine Tuesday brings," Bentsen began. "I'm guessing we're having coffee here, such as it is, only to avoid running into Montgomery."

"You got that right, Joe. We don't have anything to tell him."

"About yesterday at the Masts'. Any more thoughts on that whole show?"

"There's more going on there than perhaps we'll ever know. The old man is a hard one. Maybe that's why Abel decided he liked it better in the world."

"Could be. I didn't get what their trade was, but usually, the boys are expected to work with the old man and eventually take over. They can try another trade if they want, I understand, but the pressure must be on to stay with the family."

"That may be it. The mom has had a tough row to hoe, it looks like, and the other kids didn't seem like the cheeriest bunch," Strand offered. "Did you see the little girl with a leg missing?"

"They do clam up when there's English around, that's for sure, and Mom would have told us a lot more if the old man was absent. And no, I didn't notice the girl."

"The oldest might have said something as well, I'm thinking."

"OK, note for the file. I can't see us dragging an Amish man and his wife in for the third degree. Montgomery would have our hides even if we thought it."

"Right on that, but you know what, Joe? I don't think that's the last we've heard from that family. Did you notice me giving our card to the eldest girl as we left, the one holding the little girl?"

Bentsen laughed. "What a scoundrel you are, Fletch, but they don't have a phone!"

"Don't they all know an English friend with a phone? Just wait."

"I'm not holding my breath," Bentsen said. "Discipline in those houses can be awfully tight and in the Mast household, no one farts without permission."

～

Coffee over, such as it was, Bentsen said he'd check out everything he could about Stoddard's movements surrounding both murders while Strand said he was going to stop for real coffee and hit the road for Breezewood, a two-and-a-half-hour drive in good weather.

Interstate 79 was pretty clear but for some icy patches which caught a few less than careful drivers and sent them ditch bound. Strand made sure each one car incident was accounted for via radio and cell calls to the closest PSP Barracks, and sped on his way to the Turnpike interchange and east. He and Lafferty had agreed to meet at the Bob Evans there, a fixture on the hill for decades, and have a hot lunch and good conversation.

Strand hadn't seen Lafferty in a long time and didn't know what to expect, yet he recognized the tall man with nearly white hair and pink skin as soon as he walked through the door. They shook hands, sat down at their table in a corner, and scanned their menus as they exchanged small talk before the server came.

Once their orders were in, Lafferty said, "I have a trunkful of files for you outside, Fletcher, and we can put them in your car when we leave. I hope you don't mind doing this in advance, but the security people made me promise I'd get you signature on the custody documents here in this folder," he finished, sliding it over.

Strand looked through, saw where he was to sign, and affixed his name to over a half dozen forms, one set for each file. He noticed Montgomery's official request at the back of the file. "No problem, Mr. Lafferty," he said, picking up the pen offered and making everything official.

"Maybe it was 'Mr. Lafferty' when you were a rookie trooper a hundred years ago, but 'John' is fine now," he said smiling. "You and your Lieutenant Montgomery have quite a reputation, Fletcher," said the mostly proper Lafferty, "meaning there were noises from above that we should cooperate with the investigating authorities here."

"Glad to hear that, sir," Strand said, still uncomfortable with the familiarity extended to him, "but I'm sure you could have sent someone a few rungs down the ladder to deliver these, no?"

"Not in this case, no. With the high-level interest, and my own personal interest, I thought a face-to-face with you was the only way to proceed."

As they ate Bob Evans's best lunch fare, Lafferty asked for an update, and Strand, with only a bit of hesitation, gave him nearly everything.

"All of which means you're not very far ahead of the curve, then."

"That's about it, sir, but we are narrowed down a bit. I'm sorry to tell you your guy Stoddard is starting to get our attention."

"I was afraid it might go there, but no other suspects?"

"What's in your trunk, John, might be the treasure chest with all the answers."

"Shirley and I will likely come up for Masters's funeral, weather permitting, but do we know when that might be?"

"All up to the coroner. We're waiting for more test results on a pair of drinking glasses from the kitchen. Might be nothing, but there was no sign of a visitor, yet two glasses were out on the kitchen counter, and just washed apparently."

"This is part of your theory that Masters was dead before someone else came and killed him again?"

"No longer a theory, really. If one of those glasses has any trace of a sleep-inducing drug, that will confirm it. The insulin level already gets us most of the way there. We haven't seen his medical records yet, but there was no indication in any of his effects that he was diabetic. Couldn't have been an accident, in other words."

"I see. But doesn't that one fact, the insulin level, and the likelihood of another drug rule out anyone in the mine, including Stoddard?"

"Not necessarily, John. Any over-the-counter sleep aid, given in excess, would get the killer halfway there. Then, if the killer knew of his own knowledge about giving injections or had seen it done on a relative, no medical knowledge would be required."

"That means a person without medical knowledge could have carried this off."

"Easily, but I'm guessing our real killer doesn't go around killing people every day, so the possible amateur we're describing might have taken a lot more time to do things right. Someone with medical knowledge would have been a lot surer—and faster. See what I mean?"

"I'm not sure that I do see that."

"Look at it this way, each assailant had to enter the Masters house without arousing suspicion, and so far, it's safe to assume the first killer didn't know there'd be a second killer, and the second killer didn't know there'd been one before him. Either person could have been interrupted by the other."

"That's making me dizzy," Lafferty said, "but the medical angle?"

"Apparently, if we're right, two people decided to murder Abel Masters on the same night, for the same or different reasons. Go figure. We have no reason to think they knew each other. We know Masters was struck on the head after he'd already been murdered, which means the first killer had to know what he was doing and couldn't waste time, though he had no reason to expect Masters to have other visitors given what everyone seemed to know about his personal life."

"Meaning?"

"Meaning he lived alone, had no real friends except you and Fr. Pallison, no associates outside of work, no girlfriends, nobody who might show up unexpected."

"Using your own logic, Fletch, the first killer might have thought he had all the time in the world. You can't have it both ways. In fact, logically speaking, it could all have been done by just one killer, but there I go again, sinking my own boat—that angle would mean someone in the mine."

"Hmmm! You could be right, John, but so far, we have no idea where this might go."

"And why Stoddard?"

"Plenty of motive. Plenty of opportunity. And smart enough to come up with the means."

"Sounds weak, Fletcher."

"That's why he's not in custody yet."

∾

After Strand and Lafferty trudged out into the ankle-deep snow in the parking lot and started their engines, Strand backed the Vic close to Lafferty's sedan and piled a small mountain of files into the trunk of the state car.

The men shook hands and Strand promised to keep Lafferty up to date. "I don't know much about using this new email thing," Strand said through the whistling snow, "but as soon as I know about the funeral—it'll be at the Catholic church in Foreston—I'll let you know."

Lafferty chuckled. "This email thing, Fletcher, you'll either love it or hate it."

XXXI

ENDING THEIR FAREWELL chatter, Strand and Lafferty did not linger as the snow bore down on them. Looking at his watch, Strand went into a small panic. The calling hours at Cunningham's were 4 to 7 p.m., which meant he had time to arrive in Foreston with a half an hour to spare. Aurora would be furious with him, he knew, and so he tried to call her as soon as he got back on the PA Turnpike heading west.

After several failed attempts, probably because of the weather, he finally got through, but wasn't sure he'd be glad of it.

"Honey, I'm sorry," he said after the hellos and how-are-you's, "but if I get there with this storm, it'll be in the nick of time. Please forgive me," he added, deciding to fall on his sword before she plunged her own into him.

"Fletch, you absolutely amaze me. Today is Paulie's viewing and you're in Breezewood—great planning!"

"Sorry, hon, but when we arranged this meet, the forecast was clear and dry. Where this storm came from, I have no idea."

Through the ether, he thought he could hear her exhale. In frustration? "Fletch, if you're on the road right now with that thing in your hand and not holding onto the wheel, I'll be madder at you than if you run late! Take it easy, I get it. We'll get through it. The kids and I will be there and you come as soon as you can."

"Very sweet of you, and that means I'd better get off the phone to manage the drive. Love you!"

"Love you back—be careful, Fletch. I want you back in one piece."

Strand breathed a sigh of relief and gripped the wheel more tightly than necessary, but the roads, though treated, were what the local weather guys on the radio called "greasy" or "slippy." He wasn't sure what definition the turnpike met today.

The long ride home gave him plenty of time to consider what to do with the files now in his possession. Surely, he didn't have time to get them to the Mercer Barracks and lock them up somewhere, but for the life of him, he wasn't aware of a space big enough. Stacking them in his family room did not seem to make sense or meet even the spirit of the promise he made Lafferty about their security. Finally, he decided to leave them first locked in the trunk of the state Vic, and then locked in his garage.

It was no easy task to arrange his mind for the viewing protocols he'd have to endure at Cunningham's, so instead, he considered the stacks of bound paper in his trunk. The Official Personnel Folders and Investigation files for Masters, Rieger, Stoddard, Conlon, and the men who worked for Rieger would provide him with ample reading opportunity once Paul—his beloved Paulie—was put to rest.

The thought of Paulie also brought to mind the image of Nate Robertson, swaggering and arrogant man that he was. There was one guy Strand would love to drag off the success ladder just to see if a real medical professional existed under the tailored suit. Later, he would remember his ruminating about Robertson and see his thoughts in a wholly different light.

~

By 3:45 p.m., the Crown Vic found its way to the Strand home by dint of sheer luck and good driving. Strand put the car in the garage's spare slot and locked it up tight, then ran into the house, washed his face, brushed his hair, and straightened his tie before running back out to drive the other family car the four blocks to Cunningham's.

Already a small line had gathered, mostly friends from church and the community. Strand hastened to take his place at the head of the open casket to greet those who braved the horrific weather to comfort his family—and Bob, who stood beyond Aurora, Aaron, and Anna.

Jonathan had already sent him a text message saying some political problem demanded his attention back in DC.

By 6 p.m., it seemed clear that all who were coming had already been and gone. For the last hour, they chatted with one of the Cunningham sons and went over the proceedings for the funeral on Wednesday. Bob had elected for a service before the cremation, which meant there'd be one less thing for church-goers to wonder about. Bob's presence would give them enough.

By pre-arrangement, they met Father Pallison at Rudy's, a bar and restaurant favorite of Forestonians for decades. A let-up in the weather allowed them to make the six-mile drive out there, and they didn't regret the chicken parm and associated go-withs.

Having already covered the details for Paul Strand's funeral rite, Father Pallison brought up the Masters service to be conducted in the week following, it now appeared.

"This'll be a first in my experience as a priest."

"How so?" Aurora was quick to ask.

"Apparently, someone from the family contacted Cunningham's, who's also in charge of the arrangements, to say that they would receive Abel Masters's remains onto the Mast farm, but with a condition."

"What would that be?" Strand asked, keenly interested.

"When Cunningham's transports the remains to New Wilmington, upon arrival, they will remove the body from the casket, place it on a pine board the family provides, and cover it with a white shroud."

"What's that all about?" Aurora's curiosity was aroused.

"The Amish insist that their dead be returned to the earth—dust to dust—from whence he came. And there was a hoo-hah about him being embalmed, but Cunningham's insisted on abiding with state law on the matter given the length of time between his death and the release of his body by Coroner McCreary."

"Sounds ghoulish," Aaron jumped in.

They all laughed, but it was a nervous laugh, as if ghosts were dining with them.

"It's interesting," Pallison continued, "that the body will be permitted on the Mast farm, but outside the family cemetery."

~

Early the next morning, Strand was up before everyone else, shaving and showering to get ready for Paul's funeral later that morning. Mac stood by, waiting for three things: attention, food, and personal business outside.

There was more to Strand's dawn labors, however. He figured that while everyone else did what they needed and had breakfast, he could make do with coffee and toast, while bearing the frigid morning air, even in his closed garage, to take a quick inventory of the case files tucked in his trunk. Finding the two files on Abel Masters, he trudged back to the house feeling guilty about letting his mind drift from Paul and the morning's ritual. At the same time, he couldn't control his interest in the paperwork regarding a dead body not related to him.

XXXII

INTO THE FAMILY car the silent and somberly dressed Strands climbed for their short trip up Broad Street to the church where Cunningham's trademark Cadillac hearse was already situated in the alleyway between church and rectory, but just outside the church's side door. It had always been so, making it easier for pall-bearers to descend the few steps to the welcoming casket bearer.

Strand was pleasantly surprised by the respectable number of people present. Aside from the Bentsen's and Lieutenant Montgomery, there were a few other troopers from the barracks, and the usual gaggle of parishioners who seemed to somehow thrive on funeral services. He had seen them before, professional mourners, as it were, who lent the entire affair an additional dignity.

Most surprising was the presence of Foreston's Chief of Police, Georgie Hallon, with whom the PSP had done battle over the years. Why he was there, Strand could not fathom, but he appreciated the professional courtesy being rendered, especially when their eyes caught and Hallon nodded. It was a gesture of respect Strand deeply appreciated.

As always, Cunningham's had arranged everything to a tee. Four members of the church choir were there as the organ pumped out

"Nearer My God to Thee," an unusual but fitting hymn for this funeral. Bob must have chosen the music, Strand assumed.

Already situated in the front pew, Bob sat in a black suit, white shirt, and tie, waiting alone for the Strands to join him, which they did. Once again, Strand noticed Jonathan was nowhere in sight. *And that's fine with me.*

Officially, Fletcher Strand had been raised a Fintan Strand Presbyterian. His Polish-American mother, however, refused to cut her ties to her own church. Never had he been confirmed as a Catholic and neither did he know much about its faith precepts, except what his mother patiently taught him, Paul, and Jonathan during their secretive trips to Mass in Fintan Strand's absence. Though he often thought of himself as having something like dual citizenship, he took the step of conversion some years earlier in deference to Aurora, so that Aaron and Anna would be raised with God but without confusion about the family's faith walk.

Initially not a serious congregant, over the years he had come to appreciate the deep symbolism in so many aspects of Catholic rituals. One of the best, he thought, was the funeral rite, which provided both the deceased and the family a fitting farewell.

The church became quiet. Father Pallison began at the entrance to the church. "May the Father of mercies, the God of all consolation, be with you," he recited, and those present responded, "And with your spirit."

Standing at the foot of the casket, the priest sprinkled it with holy water, and at that point, the pallbearers garbed it in a white pall symbolizing the white garment Paul had received at his baptism, reminding one and all that a person enters and leaves Christian life in the same fashion.

Father Pallison: "In life, Paul cherished the Gospel of Christ. May Christ now greet him with these words of eternal life," and the congregants responded, "Come, blessed of my Father!"

Father Pallison: "In baptism, Paul received the sign of the Cross," and again, the congregants responded, "May he now share in Christ's victory over sin and death."

Strand stood numb, Aurora clasping his hand in hers, as the rite proceeded. After the readings from the Old and New Testaments, the Eucharist, and the closing of the Mass, Father Pallison escorted the casket, still wearing the white pall of baptism, once more to the entrance of the church. Only the small sounds of the pallbearers walking the casket could be heard.

A bit earlier in the service, Strand looked over at Paul's partner as the priest delivered a brief but warm and suitable eulogy of satisfying words. Strand hoped Bob felt them more than the other mourners did.

After sprinkling and incensing the casket, Father Pallison spoke once more:

> Into your hands, Father of mercies, we commend our brother Paul, in the sure and certain hope that, together with all who have died in Christ, he will rise with him on the last day. We give you thanks for the blessings which you have bestowed upon Paul in this life: they are signs to us of your goodness and of our fellowship with the saints in Christ. Merciful Lord, turn toward us and listen to our prayers: open the gates of paradise to your servant and help us who remain to comfort one another with assurances of faith, until we all meet in Christ and are with you and with our brother forever.

By noon, Paul had been returned to Cunningham's for the cremation process, then to be interred in a plot at the Fair Oaks Cemetery in New Wilmington, where he and Bob would at some point lay at rest together. Lunch was served by the church ladies, and by 2 p.m., it was all over.

Over. Strand stood firm throughout the funeral Mass, not believing that it was over, that his brother had gone to eternity, and there was no way to reach out and say how sorry he was not to have been a better brother to him.

When they were home at last, Strand felt empty inside, like a wonderful part of his growing up years had just vanished. In the entrance to the dining room, he hugged Aurora for all he was worth. Aarie and Anna, who'd remained stoic throughout the entire morning, began crying in unison. All four of them went to the living room, sat close together, and talked about their Paulie for a solid hour.

What Bob did that afternoon, Strand did not know, but he wished he did.

∾

Later that day, Strand attempted to put his grief aside by pulling out the files associated with Abel Masters. While camped in his beat-up leather chair in the family room, one open file on his lap, he called Joe Bentsen on his cell phone and brought him up to date. Mac lay in the fleece puff bed down at his side. As always, he looked up, hoping his master was speaking to him.

"Hey, if you want to come over and grab a few of these, we can review them together for a few hours. Aurora won't mind, and the kids won't bother us. Up to you."

"You know what, Fletch, I think I'll pass, but thanks. Any other day, yeah, but today, it's probably better for you to process things on your own. OK with you?"

Smiling to himself at his end of the conversation, Strand said, "That's why you're the best guy I could ever ride with, my friend. I didn't think of it that way, but probably should have." They clicked off and Strand put his head and eyes into the mass of paper before him, then, remembering what he forgot to ask his partner, called him back.

"Sorry, Joe, I never asked you about Stoddard. Anything there? "I wish I could say one way or the other. They did remember him at the movie theater—coming back for more popcorn is pretty uncommon, the woman said, but Stoddard could have left right afterward, and she might not have noticed."

"So, nothing rules him out."

"No, I'd say not. He's still our best shot."

"Hmmm! Wish I could say that made my day, but oh, well, who said this job was going to be like *NYPD Blue*?" They both laughed and ended the call.

Thirty minutes further into his review, Anna tiptoed in. "Daddy?"

"Yes, hon, what's on your mind?"

"Why wasn't Uncle Johnnie with us today?"

"Hmmm," he said, pulling her close to the chair and putting his hand gently on her shoulder. "It's complicated, honey, and I'm not sure I can give you a good answer, because I don't really know myself. I wish he had been," he added at the end, though in his heart, he was just fine with his brother's absence. "Uncle Johnnie is a different kinda guy sometimes, isn't he?"

She nodded and smiled. "Thanks, Daddy, I just wanted to ask."

No sooner had she made her exit than his cell phone buzzed. It was Coroner McCreary.

"Say, Fletch, I'm sorry to call you on a day like this, but I just wanted to keep you in the loop on what's going on with Masters."

"No problem, Doc. What's up?"

"First thing this morning, I wanted to schedule the release of his body to Cunningham's for a next Tuesday funeral when it dawned on me that I had no idea to whom I was going to release it."

"Oh, wow, Doc," Strand said, jumping in, "I hadn't thought about that either. You know, Joe and I spoke with his parents—Amish people—in New Wilmington yesterday, and they were totally unwilling to take him, but then Father Pallison told me arrangements had been made with Cunningham's—you might check with them."

"What I was about to tell you was that when I went through the mail later, I found a letter from Attorney Charles Niven in Foreston. He's the executor for Masters's estate apparently, and he will assume responsibility. Just wanted to see if we were all together on this. How about that for karma?"

"Damn. Well, at least we know. Thanks, Doc," he said and clicked off.

A call to Niven's office went to his secretary, who informed Strand her boss was out for the afternoon but that he could call tomorrow. Instead, Strand left his number and asked for a call back as soon as possible in regard to the Abel Masters murder investigation."

The parade of distractions was enough to let him put aside Masters's files, but he did so with reluctance. In the kitchen, he found Aurora, walked up behind her, kissed her neck, and suggested the four of them go out to dinner.

"Where are we going?" Aurora asked.

"Assuming the roads are good enough, let's go to The Spot in Harrisville."

"You're kidding."

"I'm not, but just don't drink the coffee."

XXXIII

"TOO MANY FUNERALS, Joe. I don't know if I can handle it," Strand said, half serious, as they met at the Mercer Barracks first thing Thursday morning. Lieutenant Montgomery, trim and crisp as always, walked by their desks and offered a "good morning," but did not demand an audience.

"I know what you mean," Bentsen replied. "Say, the Rieger funeral is tomorrow at the Lutheran church in Foreston. Why don't I attend that one?" He chuckled. "I'm supposed to be one of them, but with Sylvie being Jewish, I can never seem to get there. Maybe I'll get a few points with the Big Guy, eh?"

"I doubt that you need 'em, Joe, but that would be great. We still have Masters's to do next Tuesday, and for that one, we both should be there."

"That's a deal," he said, looking out the window at the mix of snow and sleet pelting down. "Today's a perfect day for coffee and file-reading. Maybe that's why Montgomery didn't bother us. He couldn't see us behind this mountain of paper."

"Right," Strand said. "I'd like to take Masters and Rieger if you start on Novak and Conlon. We can divvy up Stoddard and Rieger's people later."

"Good with me," and with that, they each began flipping pages to see what surprises might be ahead.

~

As Strand perused the Masters Official Personnel Folder, careful to keep everything in order, the dead man's career laid itself out in personnel actions and promotions confirming what he'd heard from all the sources they'd already interviewed.

Masters's professional life was an unusual one, however, in that when he finished high school and college under Lafferty's guidance, he was unlike any other investigator applicant to have applied for a position. His stellar background and academic performance pushed him to the top of the hiring lists, right behind those with veteran's preference, and because the job had fairly high turnover, he had no trouble getting sworn in.

Sometime in college, he apparently went to court to change his surname, and that document appeared in order. His insurance forms were curious, however. Listed as his parents were the Masts, as Strand had previously learned, but no siblings were indicated. Strand immediately went to his security folder to check what he listed on his SF-86, the security questionnaire clearance applicants were required to complete. There, he listed four sisters and three brothers. Strand nodded to himself, as if checking off an item on his to-do list.

"Anything of note so far, Joe?"

"Nah! This amount of paper on one person could either kill someone if it fell on them or put them to sleep if they had to read it all," he said with a low chuckle.

On to Rieger's files, Strand plowed through them a bit more quickly, and as before, there seemed nothing out of the ordinary, in either the personnel actions or the background investigation. What he found interesting was Rieger's professional journey from the West Coast to Boyers, PA, an unlikely path to career satisfaction, but it must have worked for him.

"Say, Joe, how about giving a list of these names to Gloria Moses and let's see if any of these good folks have run afoul of the local or state police since their backgrounds were completed."

"Can do. So far, this review is doing one thing—confirming nearly everything we already knew or heard about. One thing I'm surprised about is how thorough the federal insurance questionnaire is. And given the original application form, the SF-171, the security questionnaire, and the insurance forms, there's plenty of opportunity for someone to make a mistake about their history if they weren't careful. Some bureaucrat somewhere must compare all this stuff to make sure everything matches, wouldn't you say?"

"Yeah," Strand said, and put the Rieger file aside, but because of something Bentsen had said, pulled some of Masters's paperwork back in front of him and began flipping pages. After a moment, he found what he must have seen but hadn't registered. "Damn!"

"What?" asked Bentsen hoping a gold nugget had been found in all the dirt.

"You know who Masters's doctor was? Of all people, Nathaniel Robertson!"

"Oh. Not so big a coincidence that, Fletch. There aren't boatloads of MDs around the county to choose from."

"You're right, Joe, but seeing his name reminds me to follow up on something before it gets stale."

"What's that?"

"I'm going to ask an attorney to take a good look at my brother's medical records. Robertson is an empty suit, I'm sure of it, and if he made just one mistake with Paulie, I'm going to go after him."

The pair spent the rest of the morning skimming all the remaining files in front of them. One by one, they checked them off: Masters, Rieger, Novak, Conlon, Stoddard, and the warehousemen, Johnston, McKenna, Meister, Manzini, and Sharpe.

"Well, let's admit we didn't really scour these files, Joe, but if there's a thread there, it didn't jump out at me. You see anything?"

"No," he yawned, "but with all this paper, it would be easy to miss something, wouldn't it?"

XXXIV

F OR STRAND, FRIDAY proved to be more of the same, but at least
it was the last workday of what had been a horrible week for him
and his family. Because Bentsen had agreed to surveil the Rieger
funeral, he volunteered to bring all their paperwork up to date, keep
Montgomery appeased, and if time permitted, go through the files
that Bentsen had reviewed. At some point, Bentsen would do the
same for those Strand had checked.

Before he began, he called the office of Charles Niven in Foreston, and to his surprise, the attorney came on the line in short order. Strand explained the purpose of his call: he wanted information
about Abel Masters's will and the status of his estate.

Niven cleared his throat and said, "You can come over after lunch
if you wish, Detective, but I can assure you the decedent's affairs are
pretty straightforward. Shall we say 1:30 p.m.?"

Strand agreed, impressed that the man was so readily cooperative,
inasmuch as so many of his profession were much more comfortable
giving reasons why they couldn't comply.

Turning to his immediate task, he lined up the files and began, as
he had with those of Masters and Rieger, to zero in on the individ-
ual's SF-171 and their SF-86 to see if any one of them had had any

medical employment, training, or education. Thus far, nothing had surfaced.

Stoddard was next on his list, and he scrutinized his file carefully. It took several minutes and more than one run through before he found, amazingly, a most damning nugget of information. In his background investigation, Stoddard's father referenced his own diabetes and said he'd required his son, David, to take basic training at a Virginia hospital to give him injections and to learn about insulin dosing, given his blood glucose levels.

There was no reference to such training on any of Stoddard's forms, but to be fair, Strand admitted, there was no requirement to include that kind of incidental training. Had the elder Stoddard not made a point of mentioning it in a feeble attempt to boost his son's competencies in the eyes of anyone considering him, thought Strand, this possible smoking gun might have gone unnoticed. Stoddard had the requisite knowledge to kill Masters—and, probably, easy access to his father's insulin supply. *Yeah, but did he do it?*

What else might have been in the files of the warehousemen, Strand didn't know. He had focused on medical training and he found it only in Stoddard's background investigation. He made a mental note that he and Bentsen had to give the warehousemen a more careful review whenever they had an opportunity.

With an air of triumph, Strand stood and marched himself to Montgomery's office. Beckoned in, he said, "Sir, we may have it, finally. Stoddard had motive, opportunity, and now, it appears, means."

"You going to pick him up?"

"When Joe gets back from Rieger's funeral, we'll get a bite, then check in with Masters's attorney in Foreston, and head to the mine and have another go at him."

～

Strand realized his mistake the moment he made a reference to food within Montgomery's hearing. For a man as fit as he was, indeed a poster child for a trooper in a PSP uniform, Montgomery loved to eat.

"Signal me when Joe gets back and we can see what the Diner has to offer today."

"Yessir," he said turning and wishing he'd been more careful. Lunch with the Chief was always interesting, but as Strand knew, it often took longer than necessary.

Not much later, Bentsen rolled in. They collected their boss and walked the few blocks in the cold into the semi-warmth of the fabled Mercer Diner, where "grease" wasn't an item on the menu, but should have been.

"How was Pastor Keely this morning?" Montgomery opened.

"Do you know everybody, boss?" Bentsen responded, surprised.

"I've known Dan Keely for years, and I assume he gave your Mr. Rieger a good sendoff."

"He did such a good job, he almost guilted me into going back to church a bit more regularly."

"You mean more than Christmas and Easter?" Strand kidded.

They all laughed at Bentsen's expense.

"Now if you're through," he said with high dudgeon, "let me give my report, such as it is. Rieger has no family here and none elsewhere, I gather, so aside from his wife, Corrine, there were about fifty people present, nearly all of them from the mine. Joe Novak, Judy Conlon, a number of other supervisors, and, incredibly, none other than David Stoddard. We've not interviewed the warehousemen who worked for Rieger, but judging by the guys I saw sitting together, his people were there, too. What you'd expect."

"Except for Stoddard."

"Right," Bentsen responded. "He's the guy who didn't care about Rieger."

"Nothing else out of the ordinary, then?" Montgomery asked.

"Nada. Rieger and his wife had no children, lived a very quiet life with their cats, and didn't participate much in their church or the community. I spoke with Pastor Keely after the service. He hardly knew Rieger."

"Thanks for doing that, Joe. In the meantime, I called Masters's attorney and we're going to see him after lunch on the way to the mine."

"And when you're there, let's hope the Stoddard pimple pops and you can make an arrest," Montgomery said, apparently oblivious to the food setting.

"Thanks, boss, that image just gave my chili a whole new taste."

"Don't be hasty in leaving, gents. I have something else," Montgomery said. "You guys like cold cases, right?"

"Who said that?" Bentsen asked, suspecting what was coming.

"Ever hear of the Purcell murder in Foreston?"

"I have," Strand offered. "Never solved. What about it?"

"An anonymous tip was called into Dispatch yesterday. Gloria Moses can tell you about it, but it's this simple: the caller said we ought to take another look at the nephew in that case."

"Chief, that murder happened in the sixties, right?"

"Yep, 1964, to be a bit more accurate. Two sisters lived together, never married, but one day one of them was found in the basement bound with clothesline and beaten to death with a hammer. Some tried to accuse the other sister, but she was helpless in a wheelchair—couldn't even talk."

"How'd the crime come to be discovered?" Bentsen said, curious now.

"It seems potatoes were boiling on the stove, and for some reason a neighbor came to check on the old ladies. The murdered woman was eighty, I believe, and he found her in the basement. The surviving one was in the living room, apparently oblivious to everything."

"And the nephew?"

"That's just it," Montgomery said, "there was never any mention of anyone being in the house, and no one pointed to a nephew." He chuckled. "All yours."

"Can't wait," Bentsen moaned.

"And speaking of old cases?" prompted Montgomery.

"Jesus, Boss, we didn't get there—the snowstorm, remember?"

Montgomery said, "All I know is there's no report on my desk yet."

~

On the way to Foreston, the detectives commiserated with one another over the assignment of a nearly thirty-year-old case. They talked further about how to approach it, but came to no conclusion. Finally, Bentsen said, "Maybe we won't get to this one, either."

Strand chuckled. "Maybe, but I wonder how come nobody knew about a nephew?"

The visit to the law office of Charles Niven on the second floor of a prominent building on Broad Street proved uneventful and unenlightening. Abel Masters's estate was fairly substantial given his somewhat hermetic life. Aside from $25,000 bequests to the Lafferty's and to Father Pallison's parish, the Church of the Beloved Disciple, the balance of the liquid assets was to go to St. Jude's Hospital for Children.

"What about his house and other tangibles?" Strand asked.

"His house, car, and furniture are to be liquidated to pay for my fee, probate court fees, and the like. Along with his life insurance, there'll be a nice amount going to the surviving Mast siblings, each sharing equally."

"Interesting," Strand said. "Presumably, the children are listed with you. Can we have their names?"

"Sure," Niven said and found his pen and notepad. In a minute, he completed the list and handed it over. "Is that all, gentlemen?"

"In this regard, Mr. Niven, is there anything else that comes to mind about Abel Masters that might help us solve his murder?"

Niven leaned back in his old-fashioned oak and leather office chair and glanced heavenward for a moment. "Actually, there's nothing. Abel was a simple, straightforward guy who made a pretty simple testament. My job should be easy."

"If that's so, then, I wonder if we could switch gears," Strand went on, "to a matter of personal interest to me."

"You want me to step out?" Bentsen asked.

Strand shook his head. "No need, Joe. I want you here for another reason."

"What's on your mind, then, Detective?"

"I just buried my brother a few days ago after a short illness under the care of Dr. Nathaniel Robertson."

Niven waited, pensive.

"Perhaps it's just personal to me, Mr. Niven, but I've never held Dr. Robertson in high professional esteem, if you know what I mean, and quite frankly, I think he neglected my brother because he was gay."

"That's saying a great deal, Detective Strand. I have heard a thing or two about Robertson, and so you have my attention. What do you want me to do?"

"I want to engage you to obtain my brother's medical records, have them examined by a medical expert you trust, and let me know if I should pursue any legal action against this guy."

Niven nodded. "I can do that, but experts are not cheap. I think I can get you a satisfactory answer, one way or another, if you're willing to spend $1,500."

Strand swallowed. "My brother is worth it. How long will something like this take?"

"Less than a month, I'd think. Then you'll know if your brother died needlessly."

XXXV

"Just curious, Fletch, why did you want me there with Niven?"

"In case there's some issue with conflict of interest with the case we're working on and my personal interests, I wanted a witness. That's all, but thanks, Joe."

"Got it. I can see why so many docs get away with murder, so to speak, because it costs the survivors precious cash to find them out. Isn't there a review board of some kind?"

"I've always understood that if a patient dies in a hospital, there is a board that goes over the records, but believe me, I've never read their findings in the *Sharon Herald,* have you?"

"No, that's for sure."

As always, Froggy 95 blared the weather and its repertoire of country and western favorites. Like those who made their living as road warriors, truckers, troopers, or salespeople, they all kept tabs on winter weather, as it could make all the difference in a bad situation.

"Think these cell phones will be able to tell us the weather, Fletch?"

"Probably—if they can get a signal."

Once again at the mine, Bentsen moaned. "I feel like I'm employed here," he said as he rolled down the ramp and flashed his credentials at the portal guard.

"'Déjà vu all over again,' as Yogi Berra liked to say. Let's do Stoddard first, then the warehouse guys," Strand said as Bentsen pulled to a stop at the cutout. "Say, I never really got to their files. Did you?"

"Just a quick skim. Well, shame on us, we'll have to get to them later. When did your friend Lafferty want them back?"

"No later than the end of next week, safe, sound, all in order, and nothing missing, or it's my head."

"Got it," Bentsen said as they walked in and asked for David Stoddard to be called to the conference room. "Oh, and please let Mr. Novak know we're here, but we're not to be bothered when we're with Mr. Stoddard. Thanks," he said to the receptionist.

Stoddard barged into the conference room some ten minutes later accompanied by an attitude that seemed all out of place for the occasion.

"Now, listen, Mr. Detectives," he began with deep sarcasm, spittle at the corner of his mouth, "I've about had it with you bumpkins harassing me practically every day."

"Yeah, we know you come from an important family, so now you listen," Bentsen said, rising to his 6'4" height and taking a step toward him. "You're going to sit down, put that attitude in your pocket, and pay close attention to everything we say and ask, or else."

"Or else what?" he said as a snigger escaped his lips.

"Or else we'll do all of this elsewhere. Walking you out of here in handcuffs should give everyone great pleasure. Then, at the Barracks, we'll have a much longer conversation on our terms. Is that clearer?"

Stoddard kept his eyes on Bentsen, grabbed the edge of the oak conference table, and let his backside find a seat, all without another word.

"Now that that's settled, Mr. Stoddard," said Strand, speaking for the first time, "let's go back to our conversation of the other day. You know, we've checked out your claims about your whereabouts and it's a real tossup as to whether you even have alibis."

"Bullshit. That woman at the theater will remember me."

"She does, wise guy, but given the setup there, you could have made a show of getting a second bag of popcorn in the middle of the picture, dumped it, and quietly exited without her seeing you."

"So what?"

"So that means your perfect alibi for the evening before Masters's body was found just went poof." Strand stopped there, letting that sink in. "Now let's talk about your important family, Mr. Stoddard. Specifically, your father."

"What about him?" he asked, his balloon deflating, his eyes darting all around.

"According to your background investigation, your father was quite proud of the fact that for a time, at least, you helped him with one of his medical issues."

"What the hell are you talking about?" he said, regaining a bit of bravado.

"Specifically, he said that you'd taken some basic medical training so that you could prepare his insulin doses and inject him for his advanced diabetes."

"Yeah, so what?"

"So, we're going to get a warrant to search that little hovel you call home. We'll search that, your car, your desk here, everything, and if we find even one syringe, even one discarded vial of insulin, you'll be facing a long term in prison for the murder of Abel Masters."

"What? Are you arresting me?"

"You bet," Strand said, and at that, the Baby Huey facing him somehow propelled his three hundred plus pounds across the four feet of oak between them and with arms outstretched, went for Strand's face.

Bentsen had only to stand, fix his claw-like grip on the back of Stoddard's neck, and slam his head on the table to end the assault. "God only knows what you hoped to accomplish with that move, Stoddard, but assaulting a law enforcement officer is just as good a reason to arrest you as anything else."

Stoddard sprawled on the table panting and rubbing his head.

Strand sat back in his chair, straightening his tie, smiling.

"Thanks, partner, that was a well-executed play."

"You mean, you're not arresting me for murder?" Stoddard asked, gasping in surprise.

"Not at the moment, genius," Bentsen said. "For now, assaulting a law enforcement officer will hold you. The murder part will come later. Probably after we search everything you own. You've heard of the Miranda warning, haven't you? If not, here it is," he said as he fastened handcuffs—with great difficulty—to Stoddard's bloated wrists and recited the standard lines. "I think, Davey boy, you've just made the biggest mistake of your career."

～

It took almost thirty minutes for additional troopers to appear and take custody of David Stoddard. While they waited, Strand informed Joe Novak of what had transpired, and that PSP Troopers would enter the Center to tape off anything belonging to Stoddard while a search warrant was obtained and produced.

Novak turned purple. "You can't search a secure and sensitive federal facility," he shouted, reaching for the phone.

"If you're calling John Lafferty, please be good enough to put him on speaker so that he can be fully apprised of the situation here."

"You have a hell of a lot of nerve, Strand," Novak hissed, but slapped a button on his landline phone so that Strand could be a party to the call.

When Director Lafferty came on the line, Novak immediately attempted to take control of the situation. Lafferty was polite to him, but turned his attention to Strand. "Is this all necessary?"

"Sir, David Stoddard physically assaulted me while being questioned in your conference room. He is under arrest for that offense, and will be taken to the Mercer Barracks for further interrogation. As soon as we're through with this call, I'll be phoning Lieutenant Montgomery to obtain a warrant for us to search any of Stoddard's possessions here in the mine, his car, and his residence."

"It's that serious?"

"Yessir. After a thorough review of the files you provided us, we found a piece of information potentially critical to our investigation of Abel Masters's murder."

"I see. Is there any way we can minimize the disruption to the operation there, Fletcher?"

"There is, sir. Mr. Novak is appropriately concerned about us searching Stoddard's office and desk lest we come across federally sensitive materials. If you were to give us permission to search here, Mr. Novak or anyone he chooses can monitor whatever we do and ensure sensitive materials are protected. We will still obtain a warrant for Mr. Stoddard's other property."

"And how will that reduce the disruption there?"

"We could do the search in the next hour and be done. Otherwise, it might wait a day, and I'd have to post troopers here to make sure no evidence was removed."

"All right, Fletcher, you have your permission—I will email same to Lieutenant Montgomery and the two of you. Please expedite the search."

"Thank you, sir. Should we impound any items, we will provide Mr. Novak a list."

"Thank you, Fletcher. Thank you, Joe, and please give the detectives your every cooperation."

Novak's shade of purple faded to a deep pink as he hung up the phone, yet he attempted to maintain control of a situation over which he had no control whatsoever. "L-let's get on with it, then."

"First, I need to use your landline for the other warrant, then let's you and I survey the terrain, and I'll tape it off until we're through. When Bentsen turns Stoddard over for transport, he'll join me while we search."

"Will that be all, then?"

"Not at all. Then Bentsen and I will need to interview Al Rieger's people one by one."

"When will this end, for God's sake!"

"When it's over."

XXXVI

JOE NOVAK HIMSELF accompanied the two detectives to Stoddard's office deep in the pale-blue limestone shaft in which approximately 130 people worked at various tasks from filing documents, including fingerprints, to reviewing case files.

In the Case Review Branch itself, forty-five college-degreed people labored in their cubicles to make sure the file for each subject of investigation was complete, accurate, and thorough. It was a tedious job with little opportunity for idle chit-chat. These were dedicated professionals, many of them the children of people who grew up in the general area who wanted to live and work close to family.

Rare was the total outsider, someone who'd never lived or worked in western Pennsylvania before coming to work down deep, so to speak. David L. Stoddard was one such person, and Strand felt certain 95 percent of the people who worked there wondered what they had done to become saddled with the likes of him.

Of course, when Novak showed up accompanied by two detectives and two uniformed State Troopers, nearly everyone stopped what they were doing to observe the parade from one end of the hundred-yard shaft to the other, where Stoddard's office was situated. Their stage whispers could be heard above the hiss of the ventilation system.

After the troopers stretched yellow tape around a perimeter where Novak pointed, he led the way into Stoddard's office followed by Strand and Bentsen. It didn't take long for the search to yield a surprising result, and because Director Lafferty gave permission for the search, the specificity required in a warrant might otherwise have been problematic.

Strand went for Stoddard's desktop and drawers while Bentsen went for the two file cabinets on the back wall. Novak indicated that the file cabinets should hold case files, nothing more, but Bentsen opened the drawers one by one, shoved the files to the back, then to the front, to see if anything was tucked in there.

"Who has access to these cabinets, Mr. Novak?" Bentsen used the man's surname because it was apparent from their dealings Novak enjoyed the formalities and the signs of respect he could demand.

"Obviously Stoddard, but most likely, many of his Case Reviewers. These are cases brought in here for secondary review or some sort of decision-making by Stoddard himself."

"There's a lot of cases here—is this normal?"

Novak cleared his throat. "N-no, that seems excessive," he answered, and stopped himself before uttering another syllable.

Bentsen gave the drawers a further look, but then turned to the coatrack, where two wool sweaters and a heavy winter coat hung.

"Ahhh! Bingo!" Bentsen said, reaching into one of the sweater pockets. In his hand was a plastic storage packet of pills, probably about four dozen. "Want to make any bets?" he asked, turning to Strand and handing it to him for his inspection.

The latter stopped his search, having found nothing, and held up the baggie with his latex gloves. "Hmmm! I'm betting this is an illegal drug, Mr. Novak, and we'll need your statement for custody of evidence purposes."

"Oh, God! W-well, almost anyone could have put that there, right?"

"You sound like a defense lawyer already, sir, but we'll see whose fingerprints are present. Plastic bags like this hold on to them quite well."

"And on this one," Strand said as he pulled open the top-right-hand desk drawer and pulled out a Ziploc bag stuffed with what appeared to be marijuana. "Gee, Mr. Novak, what kind of government work goes on here?" he asked, attempting to inject some humor into a rapidly deteriorating situation.

"Jesus," Novak prayed, "I'd better call Lafferty on this." "You do that, but we are impounding these two items and if Stoddard's fingerprints are on these bags or on any of these pills, if they're the amphetamines I think they are, we will amend our arrest documents to include drug possession for sale."

"But federal authorities will want to prosecute here."

"Probably, but we got here first, and now we have plenty to talk to David Stoddard about."

"He'll get bail, I'm sure," Novak said. "But what do you think he was doing with that stuff here?"

"Dealing, of course," Strand said. "This is a no-smoking facility, so he wouldn't be using the pot personally, would he? This should have been at home. Now, the pills, who knows?"

"The question is, Joe," said Bentsen, dropping the formality, "just who was he selling this stuff to?"

Like a façade falling off of a building, Novak said, "That son of a bitch! My God, this is going to cause a scandal for this agency, for a lot of people, for me."

"Relax a bit, Joe," Strand joined in. "If you don't tell the press, we won't. In fact, we insist on it, as will Lafferty. There's no need to tell anyone of all those people watching this office right now."

"If Stoddard was dealing to people here, that's one thing, and your feds are going to swoop in here and the stink will spread."

"Or?" Novak hoped.

"Or if Stoddard was dealing to people working at the other facilities here underground, that'll be our territory. As much time as Stoddard seems to spend out in the walkways, almost anything is possible. He puts on his sweater, goes out for air, and makes a few bucks on the way."

"You think?"

"With this kind of thing, anything goes," Strand said, "but I'm betting he'll want to tell us about this in trade for something else."

XXXVII

FURTHER CALLS WERE made to both Director Lafferty and Lieutenant Montgomery, and all agreed, after a short round of curses, to maintain complete silence on the drug evidence, until more information could be gathered.

One thing Lafferty also agreed to, at Strand's suggestion, was to allow the PSP, accompanied by Underground Storage Company guards, to bring in drug-sniffing dogs to walk through the Investigations Center and all along the walkways exterior to the Center. The USC executives further permitted the dogs to be used along the walkways exterior to other clients in the mine, but not within their facilities. The canine search was to begin that evening after all workers had exited the mine.

The officers assigned to search Stoddard's car and his Black Road address were as fortunate as their detective colleagues. Under Stoddard's passenger seat were two bags of pills, probably two hundred in total, and his so-called home was a veritable storehouse of bagged marijuana. There was doubt, one of the troopers informed Bentsen, whether Stoddard actually resided there.

Strand sat in the Vic and couldn't stop laughing. "That dumb ass.

You know, Joe, if he hadn't lunged at me, we'd never have found this stuff."

"We can laugh, Fletch, and he's going away for quite a while, but think about what we didn't find."

Strand sobered in an instant. "Right. No insulin. No syringes. That's not conclusive, however. He could have cadged some insulin and just one syringe from his father's stash on a weekend home, done his work on Masters, and dumped the evidence."

"If that's so, we don't have much, do we?"

"But we have a lot to bust his balls on, including a threat to turn him over to the feds. We've got a nice hand of cards, Joe, so we'll use 'em."

~

The stars seemed to align on that Monday evening when Aurora prepared her best version of Chicken Piccata for Father Pallison, the Bentsen's, and the Lafferty's, who'd travelled from Washington that day for the Masters funeral the next morning.

If Strand expected the dinner conversation to be somewhat somber in view of the occasion, he was wrong. Father Pallison and the Lafferty's, all three of unabashed Irish descent, had no difficulty in finding humorous, sometimes uproarious tales to throw upon the table. Strand and his wife laughed more than they'd done in weeks.

After they covered a few details about the funeral, John Lafferty turned the talk to the ongoing murder investigation. "I know you can't say much about the developments today, but can you enlighten us at all?"

Bentsen looked across the table at his host and partner and waited for him to reply.

"John, this is a mind-bender. It's as if there are several pieces of yarn in the same sweater that are becoming unraveled. I know that that's not an answer for you, but this is the toughest set of cases we've had in years. *NYPD Blue* could not cover this in one of their shows!"

Everyone appreciated the humor with such a dark subject.

Bentsen said, "If I may, since I like food metaphors better, these cases are like a good garden onion. The more you peel the outer layers, the more you find, and the stronger the smell."

"Well said, you two," Lafferty said, "but I have to tell you, it's a real toss-up as to whether the PSP continues with these cases or we call in the Bureau—there's so much federal overlay here."

"Thinking about our conversation earlier today when you were on your way up here, John, one huge advantage—in my mind—for you to let us go on as we have been is that once you drag the FBI in, there'll be little containment of information and scandal because the national media will glom on and not let go."

"How bad do you think it's going to be for us as a federal agency?"

"I don't know, sir. It depends upon where this whole Stoddard thing goes," Strand said, then adding, "but you know, eventually people will talk out of school, and we can't put a lid on this forever."

"If we're theorizing a bit, is what's coming out of the haze the probability that Masters caught Stoddard at his drug-dealing, and that's why he was murdered? Same with Rieger?"

Strand and Bentsen both smiled. "Well, that's a pretty solid working theory, sir," Strand said, "but we're still not sure. We're letting Stoddard think we've got him for two murders. With that kind of pressure, he'll be more likely to sing us a song about his drug-dealing to avoid a whopper of a prison sentence."

"But not the murders?"

"I don't know about Joe, but even though we're building a good circumstantial case on him, maybe enough for an indictment, committing two murders successfully seems way above Stoddard's capability."

"So, what's the plan, then?"

"Well, tonight the drug sniffers will do their work in the mine and we'll see what that brings. The one bright spot for you, sir, is that Stoddard may well have been dealing to customers who worked for other outfits in the mine, but not your people. Given the fact that your folks on the whole should have a higher trust level than all those without security clearances, dealing to other feds would have been criminally stupid."

Lafferty nodded. "Thanks for that. Let's only hope. And say, gents, when can I get my files back?"

The detectives laughed. Strand said, "We'll need extracts from Stoddard's if we go forward with a murder case, but we can give you Masters's and Novak's back later this week. And by then, we should be through with those of Rieger's people and Judy Conlon's."

"Why review them if you think it might be Stoddard?"

"You never know, Mr. Lafferty," Bentsen said. "We've been known to miss a thing or two."

XXXVIII

STRAND DREADED HAVING to attend the funeral service for Abel Masters, having just gone through a burial rite for his brother the week before. Nonetheless, he and his partner agreed to meet again at the Catholic Church in Foreston for the 10 a.m. service, to observe and take note of attendees, it being a staple belief amongst homicide detectives that killers often desired to see their work through to the end.

The church's sanctuary was packed with people, including some of the same criers who were there for Paul's service, but now there were the Lafferty's, a number of regional Chiefs of Investigations flown in from around the country, and at least two hundred of Abel Masters's employees, all come to bid him farewell.

Strand and Bentsen stationed themselves at the back of the church, behind the attendees, to quietly survey reactions. Judy Conlon, Masters's secretary, sat near the front with the Lafferty's and could be seen with tissue at her eyes. A number of others were similarly moved, they noted, with no surprise given the strong employee-oriented management Masters had provided. Novak and his wife were there as well, the Acting Director of the Division stone-faced.

In the larger group, the detectives could see Rieger's warehousemen there as a unit, all dressed as if they were going right back to the job after the lunch served by the parish ladies immediately following the service. Charles Niven, Masters's attorney, was in attendance, and with him, most surprisingly, was a young woman, probably about nineteen, dressed in Amish garb, purple bonnet and all.

Before the service began, Strand made it his business to lean over and whisper a hello. It wasn't to greet the attorney, but to get a close look at the young woman. It was she to whom he had slipped his card at the Mast home.

~

Strand made up his mind not to pay attention to the songs, prayers, and the rite of the funeral service itself because he knew thoughts of Paul would crowd out what he was there to do that morning. It was not easy, but it paid off. Seeing a woman who had to have been a sister to Abel Masters was, for sure, the biggest surprise of the day. It reminded him to find a way to interview her and the brother to whom the father referred when he and Bentsen visited the Mast farmhouse that frigid day.

Seeing the warehousemen also reminded him that he and Bentsen had to buckle down and thoroughly review the remaining personnel and investigations files in their possession so that he could honor his promise to Lafferty. Given the case building against David Stoddard, he began to doubt the file review would produce anything of real value, but no murder investigation was complete until it was complete. At least that was the Walter Montgomery rule they all lived by.

Charles Niven's presence also reminded him he owed Montgomery a call to apprise him of a potential conflict of interest given his retainer of Niven to check into the records of Paulie's death.

~

When the service was over, Cunningham's professionals carried the casket with care and respect to the waiting hearse. Most of the congregants stood by quietly as this last part of the farewell proceeded to its conclusion. Strand doubted that many knew what would transpire once the hearse arrived at the Amish farm, but he noted that Charles Niven and his young companion observed it all closely.

When the doors were closed and the van drove off, Strand approached Niven and asked for a minute.

"What can I do for you, Detective?"

"Am I assuming correctly that you are here in your role as Masters's attorney?"

"Not exactly. I'm here representing the Masts simply to see that this part of the process was done to their satisfaction. At the farm, the family will ensure the transfer is done correctly."

"I'm glad someone decided that removing the body from the casket—in front of the gawkers here—and placing it on a board as required by the Amish with a shroud was unnecessarily ghoulish."

"Fortunately, we were able to avert doing that part of it here."

"The daughter, then?"

"Just a coincidence. When I saw her here, I thought I'd sit with her."

"How did she get here?"

"An English neighbor brought her. Her father does not know she's here."

"Introduce me, please?"

Turning to one side, he gestured to the pretty girl, who stepped forward. "Emma, this is Detective Strand."

She bowed her head, the bonnet concealing her face as she did so. "I remember you, sir," she said, making no reference to his business card.

"I take it you loved your brother, Abel, even though he left the community many years ago."

"Yes, sir. I was not yet born when Abel left, but he visited secretly many times and I and my sisters came to care for him as our brother."

Strand nodded. "And the brother who was working in the barn? How does he feel?"

"Levi? He was very little when Abel left, but he too wants to welcome him back today."

"Are you going against your father, you being here?"

Emma blushed deeply. "Yes, I will have to tell him someday. Mother knows."

"Did Abel ever tell you why he left the farm?"

"I-it is not for me to say, sir."

"I see. Do you think your brother, Levi, will talk to me?"

"That would be for Levi to decide, but I will say nothing more."

XXXIX

THEIR DAY NOT over, Strand called in to the Barracks to see how Stoddard was holding up, and more important to the moment, to find out if the drug-sniffing dogs found anything. Lieutenant Montgomery came on the line.

"Looks like you hit pay dirt, young man," Montgomery began. "The dogs found evidence of amphetamine tablets in three different locations on the darkest walkway away from the Investigations Center—isn't that the exit road from what you said? It seems that our friend was a little careless when doling out his sales, and dropped a few here and there, the idiot. Without the dogs, no one would ever have spotted them, small as they are."

Strand whistled. "Holy cats, Chief, that ties it all in a bow for Stoddard Your Friendly Government Dealer. Where the pills were found may suggest that he was peddling his wares to people other than those in his own Center."

"You can only hope, but I'm guessing you and Bentsen are coming in to do a little verbal tap dancing on Mr. Stoddard's lies."

"I'll collect Joe, and head right over."

Aboard the Vic, Strand and Bentsen drove the dozen miles to the Mercer Barracks where they hoped to work a bit of magic on their thick-headed detainee. On the way, they strategized their line of attack, especially if Stoddard insisted on obtaining a lawyer.

With the sun shining brightly in the western sky, they sped along SR58, and within not too many minutes, they were walking in the side door directly into the trooper's squad room. The few there hooted in their direction, their way of applause for having solved a couple of nasty murders.

"Not so, fast, my roadies," Bentsen called back to his pals. "It ain't over till it's over."

"Let's get some coffee and head into the interview room, if one of your buds will escort Mr. Stoddard into our lair," Strand said, a broad smile on his face.

They all laughed, having no idea where the afternoon's interrogation would lead.

A few minutes later, a careworn David Stoddard was escorted into the square, windowless box, and attached to the metal table via his manacles. Despite the availability of a shower, the prisoner appeared—and smelled—unwashed. An unhappy camper was he. "What's the deal with the handcuffs?"

"Is this coming from the same guy who lunged at my partner at the mine? There'll be no repeat performance, my friend," Bentsen began. "And it'll stay that way until we have some reason to think otherwise."

"So, what am I charged with, anyway?"

"When we brought you in, it was for assaulting a law enforcement officer, but now there's the drug possession for sale, actual sale. And with a little imagination, we can come up with a few other things," Bentsen said with a smirk.

"Oh," Strand added, "let's not forget to add in a couple of homicides when a few more pieces tumble into place?'

Stoddard's eyes became large blank spheres while his jaw slackened to rest on top of his several chins.

"So, Davey, my boy," Bentsen said as he circled the table, his prey trapped in place, "what's your big and important Maryland family going to do for you?"

"That's all bullshit, and my lawyer will get that all thrown out."

"Speaking of which," Bentsen said, "remember we've already read you your Miranda rights, and nothing has changed."

Looking Humpty Dumpty after the fall, Stoddard stared at them as if he hadn't heard a word.

"I'm betting the Mercer County DA could get an indictment on you with what we've got already," Bentsen said.

"You're full of crap, both of you!"

"The one who's full of it is you, pal," Strand said. "We've got you ten ways from Sunday, and no fancy family lawyer is going to make a difference, except in the old man's checkbook, if, that's if, he still knows you after he finds out what you're here for."

Stoddard nodded, almost imperceptibly.

"Did you say something?" Bentsen prompted.

"What am I lookin' at?"

"For attacking Detective Strand in the line of duty, it's a minimum of two years, but for drug possession and drug-dealing, it's a whole 'nother ball game," Bentsen said, waiting for a reaction, "which gets you ten to twenty."

"And that's only if the feds don't get interested."

"Jesus!"

"You better pray, my friend. If it's murder on top of it, it'll be life with no parole."

"Let me think for a minute."

"What's to think about?" Strand asked, then said, "If it was me and I had any information to deal with, I'd be makin' a deal as soon as I could sign it."

"What if I had information about my source for the drugs?"

"Which means what?"

"How I get them."

"What we want is how you get them, who delivers, and who you work for."

"I can give you the first, and maybe the second, depending upon what's on the table."

"And your boss in this little scheme?"

"I can't do that because I don't know," he began, his eyes darting around the room. "All I can say is it's someone from around here."

"Gotta do better, my friend," Bentsen said.

"I'll do better when I get an attorney to represent me, and when I know what it's all worth."

"It's worth nothing if we charge you with murder."

"But that's the problem, men. You may have me on the drug stuff, but never on murder, no matter what you've got. Despite what you think, I had no real motive to kill Masters or Rieger."

Strand leaned forward. "Let's try this: you're dealing, likely with a source in the mine, and both Rieger and Masters find out about it. Masters had you on the bubble anyway, and killing two birds, as they say, might have put you in the clear."

Stoddard swallowed hard. "Here's the problem for you. Why would a guy like me who's vulnerable to a lot of jail time want to do anything like murder to get bloodhounds like you snooping around? Huh? Makes no sense, does it?"

"Maybe to save your ass—rats in a corner tend to hiss and bite," Strand said.

"Bullshit. I want my lawyer."

Strand said, "Let's think this through, Stoddard, you've had your phone call—we know because we checked—and I don't see Daddy or one of his flacks on our doorstep, do you?"

"And?"

"And," Strand slammed it home, "time is of the essence. If Daddy doesn't come through, and you don't accept a court-appointed lawyer in the short term, Joe and I here will move on without you—and so any deal that might be available would go bye-bye, too."

Strand and Bentsen could both see the small beads of sweat on Stoddard's forehead, the jumpy fingers, the eyes shifting back and forth.

"What do I see there, Stoddard?" Strand asked. "Is it fear of the here and now, or is it just plain fright thinking about prison for a guy like you."

"And think about this, Davey," Bentsen began again. "Think about how you feel right now, clammy, dirty, closed in, powerless. That's going to be your daily routine, but of course, if you like things that way, just say nothing and you'll have even more years to enjoy it all."

"I'm telling you it just doesn't make sense!" His voice was loud, strained.

"Neither did attacking Strand, you dumb ass," Bentsen said. "That one dumb move was what began to unravel your whole stinking life."

"You mean I did this to myself?"

~

On the way home, Strand's cell phone buzzed. He tried to see who it might be but did not recognize the number. Seeing that it was a local area code, he answered and immediately regretted it.

"Is this Detective Strand? Hi, I'm Shelly Thompson from the *Sharon Herald,* and I want to talk to you about those murders down deep in the mine. Got a minute?"

"I've got a ton of time, Shelley, but not for you. There's no story I can give you about an ongoing investigation, and you know that."

"But the *Butler Eagle* has stories screaming murder, drugs, and what all, and it's only fair that we carry it for our readers as well."

"You're absolutely right about one thing, Shelley."

"And what's that?"

"You should get a hold of the *Eagle's* source, and get what you can," he said and clicked off.

XL

"IN HIS OFFICE, boys," was the greeting from Gloria Moses at the desk when Strand and Bentsen walked into the Mercer Barracks the next morning. As they walked by, Moses raised her hand and said in a hushed voice, "Say, Fletch, just what is the story with the lieutenant? I come in at 6 a.m. every day, and he's already here?"

"You haven't been here that long, Glor, and I'm surprised no one's filled you in. Montgomery's wife died some years ago, and this job is his life. In around 5 a.m. and out after the dinner hour. That's him."

"Wow," she said, "so he's not in that early to check on us?"

Strand laughed and said in the same low voice, "Of course he is. That's why this station has some of the top ratings in the state."

Exhaling, she said, "Well, that's a load off! Thanks. Off you go—he's waiting."

Bentsen already had his coffee, and as soon as Strand filled his cup and added just as much cream, they headed toward Montgomery's dusty and cramped sanctum.

"Sleep in this morning, men?"

"Actually, boss, we're both a bit early today. A lot to do," Bentsen said.

"Nice to hear that, Joe, and what about you, bright eyes? And don't spill any of that cream with coffee on my desk," he added before Strand could utter a syllable.

As his detectives were seating themselves, Montgomery backed his chair into the ratty venetian blinds between his chair and the window, and said, "Too nice a day to be sitting in here, isn't it?"

"Chief, you called us. What's on your mind?"

Montgomery tossed the morning *Sharon Herald* across his desk. "Seen this? Isn't this guy your brother's pal, Fletch?" Splattered across the front page was an article about Dr. Nathaniel Robertson right below a two-column photo of the smiling physician.

"Looks like a nice puff-piece throwing laurel wreaths on the local boy, eh?" Strand commented with obvious disdain. "And by the way, a *Herald* reporter called me yesterday on the way home begging for the same story the *Butler Eagle* is carrying about the mine murders. Seems there's a leak somewhere."

"Not surprised," Montgomery said, "and I'm assuming you told them nothing?"

"Right, Chief, talking with the press is a problem I don't need."

Montgomery grunted and nodded at the same time. "Back to Dr. Pretty-Boy here. Got a problem with him?" Montgomery eyed his man, one eyebrow arched.

"Yep, something I was going to talk to you about anyway, Chief. This so-called doctor took care of my brother before he died, and I'm being mighty generous using words like 'took care of,' and I wanted you to know I've spoken to an attorney to look into Paul's medical records."

Montgomery leaned forward, his black face gleaming under the overhead light, "I can't say as I blame you, Fletch. You didn't ask me, but this guy Robertson is nothing but a show-dog and something's going to catch him up. Maybe it'll be you, but why did you need to tell me about it?"

"I'm using Abel Masters's guy, Charles Niven, and I just wanted to make sure no one thought it a conflict of interest since he might be a witness at somebody's trial."

Montgomery closed his eyes behind the polished, rimless glasses perched on his nose, but only for a moment. "Noted. Do what you have to. I know you'll do what's right as far as the job goes, but in these cases, my friend, there's rarely the kind of satisfaction you're looking for."

"You have experience in this?" Strand said while Bentsen sipped his coffee and Bentsen continued to sit quietly.

Once again, Montgomery paused, then said, "Robertson took care of my wife, but in all honesty, there didn't seem to be an issue. A bad, sad case of cancer," he said, looking beyond them, "and maybe I didn't know any better, but even though he struck me the wrong way as a caregiver, I couldn't find fault. I shouldn't say so, but hope you do."

Strand sat back in his chair, taking it in. Just one more thing he and this man had had in common over the years, despite the differences in their race, religion, and where they came from, he thought.

"So, what's next with this Stoddard idiot?" Montgomery asked when he regained his focus.

"We'll give him one more day to decide on waiting for Daddy to come up with counsel, or we'll push a bit harder with him," Bentsen said.

"He knows the train could leave the station without him—and a deal."

Montgomery nodded. "Should we bring in your new fed friends, Flaherty and Kempinski, to lean on him?"

Strand said, "Not a bad idea, but let's hold off a bit."

Montgomery nodded. "What else are you doing on Masters and Rieger?"

"Shakin' the trees, boss, just straight old detective work," Bentsen said.

"Well, don't make a career out of it!"

"Got it. This morning, we're headed out to Amish country to see what else there is to know about Abel Masters."

"And Rieger?"

"At this point," Strand said, "we figure if we get one, we get the other, and Stoddard may be the key, or," he added with emphasis, "there's something going on here we just don't know about yet."

Montgomery nodded. "And don't forget to poke around in the Purcell case I gave you—in your spare time, that is."

~

"Purcell case?" Bentsen whispered to Strand out in the hallway.

"Yeah, you know, the old lady who was murdered in Foreston back in '64? Remember? He seems to think we have luck with the old dogs."

When they were back at their desks, Gloria Moses walked by and dropped a report on Strand's desk, "Isn't this the one you called about, Fletch?"

In front of him was the complete report from the drug-sniffing exercise, but because he'd already heard the meat of it on the phone, he almost didn't pick it up, but attached to it was the troopers' search of Stoddard's drug warehouse on Black Road. "You know, Joe, we should have banged on the door of that falling down wreck of a place Stoddard gave as his official address."

"Why? To find his huge drug stash?"

"No. To find out he really didn't live there—that's why the place didn't look occupied. The troopers found some paperwork on a table there indicating he has another residence—something else he's lied about."

"No shit," Bentsen said, then laughed. "Why that little rascal!"

"It's in Barkeyville. Say, didn't one of Rieger's men live there as well? Well, just another dot on our to-do list."

"On the way out the door, let's see if Montgomery can get us another warrant, and we can go check it out after our visit to Amish country."

XLI

THE DRIVE TO New Wilmington couldn't have been more pleasant given the brilliant sunshine across the long stretches of barren fields waiting for the plowmen. It was easy to tell when they were entering what everyone called Amish country.

In front of them and on either side of the main road, the fields were punctuated by clusters of an Amish family compound. Gleaming white clapboard homes caught the light. Near each home was a large barn if they were farmers, a sawmill if they were in the lumber business, or a pole building of sorts if they manufactured furniture. Often, a smaller residence attached to or not far from the main house was where the one set of grandparents lived in their old age, close enough to be helpful, but never a nuisance.

Black buggies with tan leather tops were aplenty. If during the day, it was a woman handling the reins of the one or two horses galloping along. The men were at their trades while the women and children managed everything else. There were few exceptions.

Strand always enjoyed his relatively few forays into the Amish community because their farms and equipment were neat and well-maintained. No rusting eyesores dotted the roadsides. And today would be better than their first visit to the Mast farm when they had the duty every law enforcement officer dreaded—to inform family members of a death. Those visits were never about people who died in a hospital bed. Nearly always, they followed a death by road accident, a weapon of force, or some industrial catastrophe. They were never easy, or forgettable.

Today, there was no unexpressed tension in the car as Bentsen steered the Vic onto the long lane to the large Mast homestead. Strand told him to pull the car over near the barn, which was thirty yards short of the house. "Let's see if brother Levi has anything to say."

The ground was frozen hard, despite the sun on their backs as they walked up the earthen ramp to the barn door. The only sound was Bentsen stepping onto a thin sheet of ice, and crashing through the shallow depression. It crackled like breaking glass.

A head poked out of the barn.

"Levi Mast?" Strand asked. "We're from the State Police and would like to talk to you for a minute."

Mast nodded, not with welcome, but with acquiescence, and went back in toward his work. As the detectives followed him in, they could see the monstrosity of a large mechanical device situated in the middle space just in front of the haylofts above.

"Good heavens," Strand said, mindful not to curse, even accidentally, in front of an Amishman, especially not when he's built like a bull, "what in the world is this thing?"

Mast chuckled. "This here is what we call a Sitrex finger wheel rake," he said, eyeing the device at his side with respect. Mast explained that it was a machine to be pulled behind a team of horses and consisted of a long steel shaft with metal ribs extending on both sides, and on each rib was mounted a five-foot-high wheel, each with some forty long, thin, spines extending from the hub, angled at the end, each with a point sharp as an ice pick. Strand counted eight such wheels while Levi spoke. "We use this at the end of the growing season to rake the hay, then make those haystacks you see in the fall. Makes pretty calendar picture, yah?" Mast laughed at his little joke.

Strand was surprised the man was so talkative. But then again, if you ask someone about their work, they're often happy to tell you about it. "But this is the end of winter, Levi, so what are you doing on this thing now?"

"Hah, you who do not farm do not understand. Over the winter, all equipment in the sheds must be cleaned, oiled, painted, sharpened for the next season. Not enough time to finish sooner," he finished abruptly.

"Thanks for that," said Bentsen, "I've seen these a hundred times but never in operation."

"You wouldn't want get near when it's running in the field. Very sharp," he said, touching, almost caressing one of the spines catching the light.

"Very interesting, Levi. Now, if you don't mind, can we talk about your brother?" Strand asked, impatient to get to the business at hand. Despite the frigid air, Mast seemed perfectly comfortable in a heavy denim jacket.

For a moment, his face held a blank look. "Brother?"

"Yes, wasn't Abel Masters your brother?"

"Abel, yes," he nodded, finally understanding.

"He was quite a few years older than you, is that right?"

"Yes, the oldest. First born after our Ma and Pa were married."

"I'm guessing," Bentsen jumped in, "they married very young then."

"Oh, yes," he laughed. "We choose early, marry early."

"That explains, then, the twenty-year difference in your ages."

"Yes," he laughed again, "we produce children over a long period—to work on the farm. No hired workers here," he said with some pride.

"Is that why your father seems so angry about Abel leaving?" Strand asked.

Mast's eyes went to the straw on the barn floor, as if thinking he needed to sweep it up. "Father is a strong-willed man, Mamm has said. They did not get along."

"Is that all?" Strand continued.

"Abel is smart, too smart to work for Datt."

"He could have done something else, no?" Bentsen asked.

"Yah. Maybe. But he left." He looked around them. "He sometimes met us in town, in Gilliland's parking lot he would wait. Datt did not know."

"So, you and he kept up with each other? But were you even born yet when he left?"

Mast smiled, his straight teeth one of his best features. "Mamm let him hold me when I was a baby, she said."

Strand nodded, having learned that Mrs. Mast found another way to have her say about things. "Did you see him often?"

"Once, twice a month since he came back from the big city."

"Why does your sister not want to talk to us?" Bentsen asked.

"You mean Emma? Mamm and me, we know what Datt does not know, but the girls are afraid of him.

"And you?"

"Me? I'm afraid of him, too, but I choose not to cross him—to his face."

The visit with Levi Mast ended when the three heard shoes crunch on the gravel outside. "Datt wants you to come in, Levi," said his sister Emma, who promptly turned and walked back to the house.

"Is there something we should know about your father, Levi?" asked Bentsen, who was taller than but not as broad as Levi.

Surprised, he answered. "No. If you mean was Datt rough with us? Never. Stern but never rough. When we were little, if there was spanking to do, it was Mamm who did it." He laughed out loud. "And some of us deserved it." He paused, thoughtful. "All Amish fathers are strong—heading the household and such. We are very close. My sisters, they and me too, we would never leave our family and community. It's what we know and love, Mister, so no, again, don't get the wrong idea. We have a good family life."

"Before we go, Levi, do you mind if I ask you about your little sister? What happened to her?"

Mast's face darkened, and it was a few seconds before he spoke. "Accident. Little Hannah was riding with my brother pulling the

Sitrex here. She let her feet dangle. One got caught. Bad accident."

"Brother? You can't mean Abel."

"No, not him. Too much I've said. Datt would be mad. I'd better go."

When Mast left and the detectives climbed back into the warm Vic, Strand said, "Well, that explains Masters's frequent rides out here."

"Right," Bentsen agreed. "He wasn't as alone as everybody thought."

Strand glanced at the Sitrex again as they turned to leave, hoping never to be up close to the thing again.

XLII

THE PAIR DEPARTED New Wilmington and headed east toward the clutch of houses and a few businesses that people called Barkeyville, always inspiring a number of dog jokes, none of them hilarious. First, of course, came the discussion about lunch.

"Too bad we don't have any reason to drive to Pittsburgh," Strand said, "so that we could get somebody's famous pierogi."

"Sign me up, but don't let your Polish genes get us into bigtime trouble, Fletch. You hardly ever mention pierogi, so what's gotten into you?"

"You know, Joe," Strand went on as Bentsen piloted the Vic, "every once in a while, I think about my mother and how much she endured to keep us on the straight and narrow."

"But pierogi?"

"Look, she agreed to go to the Presbyterian church with my Dad because she loved him and wanted to set a good example for us, but she hated the idea of giving up the faith she was born to. It was not easy for her or the Italian women who did the same thing back then—and they never talked about it."

"But she took you and your brothers to church, didn't you say?"

"Oh, yeah. I think my Dad knew, but decided to look the other way. He understood."

"But back to pierogi?"

"Ma made only two kinds, cabbage and farmer's cheese. And she served them without onions because onions gave my Dad heartburn," Strand said, laughing. "It was his karma, his penance, Ma said, but that's what I grew up with, and I miss them. Pittsburgh has a few places where they still make 'em."

"So, since Pittsburgh is not on the way to Barkeyville, where are we going for lunch?"

Strand looked out the passenger window as the stark countryside rolled by. "Hey, you know what, Joe, there's a great sub shop on the way. Let me tell you what a Red October is."

"I'm listening," Bentsen said, his head cocked, just as a dog's when it hears the word "treat."

"Look, it's an Italian sub with salami, ham, lettuce, tomato, onion, baked with Italian dressing."

"Oh, man, you're speakin' my language."

Twenty minutes later, they were sitting in the Clintonville sub shop, enjoying the variety of tastes resplendent in the Red October with warm dressing oozing out the sides. Satisfied after their fifteen-minute break, they flew up the road to find the Barkeyville address Stoddard worked so hard to hide.

By pre-arrangement via the cell phone that Strand didn't always despise, troopers were there waiting to execute the search warrant Montgomery had obtained for them that morning. As they pulled into the driveway, they saw a large home, very much unlike the much more modest affair once occupied by Stoddard's boss. The man lived well, seemingly well above what a Branch Manager in the mine might be expected to afford.

"I guess the drugs would have paid for this," Bentsen observed as they pulled to a stop behind the state cruiser.

The detectives exchanged greetings and walked around the house in search of an easy entry. None found, they forced the back door and entered. For over an hour, the four men searched the premises, garage included, and what they found was nothing. The house was largely empty of furniture and personal odds and ends like family photos. Stoddard's kitchen and bedroom appeared occupied, but not much beyond that. Even so, Strand and Bentsen were surprised their search failed to produce even one syringe or vial of insulin, or any other shred of evidence they could use against David Stoddard.

Comparing notes amongst themselves, the officers were satisfied nothing had been concealed from them, and in short order, they secured the house and left.

"That's a bummer!" Strand said, dejected.

"Yeah, because I can't think of any other places to look for evidence that Stoddard killed Masters and Rieger, no matter how good the rest of the pieces fit together."

~

"Well," Strand said as they began the short ride to the mine, "we've still got Stoddard for drugs, and I can't help thinking he's a part of the puzzle for Masters and Rieger. But for the life of me, I can't see how."

"Fletch, remember this isn't a one-hour TV show. *Law & Order* is great, but this is the real world, and solving some of the murder cases we get might take a few episodes," he said with a smirk.

"You're singin' to the choir, Joe. I thought we had the guy. We'll just have to keep working it."

"And hold Montgomery at bay," Bentsen said with a snort.

At the mine, they checked in with Novak and asked if the conference room was free for a chat with Judy Conlon. Gracious for once, Novak said, "Why not use Abel's office. It's private and available."

The detectives and Mrs. Conlon sat down right after she offered them coffee. "What more can I tell you, gentlemen?"

"We've learned a good bit since our first talk, Mrs. Conlon," Bentsen began, "but there's more to know, we think."

"What you told us about Mr. Masters has hung together well," Strand said, "so, this time around, we're wondering what you could tell us about David Stoddard, Al Rieger, and Masters—and their relationships. Were any of them close?"

"No. I told you Mr. Masters kept to himself, here and away from the office, from what I could observe. As far as the others are concerned, none of them ever gave me a clue there'd been any socializing amongst them. Mr. Masters didn't eat lunch with his managers, but I think some of them, the managers, I mean, ate lunch together."

"Like Rieger and Stoddard?" Strand asked.

"If they did, it wasn't often," she said, rolling her eyes.

"Any notion as to what Masters thought of those two?"

Conlon shifted in her seat and cleared her throat. "Mr. Masters would make a comment to me from time to time, maybe just to vent or to see what I thought about it."

"We get the idea you have always been the well of all knowledge here, Mrs. Conlon," Bentsen prompted.

She smiled and said, comfortably, "For whatever reason, people here tell me things they wanted Mr. Masters to know, or for me to just keep under my hat, or maybe even to see if I might comment, but I've never fallen for that. I think the reason I've done well here is that I keep myself to myself, if you know what I mean."

"So, what did Mr. Masters think about those two?"

"As for Al, Mr. Masters thought he was very competent as a facility manager, but they had nothing in common otherwise, so Al wasn't up here much except when there was a problem of some sort."

"With Stoddard?" Strand asked.

"Al thought something was amiss with Stoddard of late, and I think he was also worried he had a bad egg or two in his own shop. He was a pretty nervous guy, you know."

"How did Mr. Masters take all of this?"

"Oh, he and David did not sit well together, as I may have mentioned. Oil and water, but there was no indication, at least to me, that it was more than that."

"You know, of course, we've arrested Stoddard for drug possession and drug-dealing in the mine. What do you think about that?"

With no change in her demeanor, she said, "Well, that certainly explains all the walks Stoddard took along the mine walkways. I supposed he just had a bad nicotine habit."

"Anybody else comment on that?"

"Only that he never seemed to take the direct path from here to the gate, but he took the parallel walkway so many others in the mine used to enter and exit."

"Hmmm!" Strand said. "Thanks, that's helpful, and now that you've had time to think about it, about where Stoddard was getting his drugs, what Al Rieger knew about it, or for that matter, if Masters suspected anything—any ideas you have would be helpful as well."

Conlon nodded, thinking. "Just in the last day or two before Mr. Masters died, there was something going on. He spent a lot of time with a file on his desk, somebody's background investigation, I think, and he seemed pre-occupied."

"Whose file?"

"I have no idea. Stoddard came up here on occasion to talk about a case or two, and it may have concerned one of those. And Al Rieger was up here too about some case."

"Did either of them comment at all?"

"Only for Stoddard to say, something like, 'Now I understand why this whole privatization thing has come down on our heads.'"

XLIII

T HE DETECTIVES REMAINED in the conference room while Judy Conlon left to page Al Rieger's warehousemen one by one and brought them in.

While waiting for the first, Bentsen said, "You know, I never got a chance to get to any of the files on these guys. I thought you had. Anything interesting?"

Strand looked at him sideways. "Oh, Christ, Joe, all I did was glance at them, and for whatever reason, I thought you had. We'd better get to them and get them back to Lafferty ASAP, before there's federal hell to pay."

"It won't make any difference, I'm guessing. Nothing's pointed to any of these guys, but if Stoddard isn't our guy, then we'll have to dig a little deeper," he added with disgust.

"Right," Strand said, "except that there's not too many other places to look."

The conference room door opened, and Judy Conlon ushered in Artie McKenna. "Not you guys again," the man said, sarcasm draping his words.

"Sit down, Artie, but leave your attitude at the door."

"It's taken you guys a long time to talk to me."

"But now we have two murders, and gee, you're now in the spotlight. How do you like it?"

"What the hell do you mean?" McKenna demanded, his face getting as red as his hair.

"Nothin' yet," Bentsen said, and proceeded to quiz McKenna on his movements before and after both the Masters and Rieger bodies were found. Nothing.

"What do you know about David Stoddard?" Strand ventured.

"That prick? He was too good to talk to us, not even when he went out into the walkway to have his smokes."

"A real regular, was he?"

"I could set my watch if I wanted to. It was always when people from the other facilities were on break, and he would walk with them. I guess we weren't good enough." He paused. "Hey, how're you guys doing with Al's killer, anyway?"

"You said 'Al's,'" Bentsen said. "Why not Masters?"

"You know, Al was our boss, a good guy."

"Yeah, I saw you at the funeral," Bentsen said. "Any of you guys have a grudge against Rieger?"

"Naw. Most of us have friends or relatives working here and we've known Al for a long time. Different kind of guy, you know, always nervous about something, but a good guy."

"Anything special to be nervous about?"

"Him? Could be about the time of day. If you're wondering about Al being connected with Stoddard on the drug thing everybody's talkin' about, no way, man! No way."

Bentsen nodded, looked at Strand, and sent McKenna on his way.

～

Frank Sharpe was next, a man in his early forties and the only Black person in Rieger's branch. If Artie McKenna, short as he was, could not have manhandled Masters's body, Sharpe could. Of strong build, he could have moved a ton of bricks with ease. He sat down heavily in the seat to which he was directed.

"I don't have anything to say to you. I don't know anything."

"What a short interview! And we haven't asked you a thing, Frank," Bentsen said.

"Look, I don't mean anything by it, but we're all a good team, and I don't want to say anything to hurt anybody."

Strand spoke. "Think about this, Frank, we've got two dead men here, possibly by the same hand, so nobody's more hurt than Abel Masters and Al Rieger."

"Sorry. I meant nothing, and I know nothing."

Twenty minutes later, Strand and Bentsen agreed. They had to wait a few minutes for the next man, Elgin Meister. "You gotta wonder," Bentsen said, "how a guy like Sharpe wound up here. There are so few Black people who've ever decided to live up this way, yet some have."

"Interesting. One of these days, we might get an answer."

Conlon poked her head in the door and apologized. "We didn't know where he'd gotten to, but he's on his way."

When he finally appeared, Elgin Meister was just as imposing as Frank Sharpe but in a totally different way. He was of solid build, all muscle bulging through his blue work shirt. To Strand, he had a familiar look about him, but couldn't tell if they'd ever met before.

"Do we know each other, Mr. Meister?"

"N-no, sir," he said, and stopped, sitting himself down when Bentsen motioned to a chair.

"Were you out in the walkway when we found Mr. Rieger's body?"

"Y-yes, sir, with the other folks gathered 'round."

"Surprised at what happened, then?" Bentsen asked.

"W-why yeah, I mean, yes, sir, poor Mr. Rieger."

"Who had a reason to kill him, Mr. Meister?"

"N-no one I can think of."

"How about Abel Masters?"

Staring straight ahead, he said, "Why would anyone want to kill Mr. Masters?"

"And David Stoddard?" Bentsen continued.

Half rising from his chair, fingertips on the table, Meister said,

"He's dead!?"

Strand half rose as well, "Nobody said Stoddard was dead, Mr. Meister. Should he be?"

"Well, dealing drugs and all," he responded, settling back down.

"What do you know about that?" Bentsen again.

"Nothing."

"Do you think Stoddard brought his drugs in here to sell or did someone here help him?"

"Why're you asking me? I know nothing about it."

"You seem awfully jumpy for a guy who knows nothing," Strand said. "And by the way, you refer to them as Mister Rieger and Mister Masters. Most other people called them by their first names. Why are you so polite?"

Still staring at the space between his questioners, he said, "Maybe my folks raised me right. And besides, I haven't been here as along as the others."

"Oh?" Bentsen asked, his pencil poised above his pad.

"Just a few years."

"Who hired you?"

"Mr. Rieger."

"Anything else you can tell us?" Bentsen asked.

"Nothing."

"You can go now. We may want to talk to you again later, but please see that Manzini comes in, will you?"

"Manzini? You're talking to everybody?"

"Yep. Is that a problem?" Bentsen wanted to know.

"No, sir," he said half rising, briefly unsure of what to do next and then making for the door. As he opened it, Manzini could be seen leaning against the opposite wall in the hallway, fright the only expression to be read on his face.

XLIV

FOR ANOTHER MINUTE, the door remained closed and neither man was visible. To Strand, the door remained closed longer than needed, but he and his partner waited patiently as the seconds ticked by.

At last, Angelo Manzini strode in, not like he owned the place, not like McKenna, but as if propelled by some invisible force. He clearly did not want to be there. A wiry but seemingly strong man, his sleeves rolled up on his biceps, he marched to the chair and without a word, sat down as if he suddenly belonged there.

"Comfortable, Mr. Manzini?" Bentsen began.

"What do you want?"

"Surely, you must have been told by somebody exactly what we want," Strand pointed out. "Surely, Elgin Meister had a word with you out in the hallway, so how about telling us what that was all about?"

"N-nothing at all." He thought for a moment. "Just reminding me about the run to Breezewood we need to load, that's all."

"Hmm. I thought you'd have already known that," Strand continued. "You sure that was all he said?"

"Sure."

"How was Italy, Mr. Manzini?" asked Bentsen trying another tack.

"Why do you ask?"

"Was that such a hard question?" Bentsen paused in the silence. "How long were you gone?"

"That's none of your business, is it?"

"Do you want to come down to the Mercer Barracks with us so we can explain our business to you?" Strand asked, his voice rising just enough.

"No, no, we can talk here. I was there with my family visiting relatives in Napoli. We were gone almost two weeks."

"First time?" Bentsen asked.

"No. We've been there twice."

"Last year, too? That's expensive, isn't it, Angelo?" Bentsen purred.

"Y-yes, but we travel cheap," Manzini said, as if pleased with himself.

"You said 'family.' How many is that?"

Manzini licked his lips. "My wife and I and four kids."

"Hmm," Strand said and waited a moment. "Have any other jobs, Angelo?"

"Just this one."

"And your wife?"

"She's at home with the kids. That's best."

"That's very nice, Angelo," said Bentsen, jumping in.

"You still haven't told me why you're asking me all these questions."

"Haven't you heard, Angelo," Strand asked, sarcasm draped on his words, "we have two murdered men here and a drug dealer in custody, so what do you know about any of that?"

"Why would I know anything?"

"Funny how you and Meister seem to answer big questions with another question, but not much of an answer," Bentsen said. "You work here, Angelo," he continued, his voice and words more aggressive, "so there's a lot you know and we don't, so what do you know about David Stoddard? About Al Rieger? About Abel Masters?"

"I told you, nothing at all."

"You've been here a while, haven't you? And you hear stuff, don't you?"

"I suppose. But none of that involves me. People treat me right, so I have no gripes."

"How nice of you," Stand said, "but what about all the drugs?"

"No drugs in here, I can tell you—I've never heard of it."

"You make me very curious, Angelo, so you can plan on us talking again."

After a minute when no one said anything and Bentsen was bent over his pad, Manzini began to rise. "Can I go then?" he asked, victory in his voice.

"Go, but not far, my friend."

～

Lindy Johnston was the oldest and the last of the bunch, probably in his mid-fifties, and according to Joe Novak, the man temporarily responsible for facility management until a Rieger replacement could be identified. He had the lined face of a man who'd seen a lot in his life, and was prepared for whatever came.

Strand opened with a guess. "Sit down, Mr. Johnston," he said as the man lowered himself into the chair opposite, a look of confidence about him. "Do you mind if I ask, were you in the war? You seem to be about the right age."

Johnston nodded. "Good observer, Detective. I can see why you're probably good at what you do."

"Navy?" Strand asked, nodding at the tattoo on his inside left forearm.

"Right again, but you didn't call me in to talk about Viet Nam, did you?"

"No, sir," Strand continued, "but you seem different than the other men here."

"Maybe. Not too many vets. I took a government job as soon as I got out. First at the VA Hospital in Butler, then here."

"Because it's closer to home?"

"That, and I'd seen enough in the service, and those poor bastards at the VA reminded me too much of the friends I'd left over there."

Strand nodded. "Are you close to any of the guys in your crew?"

"Not especially. I live in Harrisville, not far from Artie McKenna, and we carpool sometimes, but no, I don't see any of these guys after work."

"I'm guessing Novak put you in charge because you're the most experienced?" Bentsen asked.

"Probably, but he could have picked Artie as well, but not the other two."

"Why not them, Mr. Johnston?"

"A couple of these guys, Sharpe and Manzini, think they're doing you a favor coming in when they're supposed to, and the other one, Meister, he's a bit different, and pretty new."

"Thanks," Bentsen said. "A real answer for a change."

"You know, of course, why we're here, Mr. Johnston. We've got two homicides and a drug dealer—not what you'd expect here at the Investigations Center, eh?"

"Yes, sir. Masters and Rieger—two good guys, and before you ask, I have no idea who or why anyone would want to kill them. Both of them, program guys, guys you could trust to take care of business, if you know what I mean. As for Stoddard, don't waste the ammunition, just feed that bastard to the dogs as far as I'm concerned."

"You have strong feelings, then," Bentsen said.

"You bet I do," Johnston said, his blue eyes intense as any could be, "I fought for my country then, and working here, I'm fighting for my country now. Guys like Stoddard we could do without."

"Before I forget to ask this, Mr. Johnston," Strand interrupted, "who knows how to set and de-activate the alarm system here?"

Puzzled for a moment, Johnston said, "Oh, I thought you knew. Masters, Novak, Rieger, all the supervisors who opened in the morning, and, of course, myself and the warehouse guys."

"Why the warehousemen?"

"Odd hours we sometimes work, deliveries, stuff like that."

Strand nodded. "Thanks."

Bentsen resumed, as if there'd been no interruption at all. "Again, any ideas who might have killed either of the men?"

"Stoddard? He had a lot to keep hidden, apparently," he began but didn't get to finish his thought.

The room shook briefly after a distant boom of some sort, and a shower of dust floated down upon them. Johnston rose from his seat as if in wartime. "You guys have a car, right? You'll have to help evacuate some of the less abled. C'mon," he directed.

Strand and Bentsen rose and followed.

Judy Conlon was at the door, "There's been a small cave-in. One of the ribs in the main passage gave way, we have to get out. Go to your car and wait—we'll bring you some of our older people."

Strand and Bentsen looked at each other. "This happen before, Mrs. Conlon?" Strand asked.

"Never in my twenty years here, but we've drilled to be ready. Let's go."

"Go where?" Bentsen asked.

"You're going to drive out and up the ramp into the parking lot until there's an all clear."

The detectives did as ordered, and already at the Vic, two older ladies with canes were waiting. The women clambered in the back seat, chattering as they did. "I've never been in a police car before," one chirped, and the other announced, "I can't believe this is happening. Look—there's rock laying in the other passageway," she said pointing to the semi-darkened area beyond the cutout where they were parked.

They could see headlights of other vehicles splay on the dark limestone wall beyond, and some men running there, but everyone else, several vehicles and hundreds of people, were moving fast toward the main gate, and the Vic fell in line.

"I don't work here," Bentsen said, "but something about this isn't right, is it?"

"No, it isn't," the chirper chirped. "This kind of thing never happens."

"If it did, no one would ever work here!" the announcer announced.

"Right on that," Bentsen said, smiling to himself. He could see Strand working on a soft chuckle despite the possible catastrophe in which they'd found themselves.

"I don't believe in coincidences, Joe, and neither do you." Strand's grin changed to something else when he thought further.

No sooner had the Vic rested in a spot amidst the throng of people and vehicles in the parking lot above the mine than a black sedan pulled up beside them. Roger Davis, the mine's general manager, jumped out of his Lexus and rushed over to the Vic's driver's side window.

"You fellas need to come back in," Davis said, then noticing the two women in the back seat, gestured for Bentsen, who was driving, to step out. "That was no cave-in in there. We'll bring the people back inside after a while—good thing it's a nice day out here for a change—but you two need to come back in now. There's a body."

XLV

I T TOOK A minute for the ladies to exit the Vic and find another place to chirp and announce. Then the detectives turned the Vic around and followed Davis back into the mine and down the main passageway to the parking cut-out. The place was eerily devoid of people and other vehicles, except at the spot where two USC workmen were setting up giant work lights.

After they parked, Strand and Bentsen followed Davis to a pile of jagged rocks about four feet high and fifteen feet across. Some of the surfaces appeared to glisten, but only where the facets still had silver paint on them. It was an unnerving scene, especially when Strand focused his eyes where Davis was pointing. There at the bottom of the pile was a shoe, attached to which was a man's leg. The rest of him was under the rubble.

"Why am I not surprised?" Bentsen asked of no one.

"Mr. Davis, get to a landline, please, and call for an ambulance, no siren necessary, a few more troopers, and let's get Dr. McCreary here as soon as possible," Strand said. Off the man went toward the Investigations Center, the closest facility.

"Wanna bet it's one of the guys we just talked to?" he asked, looking up at Bentsen as he crouched down for a better look. Then, to the workmen, he said, "Look, guys, I know this is not in your job description, but we need you to carefully lift these rocks from the victim."

"Is he dead?" one man asked.

"Pretty likely, but either way, we need to find out. If there's a chance he's alive, we need to get to it, and we'll help," Strand said, taking off his overcoat and stepping to the task. Bentsen and the other two joined him, working from the edges of the pile inward.

Soon, a good bit of the debris, heavy rocks with sharp edges, was lifted from the body with care not to step anywhere that might put weight on the man underneath. There was no movement from him, no moan, no sound. Strand and Bentsen, their hands scraped and bleeding, took care to remove the last of the jagged rocks until they could see the whole body.

"It's Angelo Manzini," Strand said, attempting to feel for a pulse, though the man's torso and head were crushed. There was some blood, but not a lot. "Nothing," he said, and stepped back. One of the workmen, noticing the detectives' bleeding hands, said he was going for a first aid kit. The other man went to the far wall and vomited.

~

It took forty-five minutes for McCreary to arrive, but before he made his entrance, an ambulance had arrived, and the medical technician assured Strand and Bentsen the man was dead. "He'll have to be pronounced by the coroner," he said, then waited at the ambulance. Strand could hear them discussing how to remove the body when given permission to do so, and do so with care not to allow bodily fluids and tissue to soil their vehicle.

From what they could see, the only apparently intact part of the victim was the leg that had been first visible. The rest of Manzini had taken quite a beating from what had probably been a thousand pounds of sharp rocks that had pounded him into raw meat.

Davis and the facility managers, assured of the circumstances of the rockfall, had apparently decided to permit employees back in the mine. Despite the screen shielding the crime scene, the mine's denizens rubbernecked their way back to work.

Bentsen said, "Probably to keep them from calling everybody they knew."

To no avail. Shortly after McCreary's arrival, Davis informed them reporters from the *Butler Eagle,* the *Sharon Herald,* and soon, the two Pittsburgh papers were queuing at the gate. "Do we have to let them in?" Davis asked Bentsen.

"It's your mine to manage, Mr. Davis," Bentsen said, then added, "but you'll have to talk to them sometime. Otherwise, they'll print God knows what based on what people here will tell them."

Davis nodded and turned to his car while McCreary called for more light directly on the body while he did a preliminary examination. Strand and Bentsen hovered nearby.

McCreary had his own light source, a powerful, small flashlight of sorts, and began assessing the damage to the dead man. "So glad you two are here. There couldn't be a murder without you guys," he said lightly, despite his present chore.

"That's what they pay us for—to wait on you, Doc," Strand said, keeping the banter going.

After several minutes, during which no one spoke, McCreary forced himself upright, took a few steps, turned to the detectives, and said, "Want the bad news?"

"Not really," Bentsen said, "but I'm sure you won't disappoint us."

"Of course, I can't make this official until I get the gentleman on the table, but the wound on his temple is dissimilar from all of his other wounds."

"Meaning?" It was Strand who spoke to McCreary but stared at the body.

"Meaning it appears to be the same kind of wound as we saw on Mr. Rieger's temple. The rest of the mutilation to this man is post-mortem. That's why you see little blood below the head."

"But what caused this little landslide?" Strand asked.

"That's what they pay you for, isn't it? You want my guess? Once you sift through all the debris, I'm betting you'll find the bits of a small explosive device detonated so that we'd all think the victim died from the rockfall." McCreary raised his eyebrow as if to underline his hunch, and at once pulled out a cigar and lit it. He nodded at the ambulance attendants to remove the body and instructed them where to take it.

"Want to stop by tomorrow morning, gents? I may have more answers for you, and if your crew can get here," McCreary added, gesturing toward the pile of rock, "you'll probably have some information for me as well."

XLVI

Outside the mine, Strand called in to Lieutenant Montgomery. "Chief, we have another body. An hour ago in the mine. While we were interviewing our last witness, the whole place shook for a second or two, and we were all directed to evacuate. One of the warehousemen we'd just interviewed was found under a pile of rock."

"How in God's world did that happen?"

"We don't know yet, but McCreary has an idea what killed him, and the explosives crew will attempt to determine what made the rock come down."

"Glad you guys are OK. No other developments, then?"

"Only more evidence about Stoddard as a drug dealer, and it seems probable his customers weren't colleagues with security clearances. Lafferty ought to be happy about that!"

"You're breaking up. We can talk in the morning."

"It just occurred to me, Joe," Strand said after ending the call, "that at the moment, we're the best people to inform the Manzini family of what's just happened."

"Yep, and check out his residential situation while we're at it."

"He sure seemed to fit the role as Stoddard's accomplice, didn't he?"

"Yeah, and if this was no accident as McCreary suspects, that means he either knew too much, or was involved, and…"

"And there's still someone else involved—and he works in the mine."

"And it's likely that we'd just interviewed him."

"So, if we cross off Lindy Johnston…" Bentsen began.

"We're down to Sharpe, Meister, and McKenna," Strand said, finishing the sentence.

~

The late Angelo Manzini lived on the north edge of Butler in somewhat of an upscale neighborhood not far from the town mall on SR308. At first, they drove by the home, not thinking it could belong to a man living on a warehouseman's government salary, but there it was.

At the end of a long driveway stood a two-story brick colonial with a two-car garage attached at the side. On the large concrete pad abutting the driveway near the garage was a newer RV, obviously large enough for a family of six from what they could see.

After parking the Vic, the detectives walked toward the front door, past manicured spaces extending the length of the home's front. After a moment, an attractive woman with styled black hair opened the door.

"Yes, I can help you?" she asked, a bit of an accent present in her words, as often happens when those newer to English mismatch voice tone and words or cadence.

Strand identified himself and Bentsen and asked if they could come inside.

"Of course. Is there something wrong?"

The interview with Regina Manzini did not go as most do when a surviving spouse has to be informed of their partner's death. With his gentle giant approach, Joe Bentsen began by telling her that her husband, Angelo, was dead.

For a moment, Regina showed no reaction. None at all. As she sat on the couch in their elaborately appointed living room, not a muscle in her body gave evidence that she was alive.

Then, in one convulsive flash, her whole upper body heaved in grief. "Say no more. I tell him this would happen. We can't go on like this, I say to him."

"What do you mean, Mrs. Manzini?" Bentsen asked.

Strand noted that Bentsen only said Angelo was dead, not how it happened. He hadn't said he was murdered, because Doc McCreary had not yet officially declared it so. While Bentsen took the lead, Strand observed her and her surroundings.

"He bring home too much money, but he not tell me how he gets it. He was doing something wrong, no? Now, he's gone."

Changing the subject, Bentsen then asked, "I take it you're not from this country? No relatives here?"

"No. Angelo bring me back from Napoli nine years now—we have three girls and a son named after Angelo. What shall we do?"

It was a question so many asked. It was the unanswerable question, yet Bentsen, never one to give up, said, "It's one day at a time, Mrs. Manzini. We'll find you some help to get through all this."

"Good idea, Joe," Strand said. "How about calling the Barracks and have someone there get hold of the social services people and get a rep out here pronto? She's going to need a lot of help now," he continued in a lower voice.

Bentsen nodded and stepped away.

"Now, Mrs. Manzini, if I may ask, did Angelo ever say how he made so much money?"

She thought about it. "No, he just say he and friend at work sell stuff to people." She threw up her hands. "That's all I know."

"We're having some people come by to help you with things. In the meantime, is there a neighbor who can stay with you?"

"Y-yes, across street. Mrs. Steves. She's home."

Hearing this, Bentsen nodded to Strand and went out the front door as it began to rain. In a few minutes, Mrs. Benita Steves— somebody's grandmother, Strand thought—bustled through the door and went right to her friend.

"Thank you, Mrs. Steves," Strand said. "Someone from the county will be here withing thirty minutes, they said."

Before they left, Bentsen asked to speak to the neighbor for a moment, but she knew nothing about the Manzinis' financial situation. She rolled her eyes to heaven and said, practically in a whisper, "I told my husband, Leo, not to get involved here. Something wasn't right, but this I can tell you. Regina and these kids are the sweetest people on earth." Bentsen having briefed her, she added, "They deserved better." She turned and went back to the couch where Regina sat, weeping quietly.

XLVII

BACK IN THE Vic, Strand said, "As unpleasant as this is going to be, I'll call Montgomery and have him obtain another search warrant. It's unlikely Manzini brought home any direct evidence of his involvement with Stoddard and whoever, but we'll have to check that box."

Bentsen nodded and said, "While we still have a few hours of light, let's do drive-by's of the McKenna, Meister, and Sharpe residences. Then, tomorrow, my friend, we'd better have another go at David Stoddard."

"And if he's stubborn, we can see if Flaherty and Kempinski have a couple of hours to spare. Maybe they can put the fear of God into him."

"Yep, right after we see what Doc McCreary and the explosives guys have to tell us."

"And one way or the other, we've got to take a closer look at their files!"

First came Frank Sharpe's modest two-bedroom rambler on the main road running through Barkeyville. The home looked exactly like one might expect of a man in his job situation, and it looked well-maintained except for an ice-encased kid's bike outside near the front door. Theoretically, both Manzini and Sharpe made the same amount of money, and unless Manzini somehow won the Irish Sweepstakes, there was no explanation for the difference in the size and substance of their living circumstances.

Artie McKenna's place in Harrisville appeared to be a small working farm, right sized for a man with a full-time job, but who increased his income in an honest fashion. Near the two-story white frame farmhouse was a barn large enough for a few implements and a horse or two. Strand and Bentsen took note of what they'd seen, and headed toward Foreston, where Elgin Meister listed his address.

"I'm not sure," said Strand, "but I think this might be one of the apartments owned by a friend of mine. We'll see."

Once back in the Borough of Foreston, they drove slowly up North Broad Street and found Meister's address. "My barber, Ed Thomas, has his shop at the back of his eight-unit apartment building. It's been here half a century. Looks like Meister has an apartment with him."

"Is Meister married?" Bentsen asked.

"Don't believe so, but now I know why this guy looks familiar. You remember me talking about Anthony's restaurant right on the main drag downtown?"

"Yeah, the place where the rolls are swimming in garlic butter?"

"Right, the one Aurora refuses to go into because she says she has to have all her clothes dry-cleaned after eating there."

"But the food's good?"

"Oh, is it! Best Italian food in the area. Aurora makes me pick it up."

"So, what's this restaurant have to do with where Meister lives?"

"The owner is Ed Thomas's cousin. Either I've seen him at Anthony's or somewhere else in town. Anyway, that's what I think."

"Hmmm!" Bentsen said. "It looks like this guy Meister lives well within his means, so no issue here."

A day at the Mercer Barracks could be fascinating, intense, or down-right boring. At their desks, Strand and Bentsen sat facing each other, coffee and stale donuts each within reach, while they shuffled through what reports lay scattered in front of them. After a minute, a slurp, and a bite, Bentsen said, "Let me check with Gloria, and we'll see if anything's back from the explosives boys."

While he was gone, Strand called Charles Niven and swore to himself when he realized the attorney wouldn't be in so early. "No attorney ever is," he said to no one while waiting for the standard re-cording to play through before he could leave a voice message. "This is Detective Strand, Charles, and I'm calling to see if there's been any development on your research about Dr. Nathaniel Robertson. Please call back when you can. Thanks."

"Nothing yet, but Gloria says a lot of this stuff floats in after 9 a.m.," Bentsen reported upon his return.

"Just as well. Let's finish our breakfast and see how Mr. Stoddard is enjoying one of our executive suites," Strand smirked.

They waited in the interrogation room for Stoddard to do his es-corted march into their presence. With a studied look of not having a care in the world, they readied themselves for whatever Stoddard had to pitch.

Clad in the standard prison garb of the day—a gray one-piece jump-suit affair, a zipper up the front, no belt, and soft slippers—their prison-er looked just as gray as his clothing, unshaven, and even shorter than before as he sat stoop-shouldered in front of them. He said nothing.

As agreed, the detectives remained silent for a full minute before Bentsen said, still leaning back in his chair, "Hear from Daddy yet?"

"No," he began with an air of defiance rapidly dissipating, "I'm sure he's busy, but he's sick, too, so I have to be patient."

"Good thing you have a lot of patience, Davey boy," Bentsen con-tinued, "but we have so much less."

"It's David. So, what do you want from me?"

"For starters, friend," Strand said, leaning in and taking a chance, "how long have you been working with Angelo Manzini in the drug business?"

Face frozen for seconds, Stoddard finally replied, "Why don't you ask him?"

"I'm asking you, dipstick."

"I'm not talking until my attorney gets here."

"Are you telling us," Bentsen asked, standing up and taking a step closer to Stoddard's chair, "you don't know what we're talking about?"

"Look, Detective, I told you I'm not talking. And I'm sure Manzini has nothing to say."

"You're darn right. He's been murdered," Strand said, taking another chance.

Stoddard had been about to make a belligerent comment until he processed what he'd just been told. Remaining defiant, he took a deep breath. His voice shaky, he said, "Well, at least you know I didn't do it, did I?" Then he lowered his eyes, as if he'd made the comment only to buy him a few more seconds.

"You know, you're right about that," Bentsen mocked him. "But so far, that's the only point in your favor, and it's not even a bargaining chip for you."

"I think you're running out of luck, Stoddard," Strand said, "so when we send you back to your cell, be grateful you're here. Manzini's killer obviously wants his pals to remain silent."

"You're bullshitting me, you know that," Stoddard said with a raised voice. "You don't scare me!"

"Relax," Strand said, getting up to leave, "we won't be releasing you to be the next victim—yet. Or should we?"

When the detectives rose to leave, rivulets of sweat appeared on Stoddard's forehead and dripped into his collar, yet he held his fixed stare, saying nothing.

≈

Request in hand, Strand and Bentsen visited Lieutenant Montgomery in the box of an office where dust balls had the best seats, a place the boss called home nearly fourteen hours a day. As always, when he was bent over his desk, what they saw first was his once dark hair silvered with age and service.

Blest with the hearing of a trained guard dog, Montgomery said, "I heard you coming down the hall, and I've been waiting for you two birds. I'll bet I know exactly what you want."

"A transfer to a really quiet place like Potter County where the only dead things are deer and bear carcasses on the road?"

Montgomery snorted. "A comedian now!" he chuckled. "Hmmm! Potter County, now don't give me any ideas."

"Now that you're in a good mood, Chief, we need you to make a call for us."

"Gee. No surprise there! You want me to call those two suits from the Bureau to scare the crap out of our rent-free resident back there."

"Got it in one. Can you let us know when they can make an appearance, so we can get our timing right?"

"Translating that means I need to call right away to fit in with your plans, I suppose," he said, picking up the phone. "Tell me how much I enjoy being your gopher." He dialed the number for the Pittsburgh Field Office and asked for Agent Flaherty or Kempinski. In a few seconds, Montgomery leaned forward as if he'd just caught a fish.

Montgomery explained to his listener what they needed, and interestingly, it appeared that cooperation was the new name of the game.

"The thing is, Agent Kempinski, we need you and your partner to do a federal tap dance on Stoddard ASAP since there's been another murder up here, as you've no doubt heard."

After still another minute, Montgomery hung up and said, "You birds owe me lunch at the diner. They'll be here in an hour, now that they might get their hands on a guy who's been storing his drug inventory in a government facility."

Strand gave his chief a thumbs up sign, stood up, poked Bentsen, and said, "That's a deal. Maybe today. We're still waiting for a report on the cave in, but while we're waiting, we'll head up to the courthouse to see what Doc McCreary has to tell us."

"Keep me posted, and if you get back in time, you can watch the show."

XLVIII

THE MONTH OF March having finally granted them a sunny day, Strand and Bentsen strolled the few blocks to the Mercer County courthouse square, found the lower-level entrance and made their way to the coroner's haven, the sweet and sour sanctum McCreary liked to call his morgue.

"Ah, gentlemen, you've lowered yourselves to pay me a visit," McCreary said, taking the illegal cigar from his mouth and tamping the ashes in his illegal ashtray.

Firing a return salvo, Bentsen said, "One of these days, someone's going to bust you, but not for smoking. It'll be for smoking the foulest-smelling cigars known to Western civilization."

McCreary leaned back in his spring-loaded county chair and laughed. "For one thing, none of the rule mavens have the nerve to enter my domain, and for another, these stinking cigars are the only ones to counteract the odor after I've been working on a, uh, a client," he said, beaming as if he'd won a debating contest. "It seems we have this same conversation every time you two show up here," he finished, chuckling with the cigar clenched between his teeth.

"So nice you two are having a good time, while three murders have gone unsolved," Strand said, enjoying the moment.

"Four, actually. While you were taking your time getting here, Montgomery called me to remind you about the Purcell murder. He's guessing and I'm guessing you haven't touched that one yet."

"Jesus," Bentsen said, we've got three dead bodies less than two weeks old and he wants us to fart around with another golden oldie from when?"

"To be precise, Joe, 1964."

"Enough, already," Strand intervened. "What have you got to tell us about Angelo Manzini?"

McCreary leaned forward, cleared his throat, then picked up his cigar and took a puff, licked his lips, put the smoldering tube in the tray, and after the proper dramatic pause, said, "Murder, no doubt about it. As I said at the scene, it was a blunt force trauma to the head. Putting on my best courtroom suit and in the witness stand, I'd say the same weapon used to kill Al Rieger was what killed Angelo Manzini."

"Not surprised, Doc," Strand said. "Any more?"

"See here," he said pointing to a photo on his desk, "there's a round impression deep in his left temple, just like with Rieger. This one is a bit clearer. I'd say it was the flat end of a steel pole or crowbar of some kind."

"But not the same kind of wound we found on Abel Masters."

"Right you are, Fletch. Masters was struck from behind. The other two had the end of the bar jammed into their left temples—they died almost instantaneously."

"And Masters, you said, was already dead," Bentsen said.

"Well, we know the obvious. Two different killers were involved in Masters's death, only the second one didn't know the first had already been there. And now, we have two more murders, both apparently by the same hand and with the same weapon. That's about it," McCreary said, leaning back again, the cigar lodged in the corner of his smile, "except you still don't know what caused the rock to cave in on top of him."

"And," Strand observed, "why did the killer bother?"

~

Back at the Barracks, it was a mixed bag of luck. No report from the explosives guys, but the FBI agents had arrived and were talking to Montgomery, so Bentsen and Strand decided to join them, despite the tight quarters in the station commander's far from impressive office.

"Glad you could make it, you two," Agent Kempinski said, derision seemingly a part of his social upbringing.

Bentsen couldn't resist. "The least we could do since you and your buddy here are going to crack the case wide open for us."

Flaherty snorted. "We'll see what happens. Just how can we help you with him?"

"Right now," Strand said, "his lips are sealed about who his accomplices were in his drug-dealing gig, and we think one of them might be our killer, so what we want from you is to scare the bejesus out of him with whatever federal charges you can dream up in hopes of loosening his tongue a bit."

"Can do," Flaherty said, "but we need to give him a time frame. What're you looking for?"

"No more than twenty-four hours. He says Daddy is going to send a lawyer, but it's not lookin' too good. After that, he gets an appointed attorney, and he's arraigned for every state crime we can pin to him."

Kempinski smiled. "I like it, let's go."

As Flaherty and Kempinski entered the interrogation room to Stoddard's surprise, Montgomery and his two detectives crowded into the adjoining room to observe via the two-way mirror.

Despite what intimidating language and threatening gestures Kempinski could bring to bear on David Stoddard, who sat there like Gibraltar, he held his ground and, in effect, called their bluff. "If you guys could charge me with murder, you would have done it by now, so get lost. I don't care who you are, I'm not saying another word until I get the best representation I can get." With that, he shut his mouth and stared at the tabletop.

In the observation room, Bentsen started laughing. He was joined by his companions until Montgomery, still with a broad smile underneath his pencil-thin mustache, said, "OK, men, we don't want to embarrass our important new friends, now do we?"

～

Eagerly, Kempinski and Flaherty accepted Montgomery's invitation to join him and his detectives for lunch at the fabled Mercer Diner, where grease glistened like the equivalent of liquid gold. Strand took the opportunity to quiz the agents on the topic of privatization.

"OPM took a bullet in the back for us," Flaherty began. If you've been reading *USA Today,* there's a story every other day about what some journalists are calling Filegate."

"I think we've heard something about that," said Bentsen.

"Right, the White House is accusing us of dawdling around with the background investigations necessary for the administration's new staffers. Of course," Flaherty went on, "White House cases get top priority, so for the most part, those cases are done."

"Then what's the problem?" Strand wanted to know.

"Be glad you're where you are," Kempinski said. "The problem is that a large number of their appointees are just not clearable."

"What?!" Montgomery said in a loud voice, and stopped chewing his club sandwich.

"Right, my friend, and OPM is caught in the middle of it. That agency does the lion's share of background investigations for the federal government—we only do the cases where the position has to have the advice and consent of the Senate."

"I think I get it," Strand said. "You guys and OPM are under pressure to get these cases done, but when it's dirty, they get nasty about it."

"That's about it, but the president can't exactly disband the FBI, can he? But they can put a stake through the heart of a backwater bunch like OPM and nobody will care."

"Good God Almighty," Montgomery said, freezing his forkful of fries midway to his mouth. "You guys think this may have anything to do with what's going on in the mine?" he asked, looking at Strand and Bentsen.

"It's the gorilla in the room, Chief," Strand answered, "but to what degree it plays a part, we have yet to find out."

"I may not be Sherlock Holmes," Bentsen said, "but to me, these killings are all of a piece—there's a thread running through all of them, and we just can't see it yet."

"Well, guys," Kempinski said with a big smile, "thanks for lunch and thanks for keeping these murders to yourselves—better you than us."

XLIX

"HEY, JOE," STRAND said to his partner once they were rid of their boss and Bureau boys, "since Montgomery wants us to detour a bit, to 'clear your heads,' he said, and dig around in that old Purcell murder, do you mind if we stop at Attorney Niven's office? He hasn't called me back, and I'd like to see if he's found anything on Robertson."

"You bet. I can sit in the car."

"Thanks, buddy. I owe you one."

In Foreston, Bentsen parked the Vic and Strand climbed the stairs to Niven's office.

"Hey, Detective Strand, I was just going to call you," Niven began, after Strand talked his way past the man's secretary.

"Hmmm!" It was all Strand could manage, one noncommittal syllable, to keep him from expressing an opinion about lawyers.

"Sit down, Detective. I have news for you," he said and went on without waiting for an acknowledgement from his client. "Whether or not this may be introduced in court, my paralegals have been comparing the patient histories of Dr. Robertson with several other family doctors in the area, and the results of that study are definitely not favorable to him."

"How so?"

"It seems that when Dr. Robertson's patients enter a hospital, either in Foreston or Sharon, a somewhat higher percentage of them never leave the facility. Yours, you'll be interested to know, is far from the first pursuit of malpractice against the man. Even when we dig deeper and eliminate the outliers, a patient of Dr. Robertson has a 30 percent higher chance of early mortality than with any other family physician within fifty miles."

"Jesus! But what does that data have to do with the care given my brother?"

"The short answer is we think his care has been, shall we say, neglected, for some time. We'll have to see what medical expert witnesses have to say, of course, but a lawsuit, perhaps a class action suit, looks promising."

"That son of a bitch!"

"There's a long way to go on this, Detective, and you already know it'll not be inexpensive to pursue it, but we also looked into his personal life a bit to determine what, if any, behaviors were present to suggest Dr. Robertson took too casually his responsibility for care."

"And?"

"It seems that one reason he hasn't spent much time thinking about his patients is that he has another full-time residence he likes to visit every other weekend, taking an extra day each time."

"Really?"

"We don't know what's going on, exactly, but Dr. Robertson has a small horse farm in Leesburg, Virginia, just off of SR15. It's quite a valuable piece of property, we believe."

"How does he afford that? Is his practice that lucrative?"

"Not if he works only nine days out of every ten and rarely on weekends."

"Then?"

"Something's amiss, to be sure, Detective, but we haven't gone that far yet."

"Any idea how long he's had this horse farm, Mr. Niven?"

"About five years or so—we're obtaining the deed now."

"You're going pretty far, sir, and I'm wondering if this is all necessary in pursuing him for my brother's wrongful death."

"You bet we're going far, Detective. And say, call me Charlie if I can call you Fletcher."

"Fletch."

"We're going far because there's a lot of smoke about this case and we'll need everything we can to go to court."

"Do what you have to, Charlie. If there's a fox in the henhouse, let's get the fox."

~

"Are people more likely to answer the door on sunny days?" Bentsen asked as he piloted the Vic to Tidball Avenue, just off of South Center Street, in Foreston. Like most March days, even sunshine couldn't erase the drab, dead things in every yard, by every curb.

"I could argue it either way, but let's test the question," Strand said as he exited the car and pointed to a house near the corner. "According to locals, the Purcell house once stood right here, and so this gray job with white trim should have been one of the next-door neighbors."

He was wrong, however, and the current residents had no knowledge of the Purcell murder, and in fact seemed startled something like that might have occurred next door to them. At one house backing onto the former Purcell residence, no one answered, but the house was well kept. "Probably both working," he muttered.

On the third try, what would have been the neighbor on the other side, the pair struck gold, sort of. "My aunt, Jennie Augustine, used to own this house, but she doesn't live here now," said Ardis Monroe, a middle-aged woman clearly caught in the throes of what some would call spring cleaning.

"And where would she be now, Mrs. Monroe?" Bentsen asked.

"Oh, just up Broad Street at Grove Manor. She'll be ninety-three this year and sharp as a tack."

Smiling broadly at both the woman and his partner, Bentsen

seemed beside himself with such a rare piece of luck. He thanked her and was about to leave, but Strand wanted a word.

"Mrs. Monroe, are we correct in thinking this house was the next-door neighbor to the Purcell residence back in the sixties?"

"You bet it was, Detective. Stood right there," she guaranteed, pointing to what was now a wye turn-in to Tidball Avenue. "I was younger then and didn't live here, but I'm old enough to remember how the town reacted when that happened."

"How's that?"

"Why, people were terrified," she said, both hands grasping the broom handle for support, "and not too long after Agatha Purcell was moved to a nursing home, the Borough bought the lot and tore the house down."

"Agatha was the older sister in a wheel chair, wasn't she?" Bentsen asked.

"Yes, they found her in her wheel chair in the living room. She'd had a stroke and was mostly paralyzed, you know. The sisters lived together, and Nella was the one who was murdered. Found her in the basement. A lot of blood, they said."

Bentsen nodded. "I don't suppose you personally saw or heard anything related to the case?"

"Well, yes and no. As I said, I didn't live here, and everyone said it was a passerby who knew the sisters had some money in the house, but that didn't make much sense when you think about it."

"Why do you say that?" Strand jumped in.

"Unless the man knew the women, why would he pick their house. Why not my aunt's?"

"I see your point, and you think it was a man?"

"Do you think a woman would go down in that basement and pound old Nella with a hammer? Really!"

"I understand. And you say you aunt's memory may be well enough to tell us about that day?"

"Oh, yes. She's always had her own ideas about that murder, but no one's paid her any mind."

L

O N THE WAY over to Grove Manor, not more than a mile away from where the Purcell killing occurred, the men hoped to find Jennie Augustine in a lucid state. "Hey, Joe, you know what's bugging me a bit? Down in the mine—that whole badge operation? I just want one more confirmation that Abel Masters died elsewhere."

"How ya gonna do that?"

"If that system is pretty foolproof, then if Abel Masters left the mine on his last day there, he would have handed in his badge."

"Right."

"And if he was murdered elsewhere, he wouldn't have gotten his badge the next morning when his body was found."

"Right. And that means with no badge on him, his body had to have been brought in by one of the vans or in the trunk of one of the cars allowed to park there."

"Yeah, but that early in the morning, and using the main entrance to the Center, not the one used by all the employees coming in, it could have been anyone who worked there, right?"

"Right—so the question for the guard at the gate will be, 'Is Masters's badge in its slot, or what?'"

Bentsen guided the Vic past Grove Manor's main entrance into the parking lot of the pristine-looking one-story brick building, and within a few minutes, they were being taken to Jennie Augustine's private room.

The detectives introduced themselves to the old woman, who was sitting by her window, nicely coiffed and dressed for the day. She seemed intent on the birdhouse just outside.

"Welcome, gentlemen, I was just watching to see if any birds have begun their spring nesting—perhaps a bit early for that," Augustine said, "but what can I do for you?"

"We just talked with your niece, and she said we'd find you here."

"You can call me Jennie," she said, her voice squeaking a bit, "and where else could I be?" She enjoyed her little joke.

"Jennie," Strand said, "we're hoping your fabulous memory will help us with a little inquiry we're doing on Nella Purcell's murder back in '64.

"Oh, my!" she said, her hand on her chest. "That wasn't too long ago, you know. May 6, it was, and a beautiful day, too."

"Your reputation is well deserved," Bentsen said. "What else do you remember?"

"Well, they said someone must have broken into the house, but as I recollect, that wouldn't have been necessary. You see, Nella Purcell was cooking potatoes on the stove—they were going to have city chicken, mashed potatoes, and a vegetable that night, she told me that morning."

"But why didn't anyone have to break in?" Strand prompted.

She looked at them as if they had two heads. "Well, it was a warm day, and no woman worth her salt would let a day like that go by without having a door or two and some windows open to air the place out, don't you see?"

"Got it," Bentsen said. "And what else did Nella tell you? Were they expecting any visitors that day?"

"Oh, no," she said, looking into the middle distance, "not unless you count their nephew."

"Their nephew, did you say?"

"Oh, yes, and I know you're going to ask me the name, but the problem with my age is names of people and things escape me," she squeaked and laughed at the same time. "But wait a minute, let me think. Hmmm! It was Nicky something, but they didn't live here. His mother dropped him off sometime mid-morning when Nella and I were chatting."

"What else do you remember, Jennie?" Strand asked with a Cheshire smile.

"Not too much. I think his mother had an errand in town and she just dropped him off for a visit—maybe an hour or so."

"Do you know if the police ever talked to him about what happened there?

"I don't know everything, young man, but honestly, I doubt it. Nella was dead, and Agatha could hardly talk. All I know is what Nella mentioned in passing. There were four sisters in all, and the woman who dropped off the boy was their baby sister—I think they lived in Hermitage or Sharon—somewhere over there," she said, pointing west. "I don't suppose it made much difference; do you think? What would a young boy know about such a horrible crime?"

"I understand, ma'am. What do you remember about the boy?"

"Not much, but glad he wasn't my kin," she said. "He was about thirteen or fourteen, tall for his age, really dark hair, but what an attitude! And a sneaky kid, always needing a few bucks, Nella told me."

"Hmmm! Why do you say that?" Bentsen asked.

"I don't know, just repeating what Nella said. Anyway, I suppose he wasn't happy to have to spend an hour with two old ladies!"

"And you think they were from Sharon?"

"As I said. They just showed up from time to time."

"And you can't recall the name?"

"Well, the mother would have been a Purcell, but I don't recall her married name. As for the boy, they called him Nicky, or something like that."

Just after the men left Jennie Augustine and were walking out to the Vic, Strand's cell phone buzzed. Pulling it out of his pocket, he said, "This ought to be interesting. It's Jonathan. Wonder what he wants. Give me a minute, will ya, Joe?"

Bentsen climbed into the car while Strand stayed out in the warming sunshine, leaned against the rear fender, and answered the call. "What's up, big brother?"

"Nothing good, from what I hear?"

"I have no idea what you're talking about, Johnnie."

"No idea, my ass, little detective. You know you're messing around in White House business."

"You mean the murders in the mine? Hardly my fault, bro."

"I don't mean them, although it's about time my little detective brother got off his ass and solved the thing so that we can all get past it and move ahead with this Administration's agenda."

"I guess that's all that matters to you," said Strand, disgust edging his voice. "But if it's not the murder spree, then what?"

"You know what! You're investigating Robertson!" The phone's speaker crackled.

"Wrongo, brother! I haven't made a single inquiry on him, but if you mean that I've asked an attorney to look into Robertson's medical practice, including his patient mortality, then this should be a call of thanks."

"What the hell are you getting at?"

"Your doctor buddy is probably a quack, and if there's any, repeat, any evidence he did not give our brother the best care possible, I'm going after him in court."

"Hey, settle down, Fletch! That won't bring Paul back; it'll only cause trouble."

"You mean it'll cause you embarrassment."

"It's already embarrassing. People are calling and asking why a fed would be coming around and then a few weeks later, a private gumshoe comes around again. You see how this looks?"

"I don't give a shit how it looks, Johnnie. What I give a shit about is how Paulie died. Get it?"

There was a long silence during which Strand wondered if the call had been dropped.

"Jesus, Fletch," Jonathan said, his tone much more conciliatory, "Paul is gone, and life has to go on. Can't you let it go?"

"Let it go? Look, Jonathan, I know you two were buds growing up, but there's an aroma here. I don't know what it is, but it's not perfume."

"We'll know everything there is to know about Nathaniel Robertson when OPM finishes their background investigation, Fletch, thank you very much."

"Hmmm! I wonder. But of course, you must see him twice a month when he's down there, right?"

Another bit of dead air greeted him. "What do you mean by that?"

"Oh, didn't you know? He has another residence—in Leesburg—which he visits regularly. And because of these little trips, he's spent less than full time taking care of his patients."

"N-no, I didn't know about a place down here? How did you find that out?"

"Never mind, Johnnie, I've told you more than I should, but hell, it'll probably be in his investigation file."

"I wouldn't know. It's still at OPM's Investigation Center for all I know."

"And all I know, brother, is that you'd be wise to be putting some distance from this appointment."

"Why?"

"I've already said enough, but you've had fair warning."

After closing the call, Strand seated himself in the Vic's passenger seat and said, "You know, Joe, sometimes a lead comes from a witness you'd never expect."

"Who's the witness?"

"My big brother."

LI

"**L**ET'S HEAD TO the mine after a bit of lunch at Harrisville's five-star eatery," Strand added before Bentsen drove off in the wrong direction.

"I thought we were going to settle down back at the office and plow through those files."

"We were, and we are, but first, let's follow the trail while it's warm."

"Going to fill me in?"

"Do you remember somebody telling us Stoddard was up at Masters's office about a special case just before he was killed?"

"Yeah, what of it?"

"That was my brother calling to lean on me because I had Charlie Niven check out Robertson, and..."

Bentsen jumped in, "Whoa, baby! What does that have to do with our case?"

"Maybe nothing, and now I'm beginning to wonder, maybe a lot."

"For God's sake, Fletch, how about some plain English?"

"Sorry. My brother is frustrated because—as I'm sure I told you—Nathaniel Robertson is up for a job in the Office of the White House Physician—and had to undergo a background investigation."

"And?"

"And my brother said Robertson's case is being held up by the Investigations Center for some reason—an extension of the Filegate issue with the FBI that's prompting the whole privatization of OPM's Investigations Program."

"Holy shit! It does get complicated, doesn't it?"

"I'll say it does. So, let's see if the Robertson file is still available—we'll have to get Lafferty's permission to see it—but it may be worth the effort."

"You're sure this isn't getting into conflict-of-interest territory here?"

"Nope," Strand said, looking directly at Bentsen. "You know me better than that, pard."

"Sorry. I just want you to keep your ass clear of any problem down the road."

"Don't worry. We're on the same page here, but thanks." Then, after a moment while each of them absorbed the implications of what they'd just said, Strand added, "Stoddard ought to be able to confirm that they were talking about Robertson—and his time is about up, wouldn't you say?—but if, indeed, this was the case Stoddard was concerned about, we want to know why.

And," he went on, "you and I don't believe in coincidences. Let's see what's in it."

"Gotcha. While we're there, let's check the box with the guard at the front gate to see about Masters's badge. We should already know the answer, but we'd better find out, all in the interest of no surprises."

Strand nodded as Bentsen steered the big Vic into one of The Spot's gravel spaces.

∽

After a quick lunch in the small room where the counter was, the men enjoyed their cheeseburgers and fries and watched with quiet glee the entire coffee preservation effort underway by the owner. It took ten minutes for their food to arrive, and even less for them to chow down and be on their way. They both had sodas.

"I'm beginning to feel as if I work here," Bentsen said, somewhat dismayed, as he guided the Vic down the long asphalt ramp and through the portal. "Have I said that before?"

"That's the thing, Joe! We do work here, and if we don't figure this out soon, we'll be looking for jobs, won't we?"

"Yeah, tell me! Did you notice, the plumes of smoke did not greet us today?"

"I guess warm, sunny days will do that."

"Say," Bentsen said to the guard as he stopped the Vic to show his wallet badge, "Can you check to see if Abel Masters's badge is in its slot?"

"Just a sec," the guard said, and walked over to the sturdy metal tree upon which several hinged pieces of plywood hung with all the badges of those who worked in the mine. After swiveling a door or two, he returned to the Vic and said, "It's still on the board, so that means he turned it in the night before when he left the last time he was here—alive."

"Christ, he's been dead two weeks now. Why is it still on the board?"

"Hell if I know, no one's told us to rescind his access."

"Hmm! I guess the killer did," Strand said, leaning across Bentsen so the guard could hear him.

~

As Bentsen drove along the familiar underground roadway and came near the cutout where visitors and some employees, like Al Rieger, were allowed to park, they could see men garbed in white cotton canvas suits, masks, and gloves diligently working at the pile of rock at their feet.

"Are you guys still at it?" Bentsen called out.

"Slow going, Joe. There's a lot of rock here and even with the Klieg lights we set up, it's hard to see in this perpetual darkness, if you know what I mean."

"Got it. Still no clue what set off the rock slide?"

"Definitely some kind of device, given the splatter pattern. Had it been a natural cave-in, all the rock would simply have piled up just below the fracture."

"I hate to ask," Strand said, jumping in, "but any idea when you'll get to the bottom of it?"

"Joe, your partner's humor is lost on us," the explosives expert said.

"Me too, brother," Bentsen replied, and they all laughed.

"Seriously, Fletch, maybe tomorrow."

"Thanks, guys," Bentsen said, and the pair turned and went inside looking for Joe Novak.

LII

"YOU'RE THE LAST guys I thought I'd see today, and I sure hope you have news for all of us," Joe Novak said, sitting behind his desk and not getting up to greet the two detectives.

"No such luck, Joe. We need to get a look at a file you might still have," said Strand to the little man for whom he had little patience.

"What file is that?" Novak asked archly.

"Whatever file it was that David Stoddard came up to see Abel Masters about just before he died."

"You're kidding, right? How would I know that?"

"Could we ask Mrs. Conlon to step in, please?" It was Bentsen, soft soap and all.

"Judy!" Novak bellowed without rising.

In a moment, Conlon came in, her very dark brown hair atop a head with blue eyes, a few freckles, and a polite smile that served her well. "How can I help?"

"This may or may not be relevant, Mrs. Conlon," Strand began, "but I think you told us that David Stoddard came up to see the director with a particular case file the day or so before Masters was murdered. Do you have some idea what file that might have been?"

Conlon stood stock still, thinking. "I remember him saying

something like that, but Al Rieger was up here concerned about one of his men, too. That's why this is confusing. As for Stoddard, he came up with files from time to time, but this time," she said, picturing her memory, "he came up, looked at me, and went in without asking, closing the door behind him. They were together for about thirty minutes, and even though that office is pretty sound-proofed, I could hear voices. I think I mentioned that's when Stoddard said something about privatization, remember?"

"Yes, now I remember. Were they angry?" Bentsen asked.

"No, but agitated."

"Say," Novak interrupted, "hold on a minute. You guys have Stoddard in custody, why are you bothering us. Why not just ask him?"

"Nice point there, Joe," Strand said, "and we'll do that, but right now, we're asking Mrs. Conlon."

Conlon remained passive, waiting.

"Think back, please, Judy," Bentsen said. "We need to know which case file that was, and what happened to it."

"Let me think about it."

"Before you answer," Bentsen said, "was it on his desk when we found him that morning?"

"As far as I could tell his desk was undisturbed, but he would not have left the night before with a sensitive file on his desk like that," she said, her voice soft but sure. "One of us locked it up, and I returned it to David Stoddard after Mr. Masters's murder so that he could ship it on."

"So, it's not here?" Strand asked.

"I'm pretty sure not," she answered, then thought some more. "I remember now. A few days later, he called up here and demanded that I call Al Rieger and have him hold the afternoon shipment so he could get an important file to Mr. Lafferty."

"And how did that go?" It was Bentsen.

"It's never a good idea to hold the van transporting the trunks. They have a schedule to meet and they don't like to keep the guy in Breezewood waiting."

"Why is that?" Bentsen asked.

"Because the Breezewood guy has to drive back into DC traffic, and I guess he's not happy if we're late on this end. At least that's what Al said. Later, when Al came up, he told me Stoddard was in quite a state about it, and handed it personally to one of the warehousemen."

"Very nice, Judy. You have a fine memory."

"Yes, thanks, Mrs. Conlon," Strand said, having no idea why he kept referring to her by her proper name. "But let's test your memory one more time. Can you remember the name on that file?"

Mrs. Conlon cleared her throat, then looked at Novak before turning back, and answered, carefully, "This is embarrassing, Detective Strand, because when you asked me about this before, I didn't tell you because it was a White House case. They're special, and I had no reason to believe it had anything to do with what happened here. I'm sorry."

Strand exhaled, but said nothing.

"And," she added, "it seemed there was more than usual interest in the case because the subject was from around here."

"And the name?" Strand asked, the hair on the back of his neck rising.

"Oh, I'm sorry. Of course. The case was on Dr. Nathaniel Robertson."

~

The old railroad clock on Novak's office wall ticked in the silence until Strand spoke again.

"Joe, we need to have a private space for a few minutes. Mrs. Conlon, please see if you can get Mr. Lafferty on the phone."

"What does all this mean?" Novak asked the room.

"Not sure yet, maybe nothing, but something started to unravel this sweater, and I think we're getting close," he answered Novak, then turned to Mrs. Conlon. "Did Al Rieger mention which of the warehousemen might have handled that file, or do you have any idea which one of his men he had a concern about?"

"No, to both questions. No, I'm sure he didn't. That you will have to get form Mr. Stoddard."

"Good enough, then. Lead us to a private space then, please," Strand said, noting to himself Novak did not volunteer his office.

"Well, I'm sure no one would mind if you use Mr. Masters's office. Come with me and I'll get Director Lafferty on the line."

"Oh, by the way, Joe," Bentsen said, turning back to face Novak, "you might want to have Masters's badge removed from the guard stand. I don't think he's coming back."

~

In what had been Abel Masters's office, Strand sat in the man's desk chair and waited for the phone to ring, while Bentsen sipped a steaming coffee.

Strand picked it up on the first ring. "Hello, Mr. Lafferty, how are you?"

"Well," Lafferty responded with not a small bit of exasperation, "at least some files are coming down here from the mine!"

"Sorry, sir, it's been a bit of a mad house here, but one of the files that's just arrived on your desk may be one we're interested in."

"Oh? Which one is that?" he asked, being cautious.

"The file on Dr. Robertson, sir."

"Yes," Lafferty sighed. "Just what kind of karma is operating here, Fletch?"

"What we did not know at the time we discovered Abel Masters was that Dr. Robertson's file held his attention for some reason, and some piece of information in it may, in fact, have led to his death."

"Fletch, that's hard for me to digest, but what exactly are you asking me for?"

"We need that file back here ASAP, and sir, I promise we'll get you the rest early next week."

"I've heard some words like that before, but this time, you'd better mean it. This case, in particular, has become a hot property, as the"

White House Security Officer has become a bit demanding about it."

"Why is that, sir?"

"They want it pronto so they can proceed with the appointment, but they're not going to be happy when they get it."

"Meaning?"

"I'll let you read that for yourself, Fletch."

LIII

"WHEW!" JOE SAID, when they got into the Vic. "Let me catch up with a note or two before we head out."

"Sure—I need a minute to process all of this myself. So, we've confirmed the fact that it was Robertson's file, but why? What the hell has he to do with all of this?"

"You got me, but one thing we know for certain is that our killer is one of the three warehousemen—it's gotta be McKenna, Meister, or Sharpe."

"Yep, but why? If one of them was helping Stoddard import drugs, the question is, were the drugs coming in one of the vans—in a trunk maybe?—or were they just helping him out by bringing the stuff in a vehicle when Stoddard himself couldn't count on parking inside when he needed to."

"For my money," Bentsen said, "the stuff was coming in a trunk. Stoddard could have brought his own stuff in a briefcase any day of the week and no one would be the wiser."

"That's probably right, Joe. I noticed that nearly everyone walking in here is carrying something—a purse, briefcase, lunch, you name it, but I'll bet the guards rarely check their contents."

"Probably true, but you know, Fletch, we'd better be careful here."

He chuckled. "Isn't it true in all the TV shows and detective novels, it's the one you least suspect?"

"Right, but this is no novel."

~

Once out of the mine, Strand and Bentsen each called home and said they'd be a bit late for dinner. Bentsen's Sylvie fussed, sighing for her plight, but with a tone. Strand's Aurora wasn't happy, but said baked chicken would be waiting for him.

With time left in the day, and limited overtime authorized, they needed to update Montgomery, and just to check another box, have another conversation with Stoddard. Off to the Mercer Barracks Bentsen headed, and with deft driving, made it there before the sun went down.

Of course, Walter Montgomery was still at his desk, his light on, and he was bent over his blotter scanning various reports when his men reported in. "What's been keeping you? Here's a report you've been waiting for."

"Gee, which one could that be?"

"Don't get smart, Strand, the bomb boys had a lot of rock to pick through."

"So, what did they say?"

"You two can read it, but it's pretty inconclusive. What fragments they found suggested little more than some fireworks on steroids, possibly a pack of cherry bombs ignited at the same time."

"You mean homemade," Bentsen said.

"Yep, and Scotty Mason, one of the guys you saw in the mine, is a farm boy from Beaver County, and he suggests this was a concoction some farmers use when dynamite is too much. I guess it was powerful enough to loosen a ton of limestone."

"It's definitely murder, isn't it?" said Bentsen, not really asking a question.

"Looks like it," Strand said.

"Wait a minute," said Montgomery, unsatisfied. "Set it up for me.

How did the killer make this happen?"

"Chief," Strand offered, "all the killer had to do was ask Manzini to meet him at that limestone rib just outside the cutout. It's pretty dark there. Having set his explosive contraption above the meeting spot, he waits for Manzini to show, bashes him in the temple, then detonates his little bomb with a fairly short fuse, and melts away in the darkness. Manzini never knew what hit him."

"Maybe. You'll have to get the bomb boys to buy off on it before a prosecutor takes us seriously."

"If it gets to that," Strand said, "but I'm willing to bet it happened that way or something close to that."

Then both Strand and Bentsen brought their lieutenant up to date on their discoveries with the Purcell murder as well as the co-incidence of the Robertson investigative file having been one of the last things Abel Masters read before going home Friday night and meeting his maker Sunday evening.

"Either way, Chief," Strand went on, "Judy Conlon locked it up—or Masters did—so we never knew it existed."

"Jesus, Mary, and Joseph," Montgomery swore, "you two want to bring the wrath of the federal government down on us, don't you?"

"Boss," Bentsen said, "you know how it goes, we didn't do this, the killer did."

"Next thing you'll be asking for a warrant to search a White House wannabe's possessions, right?"

"Not yet," Strand said. "No smoking gun yet."

"So, what's next?"

"We'll both be here first thing tomorrow scouring the files we do have—a few for the second time around—to find whatever thread it is that connects everybody here."

"Sounds like fun," Lieutenant Montgomery surmised with a broad smile. "On the Purcell thing, any way to track this nephew you mentioned?"

"You mean 'Nicky'?" It was Bentsen, a cynical tone in his voice.

"Well, now that you mention it, when we get a free moment," Strand said, clearing his throat, "we'll check the relatives of the dead woman—has to be some information around."

"About that free moment," Montgomery said, and started laughing out loud. "Hmmm! Guess I'll never find out about that burning body up on I-80!"

∼

"Time's up, Stoddard," Strand announced to the manacled prisoner in the Mercer Barracks interrogation room. The small window in the door bled a small glow of rapidly disappearing daylight, a metaphor for Stoddard's situation, Strand thought.

"What do you mean, I'm not going anywhere!" By now, Stoddard's appearance was disheveled despite the services available to him. His eyes darted, and there was a tiny twitch affecting his lower lip.

"Time's up for your attorney to show. We're going to appoint a good one for you and you'll be arraigned in the morning."

"No, wait. My dad called and an attorney is coming for me."

"What took him so long?" Bentsen wanted to know.

"I-I don't know, but it's none of your business."

"Actually, it is our business, because what else is our business," said Strand, throwing his tone right back at him, "is that there are three murders and a whole bunch of drug charges looking for a defendant, and I think I'm looking at him."

"Hey, man, those FBI guys couldn't scare me, so what makes you think you can come in here and bully me?"

"Bully you? You don't know what bullying can be, Davey boy," Bentsen said, stepping close.

"Don't call me 'Davey.' It's David."

"Sure, Davey."

"While your attorney is getting here—and he'd better be here tomorrow, by the way, because your game is over—we want to know what was so special about the file on Dr. Nathaniel Robertson."

Stoddard was caught in mid-breath, and his face froze. "That case file has nothing to do with anything," he insisted, his voice nearly shrill, "and I'm not authorized to discuss it with you, anyway."

"It doesn't matter, Davey boy," Bentsen said, enjoying the taunt, "because we'll have the file day after tomorrow."

"Look! It really doesn't have anything to do with Masters or Rieger, and for sure, not Manzini. You can trust me on this! And by the way, you already know you can't get me for Manzini—I was your guest in this dump, remember?"

"True enough, Stoddard, but you sure look good for the first two."

"Either way, you're looking for two killers, aren't you, and you're stumped." He laughed.

LIV

I N FORESTON, IT was dinnertime at the Strands'. As usual, their fourteen-year-old Aaron, whom they called Aarie, and eleven-year-old Anna were bickering as they set the table in their little dining area off the kitchen. The plates clattered and the silverware clinked as the two Strand children went as close to the edge of their mother's nerves as they dared.

Strand walked through the back door a few steps below the kitchen level, stamped his feet, and entered the fray just as Aurora, queen of her household, gave the miscreants the evil eye. In an instant, it became rainbows and butterflies.

Aurora waited for Dad to hug his kids and said, "Ah, so you made it after all, Fletcher Strand!"

"For dinner or battle?" He gave her his broadest smile as he walked over to her and kissed her on the back of the neck.

"Never mind that, Detective. Investigate that pot of boiling noodles and stir as needed."

"Noodles with baked chicken? Another Italian delicacy?"

"Don't get smart, buster," she said with a smirk. "You've had this before! And besides, we're raiding the pantry. With a little melted provolone, it'll hit the spot on a cold night."

Strand took to his task, still smiling, and said, "Looks like they're at the eight-minute mark."

"Something funny, Fletcher Strand?" Aurora asked, giving him a sideways smile of victory over the rabble.

"Nothing at all, dear."

"How are things going with your mine murders, if I can ask?"

"Hmmm!" he said and continued stirring. "This case is something like the one involving your relatives a few years ago—sorry to bring that up—where something in the past may have something to do with the present."

"Don't they all, Fletch? I mean, isn't what we were back when what we are now?"

"Oh, do I hear a saying from some inspirational speaker now?"

She chuckled. "Of course, you do, hon. It's what I always say, 'the past is always with us.'"

～

The following morning, March weather returned, its fury compounded by drifting deep snow on top of sleet frozen to the streets. Schools closed and people were advised to stay home unless an emergency dictated otherwise. As Strand dressed for the weather, Aurora sat up in bed and said, "Are you out of your mind?" It really wasn't a question.

"Just think, hon, the roads will be empty, and if Joe Bentsen can make it, so can I," he said, tongue in cheek.

"Joe lives in Mercer. He could walk to the barracks if he needed to, but you're what, twelve miles away?"

"That far?"

"Don't be a smartass, Fletcher Strand. This family doesn't need a dead trooper—you'll be nobody's hero going to work today."

"Alright, let me make a few calls and see what's what?"

"Calling God, are you, to see when the weather will break?"

"No, but I'll call Georgie Hallon to see what they're telling him about it."

"I can't believe you'll be calling Hallon. What's gotten into you?"

"I can't forget that Georgie showed up for Paulie's funeral—and for that I'm grateful."

"It's barely light out—he won't be in."

"We'll see," he said, pulling on his pants and tucking in his shirt. "Coffee?"

"Count on it."

In less than two minutes, Strand had the pot brewing Dunkin' Donuts medium roast, and soon the aroma of hot caffeine filled the room, and no doubt drifted upstairs to tempt Aurora away from her pillow. Strand smiled at the thought, and while the Mr. Coffee did its work, he turned to stare out the windows of the eating area at the near whiteout gracing Foreston's morning.

Reaching for his cell phone, he tried to call the police department, not four blocks up East Pine Street, but couldn't get a signal. The landline worked, however, and in a moment, he had the dispatcher's ear and asked for her chief. She said, "Good morning, Detective Strand, and no he's not in yet, but he should be in soon—his neighborhood lost power, so once he drops Mrs. Hallon off at her job— she works at Grove Manor—he'll be right in."

"Gee, thanks for all the information, Doris—is that what you said your name is?'

"Yes, sir. Should I ask Chief Hallon to call you?"

"You bet—but on the landline. No cell signal, apparently," he said and gave her the number.

Next, he scampered up the steps with a hot cup of coffee for Aurora, along with part of a bagel and cream cheese.

"I can't believe you'd think I'd eat all that fat, my dear man, but thanks for the coffee."

"Just as I thought, my dear wife," and without a second's hesitation, he grabbed the bagel and downed in in two bites.

"That's what you planned all along, I know you."

The phone rang, and Strand went to the other side of the bed and picked up the receiver. "Chief," he said when he learned who was calling, "thanks for getting back. Say, what are they telling you about this freeze? Will I be able to get to the barracks later today?"

"Don't think so, Fletch, but you never know. They hope to have the main roads salted by mid-morning, but if the temperature drops and it keeps blowing, not much good that'll do."

"Thanks for that, and by the way, thanks for showing up at my brother's funeral—much appreciated."

"Glad to. By the way, I hear you guys have been nosin' around the old Purcell murder—what started that, if you don't mind my asking?"

"I thought Lieutenant Montgomery would have called you, Chief. Sorry about that," Strand said, unbelieving that he and his Foreston nemesis were having a civilized, professional exchange. "Somebody called in a tip to our shop, something about a nephew nobody ever checked out."

"You don't say. I was still in high school when that happened and nobody's ever quite forgotten about it."

"Our anonymous caller certainly didn't."

"Keep me posted on this, will ya?"

"Not a problem. We're trying to fill in a lot of blanks."

"If I can help, let me know," Chief Hallon said and ended the call.

Strand cradled the receiver and turned to his wife, who sat up, sipping her coffee, wide-eyed in disbelief. "Well, hon," Strand said, smiling, "I guess miracles do occur. It's probably because he's happy we're doing his work for him."

"Uh-huh," she said, and then whispered, "the kids are still asleep, Fletch. Want to get under the covers?"

LV

THE STORM NEVER let up, a gift to everyone in the county who needed some good family time, the Strands being no exception. After a lazy morning for all of them, they rose to a house eerily silent. No furnace hissing, no nothing, no power.

Making do with candles, flashlights, and two fireplaces going, Strand made sure to let the faucets drip, just in case the outage went long. Already 60 degrees in the house, Aurora broke out the blankets, and the four of them sat in front of a glowing fire playing Monopoly, eating cold leftovers, and laughing themselves silly. Mac was beside himself with so much daytime company, he didn't know who to snuggle with first.

Fortunately, the power clicked on in late afternoon before the sun went down, and although everyone had enjoyed the day, they were grateful their routines had been given back to them.

When Strand arrived at the Mercer Barracks early the next morning, he took the expected grief from his lieutenant, who lived nearby. Bentsen sat, slurping a hot chocolate, enjoying every moment. Montgomery led the attack: "Gee, Strand, most of my troopers were out on the road doing their duty catching fender benders for all the idiots out there, Gloria Moses made it in, as had most of the other day people, and of course your partner put in a day's work, but I guess Foreston was just too far for you, eh?"

"I was advised by Chief Hallon to hunker down yesterday," Strand replied with as much false seriousness as he'd received.

"Pals with old Georgie, are we now?" Montgomery went on, enjoying some fun at Strand's expense.

"Truth be told, I had a pleasant conversation with him for once, so if you're through beating on me, I came in to do some work."

"Well, isn't that nice!"

Strand sat at his desk, opposite Bentsen, and pretended to ignore Montgomery, who was not finished. "Today's a perfect day to finish reviewing those files, gents. Yesterday, I received a very nice call from your Director Lafferty, who wants his paper goods back."

"Did we ever get the Robertson file from him?"

"Not yet," Bentsen said. "Caught in the snow storm. Might be here today, late."

"Then, let's get at it."

"Already started, Fletch. Since you were out yesterday, I started going over the files of the warehousemen. You know, McKenna, Meister, and Sharpe."

"And?"

"And nothing, so far," Bentsen replied. "But I'm only going through their Official Personnel Folders and their Investigations Files. I didn't bother with the insurance and medical stuff."

"Fair enough, I'll do the same with Masters, Novak, and Conlon—oh, and Rieger's, too."

"By the way, Fletch, good call on not coming in yesterday. As one of the troopers said, there weren't enough circuses for all the clowns who decided to go joy-riding on a day like yesterday—new records in fender benders."

"I'll bet the auto repair guys are making their vacation plans, then," Strand said, and rose to fetch himself another cup of thick black trooper's joe, while Bentsen merely flicked a thumb in the direction of the Men's and headed down the hall.

Two hours went by as Strand sorted through the four files in front of him, searching for a thread of some kind that might tie one or more of them with the killer.

Novak's file was first. Originally from Pittsburgh, he'd worked for OPM for twenty years in a number of places before landing as Masters's deputy at the Investigations Center. A wife from a small town about forty miles north, and two daughters. Why he found himself at this backwater operation, Strand wasn't sure, despite Lafferty's comments, but there was nothing in his file that stood out.

The same was true of Judy Conlon. She and her husband, who worked as a plumber, had two children, and appeared to live an exemplary life. Family, schools, and church were all within ten miles of the mine.

Masters's file, on the other hand, was a bit thicker, given his origins on an Amish farm in New Wilmington and his seemingly meteoric rise through the ranks of OPM's Investigations Program. Just as he'd found in his earlier scan of the dead man's file, there was nothing to suggest anything amiss in either his professional or personal life.

The background investigations for all three of them were thick and thorough with upwards of fifteen people interviewed on each of them, not to mention the scads of police and credit checks, school transcripts, and fingerprint results. After all that, it was nada, nothing.

Strand hoped something would jump out from Rieger's material, but nothing did. He closed the last file with a snap and watched Bentsen reach the same point in his own review.

"Good thing these feds lead boring lives," Bentsen said, nursing his cold coffee. "Except for our man Stoddard."

"Right, not even one arrest for underage drinking, for crying out loud!"

Without another word, they each went to their notes and the pile of reports that had already mounded up on the three murders and the drug case. Another hour elapsed. Eyes weary from binge reading, Bentsen stood up, rubbed his eyes, and said, "Food, anyone? It's almost lunch."

"Sure thing. Wanna check with Montgomery and see if he wants some chili?"

"That's like asking if he wants somebody to blowtorch his insides, if we're talking about the Mercer Diner."

A minute later, Bentsen returned and said, "We're on our own—where to?"

∾

After indescribable sandwiches at a nearby luncheonette, where they found Doc McCreary in a booth working a crossword puzzle and aching for what he called some "lively" conversation, they returned to the office to find that the Robertson file had arrived, signature required. Neither wanted to take responsibility for it, but Bentsen relented and affixed his name to the custody form.

"Want to flip for it?" Strand asked.

"Nah! I know you want to dig into it, so go ahead. I'll get some coffee. Want one?"

"Sure, thanks," Strand said, taking the file to his desk. Because Robertson was not a federal employee, there was no Official Personnel Folder, but a completed Standard Form-171 used by every agency as a job application. In his case, there also was his Standard Form-86, the Security Clearance Questionnaire, which in some ways mirrored the other form, but the real purpose of the SF-86 was to obtain information from a subject so that an adequate background investigation could be performed. It required listings for all education, all employers for the previous fifteen years, and residential information for at least seven years. References were listed as well as the name of a supervisor for each employment. Naturally, the investigator was not limited to sources provided by the subject, but was required to develop sources more likely to be neutral and objective.

Robertson was born in Sharon, Pennsylvania, attending local schools until his bachelor's degree from Mount Union College in Ohio, and from there, to Northeast Ohio Medical School, from which he received his medical degree in 1974. After his residency in

Youngstown, he joined a practice back in Sharon in 1979. Both parents were deceased, as was one of his siblings, a brother, while his sister, Kristin, lived in California. He married the former Deborah Hastings, a Registered Nurse, in 1976, and divorced her in 1989. No address was given.

A few things stood out in his background investigation. There was a juvenile arrest for misdemeanor possession of marijuana, which was dismissed. Although not in police files because of Robertson's age, someone had mistakenly left a reference to it in his high school records because the arrest had taken place on school property.

Next, the investigator noted that four physicians were contacted but two declined to be interviewed, each of them citing professional reasons. The other two evidently answered the questions asked, but their statements were not glowing to say the least.

Last, he searched for the statement that should have been there, but wasn't. It was that of his ex-wife, Deborah Robertson.

Unusually, in an addendum, there was a page showing the statement of a "Confidential Witness." In this case, the source said little about most of Robertson's life, but noted that when the Purcell murder occurred in Foreston in 1964, he had been at the house that morning. Strand froze. On the back of his neck, his hair stood on end. He couldn't believe what he'd just read. There was no other information and the witness could offer no corroboration to the suggestion. Was it Jennie Augustine? *Who?*

"Hey, Joe, you still awake over there?"

"What's up, wise guy?"

"Several things, and one of them is gonna knock your socks off." Strand filled him in on the reluctant physicians, and the statement of the confidential witness.

"Holy shit! Guess we're not going to have to search for 'Nicky,' now, are we?"

"Wanna bet our tipster and this witness are the same person? So, it was Nate Robertson who was with his aunties on the day of the murder, just before the crime was discovered, and there's a juvey bust for pot in here—dismissed. Hmmm! Starting to smell, ain't it?"

"Ain't it, though!" Bentsen exhaled.

"And now we have something to talk to him about, don't we?"

"Right."

"And we have somebody else to talk to as well?"

"That being?"

"Let's see if anything comes up on a Deborah Hastings or Deborah Robertson?"

"Let me guess—an ex?"

"Yep. Robertson divorced her four years ago. She could be anywhere."

"Well, let me check the City Directories for her, and if that fails, we can call the credit bureaus, all three of them, and maybe check the courthouse to see if they were divorced here, which is likely."

"Good thinking, Joe. Let's see what that divorce was all about. No children, by the way, so it shouldn't have been a big deal, but if her attorney is still around, maybe a talk with him might prove useful."

It was already mid-afternoon, but after a search of records they had available with no listing for her at all, Bentsen asked Gloria Moses to call TransUnion, Experian, and Equifax to see what might they had.

At the Mercer County Courthouse, the divorce records were on the second floor, and it took only a few minutes for the clerk to unearth Robertson v. Robertson. Strand and Bentsen sat down at one of the long oak tables and began to plow through it. Mrs. Robertson was the one who filed and claimed permanent estrangement as her reason, and was represented by none other than a local sleaze merchant named Elroy Swanson. In the file, there were a number of legal phrases designed to mask reality and preserve the dignity of one party or the other, whether deserved or not. In any event, Deborah received a nice settlement, and alimony to augment her salary as a nurse.

"Somebody knows where to send those alimony checks," Strand observed, "so she's findable. You think Swanson knows?"

Swanson was the surviving partner of Milcher & Swanson, but when the former died young of cancer, Swanson had to fend for himself. Milcher had been the star of the show while Swanson performed the less desirable legal tasks, sometimes competently.

"Isn't this the guy who spends his winters in the Florida Keys?" Bentsen asked with a groan.

"Him. His office is right on the square, remember, so let's hop over and see how the fishing is."

"I'm right with you," Bentsen said as he handed the file back to the clerk. "I wonder if his ding-dong clerk is still there."

"Hope not," Strand said, as they walked across the street, gingerly avoiding the ice pockets still clinging to the bricks laid many decades before.

In Swanson's office, still decked with an orangey shag carpeting, a dark-brown path led to the desk of the reigning ding-dong.

"What can I do for yuz," she said, not asked, as she popped her gum.

"Is Mr. Swanson in?"

"Who wants ta know?" Attitude clung to her tone like the grease of day-old pizza.

Bentsen pulled out his badge and said, "God Almighty, sister, now is he here?"

Almost swallowing the gum, Marci, she said her name was, jumped up and poked her head in the door behind her. A muffled voice could be heard, almost as if the speaker was yawning.

"He'll see you in a minute, guys—on the phone with a client, yuh know," she whined, rolling her eyes at the same time. "Have a seat. Oh, sorry there's only one chair."

Strand watched as Bentsen, for sport, just stared at her. There was nothing on her desk except the "Dear Abby" column from the *Sharon Herald.*

In a few minutes, a man whose shirt was way too tight around his mid-section bounced through the door. Still straightening his hair, none other than Elroy Swanson cleared his throat a few times, and though still groggy, his first words were, "Hey, don't I know you two guys?"

Strand and Bentsen displayed their badges and stepped forward as if to suggest the three of them go into Swanson's office. The attorney took a faltering step backwards, then smiled awkwardly, and led them into an office seedier than they remembered from their earlier encounter with him in a 1990 case.

"So, what's on your mind?" Swanson asked as he sat behind his desk, equally devoid of any work representing revenue.

"Robertson v. Robertson. You represented the wife, Deborah. What can you tell us about the case?"

"Well, you, know, there's lawyer-client privilege."

"Cut the baloney, Elroy," Bentsen said, getting to the point. "The divorce is a matter of public record and nobody's suggested your client is under investigation for any reason. We're just looking for a bit of background, that's all."

"Well, in that case," he said, clearing his throat once more and scratching his day-old beard, "there isn't a great deal to tell. Let's see. Deborah, ah, Mrs. Robertson claimed her husband had become distant, had all but abandoned their marriage, and when they were together in public, humiliated her on many occasions."

"Anything else going on there? Drinking? Drugs? Abuse?" It was Bentsen.

"I said nothing of the kind. You can draw your own conclusions."

"And where is the former Mrs. now?" It was Strand.

"Remarried now, to another doctor. Name is Thornton. Just over the line, in Hubbard. I have her address if you want it."

"You bet. Is that where she gets her alimony checks?"

"I believe so. She works at a hospital in Youngstown."

"You've been helpful, Elroy," Bentsen said, purring now. "Is there anything else?"

"That's all I have."

LVI

ONCE AGAIN, STRAND and Bentsen phoned home to give their wives the news about the uncertainty of their evening arrivals, and once again, there were sighs of acceptance. On his call, Strand said, "I'll make it up to you, hon."

"You bet you will," replied Aurora with a come-hither tone if there ever was one. Strand smiled to himself, assuming Bentsen could not hear the nuance in her words. When he hung up, however, Bentsen only looked at him and grinned the grin the two of them fully understood.

Taking US62 West, Bentsen steered toward Hubbard, Ohio, while Strand notified the local police of their planned presence and assured them it was not a criminal investigation interview.

"They were OK about it," Strand reported, "but I'll bet ten bucks they'll have a squad car drive by while we're inside."

Bentsen laughed. Within forty minutes, they were pulling in the drive of an expensive home in a cul de sac off the main road near the edge of town. The fireplace chimney smoked against the sky of a truly dreary day.

At the front door, they introduced themselves to a classically beautiful woman in her late thirties or early forties, so well kept it would have been hard to guess her age. Deborah Thornton welcomed them into her spacious living room and invited them to sit as she offered coffee.

"I hope this will not take long," she said, "as I'm preparing dinner for eight people who should arrive within the hour."

"Not long," said Strand, skipping any preamble. "We're a bit curious about your ex-husband, Dr. Nathaniel Robertson, and what happened with your marriage."

"I'm not sure I understand what two detectives from the PSP could want to know about a failed marriage," she said with a smile. "Has Nate done something?"

"Actually, we're not sure yet, Mrs. Thornton. We're investigating a series of crimes and his name came up," Bentsen lied.

"And quite honestly," Strand interjected, taking a long shot, "we were wondering if anything out of the way was going on with him. Alcohol? Drugs?"

Deborah Thornton's smile evaporated. "Not alcohol—that would have been easy to notice. But drugs? I guess I'm not surprised Nate might get himself into something," she said, biting her lip.

"Meaning?" Bentsen purred.

"A few years into our marriage, I began to notice big changes in his behavior, especially when he said we needed a little vacation home near Washington, DC, of all places! It was a nice place, a smallish horse farm, actually, and not inexpensive, but I wondered how we could afford it. But he was a doctor in a good practice then." She paused for a moment. "Sometimes we went there together for a long weekend, but even then, he'd disappear for hours without an explanation. Months before the end of our relationship, he went alone. He always seemed to be running back and forth for something," she ended, looking away.

"Could it have been another woman?" Strand inquired.

"Oh, no," she laughed. It wasn't a joyful laugh, but one of sadness if that was possible. "Nate was in love mostly with himself but for a while after our honeymoon, I thought he was in love with me."

They waited for her to continue.

"Nate was always moody, sometimes on cloud nine, other times in a deep funk, but the swings became more so. Everyone noticed—at least I thought so."

"Could there have been drug use, Mrs. Thornton? Did you ever see any evidence of him using anything?" Strand asked, thinking about Robertson needing money for pot as a teen.

"In my work as a nurse, I'm trained to notice things like that, but we never see things that are right up close, do we? Alcohol I would have noticed, as I said. He may have been taking a mild anti-depressant, I think, but nothing more than that. He was in good health, I'd have to say. Anyway, no, I never caught him using anything, and I never found anything at home."

"But you saw nothing?"

"No, but again, I always suspected something. He didn't gamble or drink much, and I was sure it wasn't another woman, so what else could it have been?"

"I guess I'm surprised," Strand said, "that you never saw or found anything—people with a habit always slip up."

"Oh, Detective," she said, "I'm not sure we're talking about the same thing. Your questions seemed to be about using drugs. I always wondered if he was selling them!"

"Why would you say that?" Bentsen asked, surprised.

"As I said, once you begin to eliminate things, you have to notice what's left," she said, thinking aloud, "and those behavior changes I mentioned. They had to do with secrecy, hiding something, like he was living on the edge of something."

Strand sat still, trying to absorb what she was suggesting.

"And even when the medical practice began to fall off, we never seemed to be short of money," she added.

Bentsen nodded. "So, the practice wasn't as good as when you first married?"

She looked down. "I'm embarrassed to tell you Nate turned out not to be a very good doctor. Patients began to drift away. Oh, my friends in the hospital never said anything to me, but there were remarks I'd overhear, especially when other physicians took over some of his cases. His mind wasn't on his work—that was the problem."

"Why was that, do you think?" It was Bentsen.

"Being a physician didn't seem to be his main focus. I don't know what it was, but it sure wasn't me, and apparently, not his practice. When I left him, his partner was still alive—he died later, I heard—but the practice was dying. There didn't seem to be enough business for the two of them."

"From the court records, it appears as if the divorce was not as easy as it could have been."

A tear appeared in one eye, rolled down her cheek, and onto her hands carefully folded in her lap. "No, it wasn't."

"What is it you're not telling us, Mrs. Thornton?" Bentsen asked.

She put her hand to her eye, as if the gesture would stanch the flow of sadness there. "Nate didn't want children, you see, but when I became pregnant, I thought he'd be elated. But it was the opposite. He flew into a tirade about my carelessness, and he didn't let up until I agreed to an abortion."

"How did that make you feel?" Strand asked.

"There's so much hype by activists about a woman's choice. Hah! In so many cases—like mine—the man still has the upper hand."

"And you wanted the child?"

"Yes. And I grew up not believing in *Roe*, but didn't judge others who chose to have it done, especially early on in their pregnancy." Then she looked up and spoke with a strength in her voice that had not been there before. "So, I agreed to the abortion, as I said, but he trusted no one to know I'd had it done, so he did it himself on a Sunday evening in his office."

"That must have been difficult for you," Bentsen said.

"You have no idea, Detective. But two days after that, I went to see an attorney, that Mr. Swanson, and began all the paperwork."

"And how did Robertson handle that?" Strand asked.

"I told him myself," she said, and her voice began to shake, "and what I'd experienced over the pregnancy was nothing compared to what came next."

"And what was that?" Bentsen asked, softly.

"He came after me with a hammer."

LVII

"**N**OW WHAT?" BENTSEN asked as they returned to their car. "Man, she let him off easy—she should have called the police right then."

"And she's lucky she was faster than Nella Purcell," Bentsen said, and the two of them looked at each other.

"We'll never know, will we, Joe? Too many people are dead now to either corroborate or contradict what happened in May 1964. Maybe we can place him there, but otherwise, we can only guess, right?"

"Right—here's my guess. Maybe our boy, Nate, needs money for something—pot? Apparently he was into it. So, he visits his aunts who are known to keep money in the house, the case file said, but Auntie Nella catches him with the money jar and threatens to tell his mother and that's that. And all he got away with was a pile of coins."

"Just after he smashed Nella's skull in with a hammer."

"Sounds like Robertson's got an anger problem," Bentsen said.

"Sounds like we still have an unsolved murder."

"But we haven't checked out the handyman someone saw around the house."

"True," Strand said, "but at least with him, the police questioned him and went no further. But no one ever talked to our boy, Nate, did they?"

Strand's cell phone buzzed. It was Gloria Moses from the barracks. "A Mrs. Augustine from a nursing home in Foreston called for you," she said.

"And?"

"She said to tell you she was wrong about something. The nephew's name wasn't Nicky. It was Nate—and they called him Natey. She said you'd know what it was all about."

"Well, that puts a nice bow on it," Strand said when he clicked off.

"Christ, wish we had a smoking gun, but we don't," Bentsen said, "and pinning him for the Purcell murder nearly thirty years ago doesn't do anything for us with the bunch of bodies in the mine, does it?"

"Maybe not, but I'm still curious about Robertson's place in Washington and his need to go back and forth."

"Well," Bentsen mused, "we don't know about that, but we can sure scare the crap out of him with 1964, can't we?"

~

Armed with coffee and somebody's stale donuts, they sat in Montgomery's office the next morning, and told their tale about Elroy Swanson, Deborah Robertson, and Jennie Augustine.

"Just tell me, Fletch, you're not hot after Robertson because of your brother, are you? You know I have to ask."

Strand could feel his color rising, but waited a moment to choose his words. "I know, Chief, you had to ask, but you know that with me, you didn't. Since you did, here's my answer. "Would I be happy to get the son of a bitch on a crime he committed? You bet. Would I go after him when I knew he didn't do it? No way in hell. Every morning, Chief—and I believe Joe feels the same way—when we're shaving, we can look ourselves in the mirror with a clear conscience."

Bentsen nodded.

"No offense, Fletch. But in case others ask the same question, I want your answer in my back pocket."

For a moment, they sipped the sludge that passed for barracks coffee in silence. Bentsen worked on his donut in the same way a beaver works on toppling a tree.

"Now that that's out of the way, what's next? Not just on Purcell, which everyone has forgotten, but on the mine murders—that's what the *Sharon Herald* keeps calling them. There's no end of calls and questions from them. You guys need any help?"

"Nah!" Bentsen said in the middle of a chew.

"Ditto that. Joe and I think one thing we could do is find Robertson and ask him a few hard questions. You never know. He'll never be expecting anyone to quiz him about what he was doing on that May day in 1964, when he was visiting his Auntie Nella."

"I'm almost sorry I gave you the Purcell case to play with," Montgomery said. "It's been too distracting while the mine murders simmer. So, here's what I think, not that you asked," he said with a lieutenant sound to it, "you can try your tricks on Robertson this morning if you can find him, but I think we should have a few troopers bring in two of your guys from the mine this afternoon and the third guy, tomorrow morning." He eyed his detectives, waiting for affirmation.

Strand and Bentsen looked at each other. It was unusual for Montgomery to insinuate himself in their cases, but if he wanted to take the responsibility, so be it. He said, "Sure," at the same time Bentsen nodded again since he couldn't talk while chewing the last of a Bavarian crème–filled.

"Then the question of the hour is who do you want first?"

Thoughtful for a moment as Bentsen flipped through his notebook, Strand said, "Um, of the three, let's have Sharpe and McKenna today, if that works, and Meister can report here tomorrow morning."

"That's a plan, then," Montgomery said as he picked up the phone. "Shall we say about 2 p.m. this afternoon?"

"And we should let Stoddard know his attorney had better be here with him after lunch tomorrow. That bastard has already had too many days' grace."

"And your thinking is?" Montgomery asked.

"Stoddard had a helper—one of the three men we have on the hook. And if Stoddard didn't kill Masters or Rieger—and he probably didn't—and he sure didn't do Manzini, we've got to zero in on one of them, right?"

This time, it was Montgomery who nodded.

"And even if Stoddard is the key, there's still the 'why,'" Strand added. "Stoddard is holding out, that's for certain, only we don't know how much he's got left in his bag."

Bentsen looked up. "Hey, man, it'll all come together, if we just have a bit more patience."

Strand turned his way, giving him a puzzled look.

LVIII

I N DOWNTOWN SHARON, across from the esplanade where Reyer's Shoe Store stood, there was a two-story office building which housed a law practice on the first floor and a suite of offices belonging to Dr. Nathanial Robertson on the second.

As Strand and Bentsen mounted the broad stairway—there being no elevator—Strand said, "I didn't see any cars in the lot, did you?"

Bentsen cleared his throat and responded in a stage whisper, "Just look around you, Fletch. Not just Robertson's practice, but the whole place seems to whisper time blowing by."

"Awfully poetic for a donut-snarfing cop!"

Bentsen grunted. "Just giving you my inner self, Fletchy boy!"

At the top of the stairs, there was a wide landing which seemed to serve as a lobby of sorts. The door on the left appeared to have borne some signage at one time, but now it appeared to be a door guarding empty rooms and dust.

On the right, the solid wood door sported *Nathaniel Robertson, MD* in bold, black painted letters. Below it, in smaller type was the invitation to enter, which they did. Inside could have been a near-duplicate of the offices of Elroy Swanson, the has-been attorney in Mercer. No shag carpet graced the floors of this office, to be sure, but as Bentsen had observed, time had worn the furnishings bare.

Behind the reception desk in Robertson's domain, however, was an elderly woman sorting through stacks of records and what appeared to be billing paperwork.

Looking up, the seventy-something woman broke into a small smile and asked, "You're here to see Dr. Robertson?" She almost seemed glad to see them.

"Indeed, we are," Strand said while whisking out his badge in one seamless motion. "I'm Detective Strand and this is Detective Bentsen, and we'd like to see him as soon as he's available."

"I see," she said. "You are fortunate, gentlemen. Dr. Robertson has a light schedule today and if he's not in the middle of a call, I'll ask him to see you." She stood, exuding competence and control with every motion. With this woman there was no chewing gum or fingernail file to compete for her attention when greeting the public.

When she left the reception area, Bentsen said, in as low a voice as he could manage, "You know what, Fletch, the puzzle pieces here do not seem to go together. Know what I mean?"

"There you go again, speaking in another tongue, but yes, I know exactly what you mean. A run-down practice in an office that hasn't been updated in a decade, but a woman at the front desk who could run a corporation."

She returned after a minute or two and said, "Dr. Robertson will see you shortly, if you gentlemen will have a seat?"

Bentsen couldn't help himself. "Ma'am, you strike me as having been with the practice a long time."

"Yes," she said with a broad, but cold smile.

"You're a very loyal employee, then."

"Not loyal, young man," she said, pleased to correct him. "I'm family, you see. Dr. Robertson is my nephew—I've known him his whole life. My name is Moira Purcell. I'm his aunt."

Strand and Bentsen exchanged quick glances, and Strand, who was sitting next to his partner, put his hand out, as if to say, "Later, Joe." Different though they were, Strand knew his partner's thought processes and in an instant, felt certain Bentsen wanted to ask about the old murder, directly or indirectly.

"How fortunate for your nephew, Ms. Purcell. Do you mind if I ask you about the office across the way? It seems vacant."

"Oh, yes, until last year, my nephew had a partner, Dr. Carl Joseph, but he died, and what a pity it was, too, for him to pass so quickly and so young," she said, seemingly preoccupied with the man's passing.

"Young like your nephew, you mean?"

"Exactly," she said, returning to the conversation. "The two were roommates in med school and remained friends. They were the same age with the same interests, but then Dr. Joseph was diagnosed with pancreatic cancer—at least that's what Dr. Robertson said, and he cared for him until the man's last breath. It was over quite quickly." Once again, she seemed to be thinking about Dr. Joseph and how he died.

"Dr. Robertson was his medical provider?" asked Bentsen, surprise in his voice.

"Oh, of course. They were close, you see, and Dr. Joseph had never married, so it seemed to make sense to them both that Dr. Robertson saw to his care."

"Doesn't something like pancreatic cancer usually demand somewhat more specialized care than, say, what a family practitioner might offer?" asked Strand, probing.

"Usually, that's so. Of course, Dr. Joseph went to see the usual specialists, I was told, but there was little hope, so Dr. Robertson took over and saw things through to the end. Poor man, it seemed like he had so much to say, but never got a chance to say it."

~

The door opened, and out stepped another piece of Bentsen's puzzle. Standing before them was a very fit, professional-looking man in a pressed suit, fresh shirt and tie, and groomed as if he'd just left a men's hair salon. Oily was the first word that popped into Strand's mind, but he put that aside and extended his one hand, displaying his badge again with the other. Bentsen did the same.

"Come this way, gentlemen. In a way, I was expecting you," his melodious words said.

"How's that, Doctor?" Strand asked, when they were inside his comfortable office and seated.

"Aren't you here about your personal matter? I guess I'm confused, Detective," he continued, his voice like oil on a hot skillet, "because there are two of you. I'm truly sorry about your brother's passing, Detective, but has this become official?"

"This visit has nothing to do with any matter personal to me or my brother, Doctor," Strand said unequivocally, coldly. "This is about a murder."

"Oh, gosh, that makes more sense, then. So, this must be about those murders in the mine over at Boyers? Really? Just because I was Mr. Masters's physician?"

Strand could feel Bentsen's posture straighten. "S-so, what can you tell us about Abel Masters, Doctor?" he asked, switching gears at a hundred miles an hour.

"Nothing for me to tell. He'd been my patient for a number of years, and at one time, we socialized a bit, you know, dinner now and then, but I hadn't seen him for some time before he—before he died."

"You don't seem shocked about his death, then?"

"Well, it's been a few weeks, hasn't it? One learns to get over the final actions of life and death in my business. Isn't it the same way in yours?"

"I never get over murders that go unsolved," Bentsen said jumping in for the first time.

"It's different for me. I seem to see a lot of death," Robertson said without irony, then, glancing at Strand, regretted his words. "I'm sorry, Detective, I didn't mean it to sound so casual."

Strand just nodded, taking in all the man's words. "Then, you can add nothing to what we know about Mr. Masters's murder?"

"No, I'm afraid not," he said, sounding casual about it, after all.

"So, just to be clear, then," Bentsen said, "you didn't see him within a day or so of his death?"

"No, Detective, I didn't."

Strand sat back in his chair, then leaned forward and said, "Then, perhaps we can talk about something you should know something about."

Robertson sat straight in his executive chair, surrounded as he was by maroon leather tucked together with brass fittings. "Oh?"

"Nella Purcell," Strand said, watching for a reaction.

"Wh-who? I mean, A-aunt Nella?" His voice rose a full octave. "Why—that incident occurred what, how many years ago?"

"Not an incident, Doc," Bentsen said. "A murder. Twenty-nine years ago. You would have been what, thirteen or fourteen then?"

Robertson cleared his throat. "Yes. How could I forget? I was almost fourteen. Let me think now," he said, his eyes seeming to search the ceiling. "It was a warm day when my mother dropped me at their house in Foreston," he said, suddenly resuming his stage presence for a part often rehearsed, apparently. "I was there for an hour, spent some time with my aunties and left when my mother picked me up."

"What did you do while you were there?" Bentsen asked.

"What did I do? Why, I don't remember."

"C'mon, Doc, you just said you couldn't forget it? Who could? Your Aunt Nella having her head bashed in? What happened there?"

"I-I don't know anything about th-that," he insisted, his facial muscles seeming to relive exactly that memory. His eyes were focused in the middle distance between them.

"Well, did you sit and chat? Outside, since it was so sunny? In the living room? In the basement, Doc? Where was Aunt Agatha?"

"N-no, I can't bring it up."

"After all these years, I'll bet you relived that hour a thousand times, didn't you?"

"Yes—I mean, no!"

"So, what do you remember?" insisted Strand, unwilling to let go.

"Nothing. Nothing," he said, his hands gripping the maroon leather arms of his chair, his knuckles white. He was breathing heavily, but winding down, like an engine out of gas.

"You sure nothing comes to mind?" purred Bentsen

"No, nothing. I don't want to talk about this anymore."

"OK, for now, Doc," Bentsen continued. "Where had your mother gone, by the way?"

"To a jeweler in town for something or other, maybe to get her rings cleaned," he said, his voice still trembling, his mind still remembering.

"You seem nervous because?" Bentsen asked.

"N-not nervous. No one ever talked to me about the whole thing, you see, and now after all these years, you show up here."

"Uh-huh," Bentsen said, "but why does that make you nervous?"

"I'm not, really. Just totally surprised, out of the blue like this. Why now?"

"It's this way, Dr. Robertson. We think someone, perhaps nearing their horizon line if you know what I mean—something you seem to see a lot of, you said—may have thought to clear their conscience and called in a tip."

"A tip? You're kidding." He paused. "On a crank call probably from some old woman, you're here suggesting something offensive?"

"Hey, Doc," Bentsen said, "we didn't say it was a woman, and we didn't say you had anything to do with it. We're just here because the caller said we ought to talk to you."

Robertson leaned back and stared at them, wide-eyed, but recovering quickly, he said, "This is nonsense! I don't know anything about what happened to my aunt, and that's all there is to it."

Strand spoke up. "So, then, it wasn't you who took their money from the canning jar in the basement and panicked when Auntie Nella discovered you? It wasn't you who beaned her with a hammer when she threatened to tell your mum?"

"What?" he all but shrieked.

"And you didn't need the money for pot, Natey?"

"No, no that's not true. We're done here," he said, rising. "I want my lawyer if you're going to ask me any more questions. And I'm not 'Natey.'"

"You mean the guy downstairs, Doc?" Bentsen asked. "He doesn't appear to get much practice in his practice."

"And you're going to need someone with a whole lot more experience in criminal matters, don't you see?" Strand asked.

"W-why is that?" he asked, standing, but wanting to sit.

"For some reason," Strand said, getting up to go, "we thought you liked hammers?"

LIX

O N THE WALK to lunch at The Wave, a few doors down on State Street, Bentsen said, "That wouldn't have gone better if we'd written a script."

"I think we left him in a panic. He knows that we know. When he calms down, he'll realize we can't prove anything and begin to relax."

"But it'll work on him, won't it?"

"Just what we want," Strand said. "We'll check in with him in a few days and see just how relaxed he is."

"Did you notice, Fletch, there were no patients there, before or after our visit. And the lawyer downstairs. No clients either."

"Yeah. It's like the place is only for show."

"Wouldn't you like to talk to his aunt, though?"

"For sure," Strand said, "but if those Purcell women were his aunts thirty years ago, how can Moira be his aunt, too?

"Hmmm! Thirty years ago, Moira would have been forty-ish when he was about fourteen, so Nella and Agatha were the oldest and Moira and Nathaniel's mother were the youngest. And Moira is the only one of the sisters left, isn't she?"

"Right, and that makes me wonder how she feels about Nella's death. Maybe we can talk to Moira on a return visit."

"Sounds good, but you're making me hungry," Bentsen said, focused elsewhere. "Let's see what The Wave can whip up for us."

The Wave had been a downtown institution for a few decades, in and out of trouble with the Board of Health, some said, but never with the patrons. The owners enjoyed a strong blue-collar and white-collar trade who thrived on good Italian food. Busy as the place was, Strand soon salivated over a chicken parm sandwich while Bentsen inhaled a meatball splash.

In between bites—chomps in Bentsen's case—they talked about Robertson and his office situation but came to no conclusion. "You know, Fletch," Bentsen said, finally, "if his ex's suspicions were right, and Robertson was—is—dealing in drugs, that would explain a lot of things we just observed, wouldn't it?"

"And don't you see, Joe, that now we might have a connection to what's going on in the mine?"

"I can see that, but it's only experience that lets me see that. There's nothing tangible we can reach out and touch."

"If we're right, Robertson has been at this for a long, long time. Small stuff, mostly, and over-prescribing pain pills to some of the low-enders who came to him, but even those patients dried up, hard to imagine as that is."

"Maybe not dried up at all, Fletch. Maybe he found a way to stay in business, so to speak, but not allow it to touch him as a doctor in town. Know what I mean?"

"You mean he was just one little spider, but found a way to spin a much bigger web?"

~

At the barracks, as arranged, Strand and Bentsen sat down once more with Frank Sharpe, who was there waiting. They expected him to have another chip on his shoulder, but they were wrong.

"Hey, guys, I'm sorry about my crappy attitude the other day. I don't know why I had such a hard time with you guys. Maybe it's because you're cops, and because there are few Blacks around here, we seem to get a lot of attention."

Bentsen sat down next to him. "I get it, Mr. Sharpe, but humor us on this, will you?"

"What is it you want to know?"

"Two things," Bentsen said. "One, let's go over your whereabouts at the time of Abel Masters's and Al Rieger's murders. And let's add Angelo Manzini to that list."

They spent the next ten minutes detailing where Frank Sharpe had been at each of those times, and quickly went over it one more time. Tension rose in the room.

"You see what I mean, Detective? Are you gonna be asking Artie and the others the same questions as me? Over and over again?"

"Most definitely, Mr. Sharpe," Strand said, "but in this particular instance, I don't think the spotlight is on you."

Sharpe exhaled, visibly relieved. "Hey look, I'm not sayin' I've been a perfect citizen in my life, but my wife and I have tried to live a quiet life up here. Mr. Rieger, he gave me a good job as a printer when the Center did its own printwork, and he took care of me and the others when that work went away."

"We hadn't heard about that. Was Al Rieger a good guy?"

"Oh, yeah. A little different, but as long as we did the job, he took care of us. I don't think anybody had a problem with him."

"What about Artie McKenna?" Strand asked.

"Artie? A wise guy, right?" he said with a knowing smile. "But a good guy, too."

"Well, Mr. Sharpe," Strand went on, "you can see why we're a bit fussy about what's happened down deep, as they say. Murders and drugs, drugs and murders."

Sharpe nodded. "I know," he said, looking down, "but you gotta know I ain't had nothin' to do with any of it."

"Any of what, exactly?" Bentsen asked in purring mode.

"Well, the drugs, you know. And Mr. Rieger getting killed. Like that."

"If you didn't have anything to do with it, then who did, would you guess?"

Sharpe looked from one to the other of them. "I told you before, I don't want to pin a target on nobody."

"You might want to think about that target thing, Mr. Sharpe, before somebody pins one on you."

"Why would they do that?"

"You can figure it out, can't you?" Strand asked. "The drugs have to be getting in here somehow, and undetected. You know, some way no one would ever suspect."

"Yeah," Bentsen joined in, "like the trunks from Washington."

"What a perfect setup, if you ask me, Mr. Sharpe. Somebody puts the stuff in a trunk in downtown DC, and what do you know," Bentsen said, not purring now, "it shows up here in the mine."

"All they need is one guy down there, and one guy up here. Now, who would that be?"

"I'm telling you, I don't know. Maybe it was Manzini?"

"Good guess, Mr. Sharpe," Strand said. "It seems the late Mr. Manzini was part of it, but there had to be somebody else, right?"

"Why is that?"

"Because Manzini is dead, that's why, and he didn't drop those rocks on himself, did he?"

"N-no, I guess not."

"In fact, Mr. Sharpe," Strand said, "Manzini was dead before those rocks hit him. Did you know that?"

Sharpe's eyes went wide. "Oh, God!"

"Oh, God, what, Mr. Sharpe?" Strand didn't let up.

"Nothing. All I know is that he and El Meister were buddies. Artie and me, well, we didn't eat lunch with them or break with them."

"And what about David Stoddard? Who was he buddies with?"

"Him? He was buddies with nobody, but he did stop and talk with them—Manzini and Meister. I've seen him a few times with them, but they never did stuff together that I saw."

"Well, Mr. Sharpe," Strand said, "apparently, they did something together."

LX

WHEN SHARPE LEFT the room with one of the troopers, Bentsen said, "Well, that narrows it down, doesn't it?"

"I suppose it does, but there's still more questions than answers even if Meister is our guy."

"Right, what we don't know is what triggered all of this right now, at this moment? Why now?"

"And why at any time when you think about it, Joe? These guys had a great gig going on here. Why mess it up?"

"I keep thinking Rieger realized something and told Masters."

There was a tap at the door and a trooper poked his head in. "You guys ready for Mr. Wise Guy?"

They both laughed and nodded as in walked the ultimate smartass himself.

"I don't know what you birds think is so funny," McKenna said. "You drag us all the way to Mercer from our homes and jobs, and for what? Just to go over the same crap all over again?"

Strand and Bentsen just looked at him, a little teakettle boiling down.

"And I still want to know why the FBI isn't in on this, anyway!"

Strand, the man with far less patience than his giant of a partner, said, "I thought we went through all this, Artie my man, and even Al Rieger told you to can it."

"So, what's the answer then?"

"Look, jackass, about twenty feet from here sits your pal, David Stoddard, and at our request, the FBI came in and had a chat with him. They're our buddies, if you didn't know it, and we could ask them to have a chat with you, and then we'll see who gets to demand answers from who!" He paused as McKenna appeared to shrink within his blue denim shirt. "So, are we ready to have a nice chat before the Bureau boys come in for their chat?"

McKenna cleared his throat, more than once, which allowed the red to drain from his face. "OK, OK. Look, I know I'm a wise guy, but somebody has to ask some questions."

"Right," Bentsen said leaning into his face, "and that's where we come in."

"Alright, alright. So, why am I here again?"

"We have such bad memories," Bentsen said, "so we wanted to hear once more about where you were around the times Masters and Rieger were murdered, and just for good measure, tell us where you were when Angelo Manzini got his."

At the last, McKenna cringed. "Look, I've already told you all I know about Mr. Masters and Al Rieger—and I had no reason to cause either of them any harm."

"And?" prompted Strand.

"But Manzini is something else again."

"How so?" It was Bentsen.

"If you think I'm a wiseass, you should have spent some time with Manzini. Cock of the walk, he was, and you'd have thought he and Meister owned the place."

"Really? Why would you say that?"

"Manzini made no secret he had something going on—you know Italians, they like to talk. He was like a schoolkid with a secret these last couple of years. Really obnoxious."

"So, he and Meister were buds?"

"I didn't say that. They were thick, but not buds. I'm not sure how to describe it. You could see them talking, even eating lunch together, but I never saw them laugh together, you know what I mean?"

Strand nodded. "And what about Stoddard? How did he fit in here?"

"Well, he didn't fit in with me or Frank, I can tell you that, but sure, you'd see Stoddard talking with the other two—never in the Investigations Center where they might be noticed, but out in the walkways to the front gate. I only saw them once or twice—Stoddard would pass them while Manzini had his smoke, say a few words, and move on. Strange, it was."

"No idea what might have been said?" Strand asked.

"Not a clue. Sorry."

"OK," Bentsen said, purring, "let's talk a little more about Elgin Meister. What's his story?"

"He and Manzini were thick—at least they ate together and took breaks together, you know, out in the walkways."

"How did Meister act—the same?"

"Him? Just the opposite. Quiet—still waters run deep, you know. He's not a guy I would cross."

"Why do you say that?"

"I don't know what he did before he came here, but it must have been tough work. Did you notice his build? He's only been here a few years, but he was OK with us because he always volunteered for whatever nightwork we had, or driving the van, stuff like that. He was single, you know, and was willing to work whatever hours."

"So, a favorite of Rieger's, then?"

"You'd think so, but Al, who liked to check on people, probably checked on him more."

"Why would that be?" Bentsen wondered.

"Why? Because Meister was always off by himself. Whenever Abel Masters would come around on his weekly tours of the place, you'd never find Meister. It took me a long time to notice that, but it always seemed odd."

"Back to our main question, Artie my man, let's talk about where you were just before the explosion that killed Angelo Manzini."

"Right after I talked to you guys that day and Lindy Johnston went in for his interview, I went back to the warehouse looking for Meister."

"Any special reason for that?"

"He was scheduled to take the van to Breezewood, but I couldn't find him."

LXI

"OK, DAVEY BOY," Bentsen said, "we've given you enough time. There's a court-appointed lawyer on the way over, and we're going to have some serious conversations now."

"Oh, no, we're not." It was Stoddard, manacled to the table where Artie McKenna had sat not fifteen minutes before. "I got word today. You can send your lawyer wherever they came from. My lawyer is on his way from Pittsburgh and he should be here within an hour."

"And who did Daddy buy you for this occasion, Davey boy?"

"Hey, knock it off, it's David. And my lawyer's name is Reinhard Koenig. Heard of him?" he asked, and chuckled with satisfaction.

"Oh, Christ," Strand said. "Not him! Remember that guy, Joe? He was the one who defended Marty Knotting in that big mess a few years ago."

"Right, a noisy guy in the courtroom, I believe. Too bad for his client, though."

"Why? What happened?" Stoddard said, his sausage-like fingers playing games with each other.

"Some people he'd done nasty stuff with found him in Williamsport, and that was that."

"What do you mean?"

"I mean poor Marty never got to see daylight," Bentsen said, just as satisfied as Stoddard had been earlier.

"Yeah," Strand said, "his buddies buried him in cement—alive."

"Jesus!"

"So, when your fancy lawyer gets here, just remember if you want any kind of deal, you're going to have to make it worth our while, or else you might meet some of your friends inside. Know what I mean?"

A trooper opened the door to the interrogation room, and looking at the detectives, said, "There's a guy out front, says he's the attorney for Stoddard here. I'll bring him back."

Within a minute, a tall, striking man in a well-cut pin-striped suit strode in, slapped his Moroccan leather briefcase on the table, and said, "Enough chatter with these people, David. I'm here to take care of things as your father asked me to do."

Without extending his hand, Strand said, "We've just been telling your new client here about what happened with the one you went to bat for a few years ago."

Koenig's face showed a brief look of puzzlement.

"You know—Marty Knotting?"

"Pretty sad state of affairs that the prison system couldn't protect one of its residents!"

Bentsen stood up, nodded to Koenig, and said, "I guess we need to let the two of you become acquainted, but Counselor," he said, eyeing the attorney, "we've lost a good deal of time already on this."

"Right," Strand said, "there are three people dead, and your client knows a good bit about one or more of the murders. We'll listen, but Stoddard here better have plenty to say."

"No need to threaten anyone, gentlemen. If you'll let me get up to speed on this, perhaps we can talk first thing tomorrow morning."

Bentsen sighed. "Hope that's not too late for your client."

"Why do you say that?" Koenig asked, opening his briefcase.

"Because," Strand said, "while Daddy dithered getting you here, our ongoing investigation has already developed information your client can no longer trade." He smiled. "That's why."

~

Into the squad room Strand and Bentsen shuffled and sat down heavily at their desks. "Of all people to crawl out of the woodwork," Bentsen said, slamming his hand on the desk.

"Right," Strand sighed, "and let's hope King Koenig falls off his throne—again."

Neither were pleased. And neither of them expected to see their lieutenant head for them at speed.

"Quit looking like the world has ended, you two. You had no choice but to wait until Koenig showed up. Just our luck Daddy found a top gun like him to stonewall us even more than what Stoddard already has." Montgomery grunted, then looked around at the empty room and asked, "So, what's next, Sherlock and Dr. Watson?"

Strand looked at his watch. "It's probably too late today to get warrants, but I think we have probable cause to detain Elgin Meister and search his residence as well as his locker at the mine. And two, I think we have enough to bring Nathaniel Robertson in for further questioning on the Purcell murder."

"Now, that's a mouthful," Montgomery said, fingering his moustache. "If you think either of them is about to flee, I can roust a judge right now as soon as Gloria types out the warrants, or we can wait till the morning."

Bentsen sat up straight and said, "Well, Meister has no reason to think we're coming for him, and he's scheduled to come in tomorrow morning anyway. Just to be sure, we might have a trooper outside his door tomorrow morning to help him find his way over, don't you think?"

Montgomery nodded. "Makes sense, Joe. What do you think, Fletch?"

Strand shrugged his shoulders. "Part of me agrees with Joe—no hurry on Meister, or Robertson for that matter. Another part of me thinks this whole thing is coming to an end, and I sure don't want to miss anything now."

This time, Montgomery looked at his watch. "I'll get the warrants going—one of you will have to check them out—it's pretty unusual for us to have two separate and unrelated cases coming to a close at the same time, isn't it?"

"With Meister, it's going to be about drugs and, possibly, a murder weapon, and Joe and I feel pretty sure he's one of Stoddard's accomplices, but we don't know who Stoddard works for, and that's what we'll be chatting about tomorrow."

"As for Robertson, boss," Bentsen said, "it's a crapshoot, and patience won't do us any good. There've been suggestions of drug involvement, but we have no smoking gun. And as for the Purcell murder, we'll never be able to prove a thing, anyway."

"There's another possibility we haven't talked about, however," Strand said.

"What's that?" Bentsen asked.

"Robertson's partner—didn't that death sound odd to you, Joe? I'll bet if we dig a bit more, we can get an exhumation order and answer more than one question about Carl Joseph's death."

"Was that supposed to be a joke, Fletch?" Bentsen asked, rolling his eyes.

"No joke, Joe. I'm beginning to think this guy Robertson is no joke at all."

LXII

STRAND DROPPED BENTSEN off at his Mercer home on Pitt
Street, waved to his wife, Sylvia, as always, then pointed the
Vic toward SR58 and home. On the way back to Foreston—and
dinner with Aurora and the kids—Strand's mental processes kept
churning the events of the past few weeks. Montgomery suggested
the Robertson case was unrelated to the mine murders, but was that
true? It was a stretch for sure, Strand thought, since nothing had
surfaced to tie Robertson to the mine murders, nothing at all. He
told himself to put it all aside, that it would sort itself out if he just
had patience, as Joe had said. Tonight, he was going to have an evening with family and that was all that mattered.

At their Pine Street home, little daylight remained as he pulled
the Vic into their drive off the back alley, but as he did so, something registered about what he'd just observed on the street in front
of their house. Pine Street was a pretty busy thoroughfare, running
as it did between the police and fire stations three blocks to the east,
and the Post Office and downtown two blocks to the west. There
was a good deal of traffic during the day, much less in the evening
hours—this was Foreston, after all! Although legal to do so in places,
rarely would people park their vehicles there on a winter's evening.

Instead of cutting his engine, Strand slowly backed out of the drive with only his parking lights on, then eased the Vic eastward through the alley, crossed Monroe, and continued through the alley still in parallel with Pine. Reaching Harvard, he turned right, then right again, and slowly cruised westward on Pine, back toward his own home. Within a block, he saw it.

Parked across from the old brick pile next to their own was an unmarked white van. No lights, no exhaust. Driving slow enough to catch the plate number, Strand repeated it to himself just as his car drew abreast of the van's passenger door, less than six feet away. All the van's windows were fogged, yet behind the wheel he could make out the shadow of a man sitting, staring straight ahead.

As Strand drove past, he kept the van in his rearview mirror, and about fifty yards later, the van began to move. At first, Strand wasn't certain because no lights were evident in the vehicle, inside or out. It went in reverse and made a Uey using the junction of Monroe and Pine as its turning circle, then sped off in an easterly direction.

Strand decided not to chase it or call the Foreston PD for help, since he had the plate number and could check it in the morning. The only white vans in the universe of their hunt since Abel Masters's murder were what he and Bentsen observed in the mine, and what Ethel Richland saw in Masters's driveway in the wee hours before his body was found. Was this a coincidence? He had learned long before not to believe in them.

~

In Aurora Strand's cozy and warm kitchen, he could smell something Italian simmering for dinner.

"It's veal parmesan over buttered egg noodles," his wife said while hovering over the stove, "and you're going to have a garden salad, Fletcher Strand, and enjoy every last leaf of it."

"I am your humble servant," he said, holding her shoulders and kissing the back of her neck, just as he always liked to do—and just as she always expected him to do.

"Fletch, you are one distracting son of a gun. You know that, don't you?"

"I sure hope so," he said, smiling while he shed his overcoat and shoes.

"You seem to be in a mighty fine mood for a guy with unsolved murder cases up the kazoo," she said. "Things going well, are they?"

"They are—I feel things are coming to a close, and I'll be relieved when it's all over."

"The fog is lifting, is it?"

"Beginning to. Say, hon, did you notice that white van sitting across the street? Was it there earlier?"

"Hmmm! Now that you mention it, I noticed it when the school bus rolled by—it stops right there, you know, and there isn't a lot of room to pass if someone parks where the van was."

"See anyone in the van or doing work for somebody on the street?"

"No—no one, but then, I wasn't looking for anyone."

Strand exhaled. "Well," he said, thoughtful, "if that same van shows up close by here tomorrow, I want you to call the PD first, then me."

"What do I tell the police? That you're curious about white vans?"

"No, smarty," he said, more serious now, "just tell them there's a guy just sitting there and he's making you nervous, what with the kids and all."

"Fletch, are you sure?"

"I'm not worried about you or the kids, but I don't want to take any chances."

"Then you are worried," she said, turning to face him.

"Look, if this is who I think it is, he won't be coming after you or the kids. It'll be me. I'm his problem. Now, let's have that delicious dinner before I get other ideas."

∼

After a mouth-watering repast in their sometimes-chilly eating area just off the kitchen, Anna and Aarie cleaned up the dishes while

Strand made sure the family's newest member, Mac the Beagle, made a necessary trip not too far out the back door. With his young bones, the pup enjoyed its first winter, and despite the snow's depth, Mac took a million sniffs before he found just the right spot, then scampered back in as soon as his wobbly legs could carry him.

"Let's go sit and watch some TV," Strand said to the dog, who clearly tuned in to his every syllable. Into the den the two marched, and there the kids were already camped with schoolbooks and notebooks in evidence. The TV was on *Wheel of Fortune,* and soon, Aurora came in to join them. It was, all in all, the kind of evening Strand could never get enough of.

Within a few hours, the kids drifted off to bed and books upstairs, and Aurora, too, slid away by the time the old clock struck 9:30. Not having watched any TV at all, Strand remained slouched in his favorite chair in the corner, his left hand over the arm, scratching Mac's neck as he lay in the woolen pouf on the floor next to him. The day's events and conversations kept rolling around in his head. Soon, he slipped into a light, fitful sleep under the Afghan that Aurora had thrown over him when she left for bed.

Something Joe had said more than once over the past few days kept coming back at him, like acid after a bad meal, only he couldn't bring the word or phrase to mind. What was the word? *What was it Joe said!?*

LXIII

A ROUND 4 A.M., Strand shook himself awake, shivering. Their family room, once a porch and not well insulated or heated, could at times feel like a campground on a cold November night. He looked over the side of the chair, and even Mac had figured out there were warmer places to sleep.

Yawning and rubbing his eyes, suddenly he stopped. He remembered the word Joe Bentsen had used. Though pronounced the same, it had two different meanings, and it was just one that made Strand feel he might know the thread which bound all those men in a way that ultimately had to lead to their deaths. *Could it be?*

He turned out the lights—and peeked out the window facing Pine Street to see if a white van was parked there. Nothing. Shuffling up the stairs and into bed, he slept like a baby, rising at dawn without the slightest hesitation.

"What's going on with you, Fletch? You never get up at the first alarm."

"But today, I have patience, darling. Patients."

"What?"

"Nothing, dear. I'm off in a few to pick Joe up and start a great day—and watch out for that white van."

"There is something wrong with you," she said with a grin, "and I love it. Come back to me safely, Mr. Patience."

~

Strand steered the State Vic into the Bentsen's' driveway. Out the front door lumbered his partner, coffee in one hand and egg sandwich in the other. Sylvie, as Joe called her, was at the door waving and pointing to what Joe carried with him.

"Sylvie sent this for you—hers are better than Mickey D's, but sorry, no coffee—you'll have to wait till we get to the barracks."

"Thanks, Joe. These," he said, referring to the sandwiches, "will get us off to the right start on what should be a most promising day."

As ordered, warrants were signed by Judge Hanscomb and ready to serve, one each for Elgin Meister and Dr. Nathaniel Robertson.

Strand did not seem all that excited about the warrants, however, his thoughts still swirling over Joe Bentsen's patience.

"Hey, Joe, let's take a minute before Stoddard's lawyer gets here and take a quick look at some of the files from the mine personnel."

"Jesus, Fletch, are we trying to memorize them or what?"

"No, we're going to glance at what we didn't before—their medical information."

"Just what are you getting at, my man? We've got a ton of stuff to do today."

"But this, my bigfooted friend, might cut us right to the chase."

"OK," he sighed and shoveled in the last bite of Sylvie's sandwich, "what do you want me to do?"

"I'll take Masters, Novak, Conlon, and Rieger, and you take the rest. Go right to the medical and insurance section—I think there are about three or four pages in each file. We're going to check their listed beneficiaries as well."

"Got it. Anything we're looking for?"

"We want to know if Nathaniel Robertson is the listed provider for any of them besides Abel Masters."

Each got busy with their piles.

Bentsen popped up with a "Bingo" when he checked Stoddard's file, then Manzini's.

"This is it, I think," Strand said, with the look of an athlete having run a good race. "Yeah, I can see it."

"Clear it up for me, then," Bentsen said.

"Clear it up for me, too," Montgomery joined in as he walked up to their adjoining desks.

"This is the thread we've been looking for. So far, we seem to have stitched together a working theory that says Stoddard was peddling drugs, first pot by himself, probably, then harder stuff smuggled in to the mine via the trunks from DC using Manzini."

"And? Get us to Robertson," Montgomery said, leaning forward with keen interest.

"Right now, this is speculation, of course, but let's say Stoddard became one of Robertson's patients and over time when the good doctor went over his blood work, he saw THC. At the same time, Robertson bought himself a rural property in Virginia where, perhaps, he could receive and transport drugs up here for sale through a small network of his own."

"Keep knitting," Bentsen said. "I like it so far."

"Stoddard using drugs as a federal employee with a security clearance was truly dumb, not because he could lose his job, but because a predator like Robertson could come along and blackmail him about it. In an instant, Stoddard not only became part of Robertson's network, he was the key link to the trunk system, a foolproof way to transport large quantities of whatever you can imagine across three states, and have it staged and ready for distribution."

"So, where does this Elgin Meister guy fit in?"

"I'm not a hundred percent sure yet, but glad you mentioned that. Is Gloria available to run a plate for me? A white van may have been staking out my house last night, and I'm willing to bet it's a van identical to those used in the trunk transport service, but this one is privately owned."

"By Elgin Meister?" Montgomery asked.

"Got it in one, Chief."

Strand glanced at his watch. "By the way, shouldn't Meister have reported in here by now?"

~

Montgomery poked his head out of the troopers' bay and called for Gloria Moses, the dispatcher. "What did you get on that plate number?"

"Registered to Elgin Meister, Foreston, PA."

Montgomery cast his eye toward Strand, "Well, there's one of your answers." Then back to Moses, "Check with the trooper assigned to herd Meister in here this morning and let us know what's going on."

"I will, Lieutenant, and by the way, Stoddard's attorney, the one from Pittsburgh, is in the waiting area to see his client."

"Check with the trooper first, then show Koenig into the interrogation room while somebody fetches Stoddard. Let Koenig know Strand and Bentsen will join them in fifteen minutes or so."

"Got it, sir."

"Thanks, Gloria. Looks like a busy day, eh?"

Moses smiled and disappeared.

"Alright, men, looks like a plan is in the making—not of our making—and we're going to have to roll with it."

Strand took the last bite out of a cold egg sandwich, threw his coffee cup away, and grabbed his notebook. Bentsen pointed to the restroom and headed that way.

LXIV

I N THE INTERROGATION room, Reinhard Koenig had on an older suit, no doubt to match an audience where dapper would be a
waste, thought Strand. He wasn't offended, just amused.

"Is your client ready to talk turkey, counselor?" he asked.

"Not unless you are prepared to use whatever influence you have
with the feds about any charges they might bring."

"Ultimately, that would be up to Deputy DA Carstairs, but I
think it's safe to say we can proceed here, and if there's a problem on
either side, we can call a timeout."

"Fair enough. First, however, could we please untether Mr. Stoddard from the table?"

"Only if your client," Bentsen jumped in, "can promise not to
assault me or my partner, the offense which got us to where we are
right now."

Koenig, who was still standing, eyed his client with a look that
could only be described as, 'How could you have been so stupid?'
"Agreed," Koenig said, placing his hand on Stoddard's shoulder.

"So, what have you got to trade?" asked Strand, getting right to it.

"I'll give you the other guy in the mine I worked with."

"You mean Elgin Meister? Too late, Davey boy," Bentsen said.

"I warned you—we both did—the time would come when what you were willing to offer would be worth zero, nada, nothing, zilch. Remember that?"

Stoddard sat still, staring at the far wall, his trembling lips the only sign of life. To Strand, he seemed as if he was about to cry.

"Y-yeah, I guess I remember, but I had to wait until my attorney showed up."

"Did you think, Davey," Bentsen asked, at it again, "we were just going to stop our investigation until Daddy could line up somebody like Reinhard Koenig here?"

"No, I guess not."

"You could have had a court-appointed attorney to represent you until this guy appeared, but nooooo, as John Belushi likes to say. You could have had your cake and eat it, too," Bentsen continued, "but unless you have something else to give, I think," he said looking at Strand, "that we're done here."

Koenig gave his client another of the same looks. For just one second, Strand felt for the guy having to deal with morons for clients.

Strand and Bentsen moved toward the door.

Koenig bent down and spoke in Stoddard's ear.

"Wait," Stoddard said, "what if I gave you who I work for?"

"Well, maybe," Bentsen purred. "What do you think, Fletch? Should we cut this idiot a break?"

"It had better be good, or we'll just call Carstairs and let him know he can throw the whole book at him," Strand said, looking at Bentsen, not at Stoddard.

"OK, boys," Koenig jumped in. "Mr. Stoddard has something worthwhile if you're interested."

"First, let's finish with Elgin Meister," Bentsen said. "I'm curious, so start talking."

"About what?"

"About murder. Three, in fact."

"Why would I know about that? We've already talked about this," Stoddard pleaded.

"C'mon, Joe, let's go. The air's getting stale in here, and Carstairs told us he'll deal until 9:30. It's just past that now."

"Right."

"Don't go. Give me just a minute to speak with my client," said Koenig, the voice of reason.

With a shrug of disgust, Strand said, "You've got three. This is already a waste of time. We'll be outside."

Strand and Bentsen stepped into the hall where Lieutenant Montgomery and a uniformed trooper were waiting.

"Elgin Meister is nowhere to be found, men. What's next?"

"Stoddard just confirmed what we suspected, so there's nothing stopping us from issuing an All Points on him for possession of dangerous drugs with intent to sell. It's not just a search warrant now, but an arrest. Chief, can we let a couple of troopers execute the search warrant on Meister's home, his work locker, and whatever else we can find? At the same time, can we get Gloria to alert all nearby departments—and in Ohio as well?"

"You got it. Anything else?"

"We'll give our chucklehead here one shot at a deal—we want his boss—right after he gives us everything he has on Meister and the three murders in the mine."

"He's all yours. And when you're done?"

"Depends on what Stoddard says. Either way, we'll head over to Robertson's office and home and execute the search warrant ourselves, and perhaps, make an arrest."

"Keep me posted."

Back in the interrogation room, Strand and Bentsen interrupted an intense, whispered exchange. Finally, Koenig shrugged, and said, "It's your party, David, go ahead."

"Where were we?" Stoddard's demeanor was a mix of fear and relief.

Bentsen said, "I can't believe you can't remember. Elgin Meister?"

"I can't prove it, but I'm pretty sure he went to Masters's house to kill him that night, but seriously, I have no idea why he did it."

"Do you expect us to take that and run with it?"

"No, I just know he thought Al Rieger saw or heard something between him and Manzini, and he suspected Rieger was going to tell Masters. Meister is paranoid."

"And what, Davey boy, the clock is ticking." Bentsen said.

"And for the same reason, he killed Rieger."

"And Manzini?"

"I guess so. He told me he had his little bomb rigged for Rieger, but he didn't need it, so when you told me what happened with Manzini, I'm just guessing he used it on him."

"All just guesses, Davey boy. Any direct proof of what you're saying?

"Like what?"

"Like you actually saw something, or he told you something?" There was little patience in Bentsen's tone.

"You know, David," Strand said, "Meister doesn't strike us as the sharpest tool in the barn, so what's to stop us from thinking Meister killed those men on your say-so since you had a lot more to lose than they did."

"N-no, I'm telling you, I did no such thing."

Koenig leaned down and again whispered in Stoddard's ear, to no avail.

"Your client," Bentsen said, looking first at Koenig, then at Stoddard, "is an accessory to murder after the fact. Had he said something to us at the right time, Manzini would be alive right now."

"You said I could get a deal!"

"We were talking drugs, David," Strand said, "but now we're talking murder—just as we suspected all along."

"Wait a minute!"

"Yes, wait," Koenig said, "he has more to give you—for consideration."

"Maybe," Strand said, "let's hear it."

"Davey boy," said Bentsen, "I don't believe you for a second, but start talking and let's see where that gets us."

Stoddard looked up at his attorney, who shot him an "up to you" look.

"I worked for Dr. Nathaniel Robertson. He recruited me to set up the whole trunk thing, and I sold his pills for him."

"You're doing good, Davey boy, we can fill in the gaps later, because we were on our way to see your boss, anyway."

"You knew about Robertson?"

"We were beginning to put two and two together, yes, David," Strand said, "but we needed to find the thread. You were his patient, weren't you?"

"Yeah, me and Manzini."

Strand looked at Bentsen, smiled, and said, "Patients, Joe. Patience, right?"

"What's he talkin' about?" Stoddard asked Koenig.

"So, Robertson recruited you, and you recruited Meister and Manzini, is that right?"

"Yeah," Stoddard said with a satisfied smile, "it was a great plan while it lasted, wasn't it?"

"Yeah, David, until you and Meister had to kill three people to cover it up."

Bentsen got up to leave. "And you didn't think those killings might shine a light on things, Davey boy?"

LXV

S TRAND AND BENTSEN sped over to Robertson's office, and because there were never any patients waiting, found a spot closest to the front entrance of the less than impressive building.
Trotting up the stairs, Strand felt the entangled patchwork of drugs
and murder was finally going to resolve itself. He was wrong.

At the top of the landing, they turned right and walked through
the door, which was standing open, as if inviting them in. No one
was in the outer office, neither a patient nor Moira Purcell, so they
crossed to the next open door, that of Dr. Robertson's office. Inside
was a scene neither would easily forget.

There, in the center of the room, at Robertson's desk, was the doctor's lifeless body, head lolled back on what had once been a beautiful
Moroccan leather executive chair. The fresh blood near his head and
sluicing onto his dead shoulders was the only movement.

Worse than the vision confronting them was the sight of Moira
Purcell standing next to her nephew grasping what appeared to be
a steel bar about eighteen inches long. It, too, was covered in blood,
and blood had already covered the fingers holding it.

The beautifully dressed and groomed Purcell stood there staring at her nephew and completely oblivious to the two detectives

standing nearby.

"Ms. Purcell," Strand said in the softest voice he could manage so as not to startle her, especially given her grip on a deadly weapon. After a moment he repeated her name, and only then did she turn in their direction, dropping the steel bar to the floor as she did so.

"Ms. Purcell, what happened here?"

"I-I don't know," she began to say, then said, "I've been wanting this to happen for a long time."

Bentsen stepped back, reached for his cell phone, and called for a forensics team, an ambulance, and the coroner. "No sirens are necessary," he said to the dispatcher. "No one here is going to recover from anything."

~

"Joe," Strand said when he heard Bentsen finish his call, "can you find some paper towels or something?" Turning to the older woman standing there, apparently in shock, he said, "Ms. Purcell, let's step out to the reception area, and perhaps you can compose yourself."

Strand led her with a hand on her elbow, careful not to disturb anything else in the room as they stepped out of Robertson's office.

Bentsen found some paper towels, soaked them in warm water, and joined his partner in the waiting room. As he stepped closer to the seated pair, Purcell began to cry and was going to put her hands to her eyes, but Strand stopped her from doing so, gently. He gave her the paper towels, and said to Bentsen, "They'll want to check this blood just to close the loop on this, but at least her fingers won't stick together in the meantime."

Bentsen nodded and said, donning blue gloves, "While we're waiting for the gang to arrive, I'll take a quick look around Robertson's office."

"See if you can find a patient list."

Moira Purcell remained rigid, unseeing.

"Are you able to talk, Ms. Purcell?" Strand asked.

Slowly, she shook her head.

"You know what, then, I'm going to call a second ambulance. You may need some medical attention."

Once again, she moved her head, imperceptibly. Strand thought she'd agreed, but wasn't sure. There'd be plenty of time for questioning her later. "Please stay right where you are. I'll be right here doing a search of...of things." For some reason, he didn't want to come right out and say, "your things."

"Joe, whoever you called, call them again, will ya, and let's get a second ambulance for Moira here."

"Got it."

While Bentsen remained in Robertson's office, Strand worked the reception area, beginning with Purcell's desk, and keeping an eye on her at the same time. He hadn't gotten very far when her voice penetrated his concentration.

"Why are you doing that, Detective Strand?" On her face was the look of someone awakening from a coma surprised to find a stranger in her presence. She was a bit groggy, but regaining her senses rapidly, he could easily see.

Surprised, Strand raised himself to full height to assess her and her physical state. "Why, I'm doing exactly as I said I would, Ms. Purcell. By the way, is there anyone I should call for you, perhaps to meet us at the hospital?"

She appeared to be deep in thought, as if considering choices. "No, sir. No one. And for your information, I do not need any EMTs poking me."

"No husband or close friend, ma'am?" he asked, ignoring her last remark.

"My husband has been gone for a few years now, Detective."

"I'm sorry, Ms. Purcell, but I'm also confused," he said, as he sat down beside her. "Did you say you were one of the Purcell sisters?"

"I did, didn't I?"

"But you go by Purcell?"

She turned to look at him full on, resolution and some other emotion written all over her face. "I was married to Bill Hastings for several years. He had a daughter I considered my own, but he was a bully and I left him, and took my maiden name in the divorce."

"Hastings? Are you, then, the step-mother to Deborah Hastings?"

She nodded with and with a half-smile, said, "Very good, Detective."

"Ms. Purcell, before we proceed further, given the circumstances, I need to warn you of your rights under the law. Joe, can you come in for a minute?" When Bentsen rumbled in, like a locomotive cutting its throttle, Strand read her the Miranda warning and asked her if she understood.

"Indeed, I do, Detective." Amazingly, she sounded in full control of her faculties.

"Did you suspect your nephew of murdering your sister, Ms. Purcell?" Strand couldn't believe where this was going.

"Of course I did, and I was pretty sure he'd done it, but no one could ever prove it."

"What made you think so?"

"For days, maybe weeks after Nella's murder, he walked around with a look of supreme satisfaction, like he'd gotten away with something big."

"Is that all?"

"For me, that was enough. His mother knew, too. Only once did we ever discuss it, and it was when Natey was finishing med school, and she begged me never to bring it up with anyone."

"And you agreed?"

"At that point there was nothing to be gained, don't you see?"

"But you came to work here? Why?"

"It was after he did what he did to my step-daughter—the bastard took my grandchild! I wanted to keep an eye on him, and I waited."

"And he never suspected you as being possibly disloyal to him?"

She cackled. It was a sound Strand could never have imagined coming from what seemed to be so refined a person. "His ego was too big for that!"

Strand nodded. "And did you ever talk to anyone about Nella Purcell's murder?"

With a much broader smile, she said, "Of course, I called you people."

Strand and Bentsen both uttered a low chuckle. Their tipster!

"I've been waiting for this day, gentlemen," she went on, "because don't you see that sooner or later my nephew, the bastard, would get his." In a few words, she went from sweet satisfaction to syllables pushed out through gritted teeth.

"You do realize, don't you, Ms. Purcell, that we see two motives for you to murder your nephew—your step-daughter's child, and your sister, Nella. Is there anything more you wish to say before we formally arrest you for the murder of Dr. Nathaniel Robertson?"

"What? Arrest me? Why, I didn't do anything?"

"But you were standing next to his body holding the murder weapon, and there was blood on your hands!" It was Bentsen, who'd been trying to keep his good manners. "And you all but made a spontaneous confession—we both heard it."

"Why, I walked in as the killer finished his dirty work. I stood there in shock as he handed me the steel bar. I can't believe I took it from him! I don't know what I said, or why I said it." Her plaintive voice underscored her next words. "Don't you understand? Why would I kill him? I always knew someone would do it for me."

"Given what we've seen and heard, Ms. Purcell," Strand said, "your statement is not credible."

"Nothing incredible about it, Detective Strand. It was one of his patients who murdered him. Mr. Elgin Meister. He enjoyed it."

LXVI

W HEN THE AMBULANCE arrived, Strand instructed the EMTs to determine Ms. Purcell's state of shock and whether she might be fit for further questioning. If admitted to the hospital, a trooper will stay with her, the detective ordered. The techs nodded in unison, and began to tend to Moira Purcell, still seated in the reception area.

Out of her earshot, Strand said, "We need to be careful here, Joe. We've Mirandized her, but despite her two motives, I'm certain she didn't kill her nephew."

"Why are you so sure?"

"That steel bar weighs about fifteen pounds for one thing—hard for an older person to lever, but most importantly, if she killed Robertson, it's a helluva coincidence she chose exactly the same weapon used in three other murders, the details of which I'm certain she had no knowledge."

"And?"

"And Elgin Meister—he's the one guy left in our elimination contest who could have killed any or all three of the first victims—and she had no way of knowing that either."

"I see your logic, and while we're waiting for Doc McCreary and his techs to show up, how about humoring me for a minute?"

"Sure, I'm full of humor."

"You sure are, wise guy," Bentsen said, scratching his head, a severe disruption to the hair thinning there, "but let's say Meister is our guy. Walk me through it, at least as far as you've figured it."

"It's not totally clear, but here's a guess: Mrs. Richland mentioned seeing a white van in Masters's driveway sometime in the wee hours of the day we later found his body, and we now know Meister has a white van. What we also now might safely conclude—most probably—is that Robertson actually murdered Masters with an insulin overdose, but Meister didn't know that, and came to do it again."

"That works."

"When Meister entered the Masters house, he thought the man was sleeping, when, in fact, he'd been very recently murdered."

"The two must have missed each other by minutes, then. Hmm! But wait, Fletch, why in the world would Robertson and Meister want to kill Masters?"

"That's the best question of all, Joe, and for that we have no answers—yet!

"Then what?"

"Meister bludgeons Masters, stuffs his body in the van, possibly in a partially closed trunk—so that no one would see a body—then drives into the mine well before 6 a.m. that Monday, and deposits the body after entering the main door where no one else goes until later in the morning. He turns on the lights, but forgets to turn them off."

"But how does he get the trunk with the blood into the warehouse?"

"That took some working out. Meister knew something about human nature, and that knowledge gave him the ability to do all of that without anyone noticing a thing."

"C'mon, Fletch. Cough it up."

"Somewhere early in this whole adventure, one of our witnesses mentioned that most of the people coming in in the morning are creatures of habit. They show up when the startup supervisor unlocks the warehouse man door at 6 a.m., and then—and the guard at the front gate will likely verify this—there's probably a gap of time when no one appears until later. Meister worked in the warehouse, and over time, was probably very familiar with these patterns."

"I can see it."

"And that's when he simply moves his van to the warehouse door—remember Stoddard said it was open?—dumps the trunk, we can guess between 6:15 and 7, then he drives his van out to the lot and walks in like everybody else."

Bentsen nodded. "So far, so good, but I'm still stuck on a couple of things. The guys at the portal gate had no record of Meister driving in, and still, I have no clue why Masters was murdered."

"As for your first point, that's always bothered me as well, but there's a simple answer."

"Which is?"

"The guys at the front desk saw Meister in a white van—just like they always do when the white vans go in and out with him behind the wheel. They probably waved to each other, and the guard forgot to note it. Then, when we asked about it, they were afraid to admit their record was incomplete. Human nature, Joe, and Meister probably counted on his buddies not paying any attention to him."

"And the second?"

"Don't know, but hold that thought for a minute. As to poor Al Rieger, what we supposed earlier is probably true. Rieger saw or heard either Meister or Manzini do something they thought gave them away, so Meister, the paranoid one as someone described him, decided to eliminate the possibility of Rieger doing them any harm, and just for good measure, Manzini."

"Right. And dead men don't talk."

"Why he killed Masters, I have no real idea, but we can speculate that Rieger must have suspected something and Meister thought he told Masters—that's pretty weak, I know. And Manzini's big mistake was flaunting his newfound riches, right? Notice how Meister lives—like a poor bachelor—and he probably resented Manzini's stupidity and didn't need the liability."

"Wait, back to Rieger a minute. I don't recall anyone suggesting

Meister left the mine after Rieger was murdered. How do you explain that?"

"Simplest explanation of all. He never left the mine that night. He knew how to turn off the alarm system, and so, after murdering Rieger, he went back inside, locked himself in, and slept there till morning. When he left the next day, he handed in his badge—and if the guard noticed, all Meister would have to do is apologize and say he just forgot to turn it in."

"Somehow, we missed the connection between Meister and Robertson."

"That's easy, too. Meister filled out his personnel forms when he began working. Sometime afterward, he switched doctors, and neglected to update anybody, or he just lied by omission."

"That all takes me back to Stoddard. Remember what we said before? Think about it. Had he not tried to assault you, we might never have been able to peel this stinking onion."

"Right, and an egotistical prick like Stoddard might well have been pretty happy with the elimination of Manzini and Robertson—the top and bottom of their network—which would have left him as the natural inheritor of a small drug empire. And eliminating Masters, a guy he hated, was icing on the cake."

"And the damnedest thing of all is?"

"We can hardly prove any of it."

LXVII

"IF YOU HAVE the murder weapon, gents, you can prove a helluva lot," Doc McCreary said as he walked in with one of his techs. "But first, they ought to nominate you two for the Murder Incorporated Award," he said with a chuckle, "since you seem to generate a good bit of work for so many public servants in two counties."

"Haha," Bentsen said, "we just want to keep you from sitting in your dungeon smoking too many of those godawful cigars."

McCreary shook off his soaking raincoat. "Hope you brought your water wings. It's crazy out there." He exhaled, walked over to where the two were sitting, and said, "So, fill me in on the latest before I go meet the guest of honor."

"On the last point, Doc," Strand said, "you're already acquainted with the late Dr. Nathaniel Robertson, so here's the two-minute rundown," which he proceeded to do, including the part about Moira Purcell's apparently bogus confession."

"Oh, jeez, on all counts." He got up to go, then turned back to them, and said, "Hey, I'm serious about that murder weapon—you get that, and you can probably tie them all together."

"Oh, Doc, didn't we tell you? The murder weapon is laying on the floor near the body."

"Right," Bentsen added, "and Purcell's fingerprints will be on it, as well as the victim's blood."

McCreary chuckled. "Sometimes the angels do us a favor, boys. If we're lucky, there'll be microscopic traces of every victim's blood somewhere on that weapon. Is it a steel bar of some sort, as I imagined?"

"You're hittin' on all cylinders, Doc," Bentsen said. "Now, let's get lucky with it."

~

"Joe," Strand said when they stepped out onto the stair landing, "I think we both need to make some calls. How about you calling in to update Montgomery and find out if there's been any progress on locating the white van and/or Meister? I guess we can state with certainty he was here in the Sharon area less than an hour ago."

"You got it. And you?"

"I've got two calls to make. Fill you in later."

Hoping for a clear day that would lend itself to a cell phone signal, they hustled down the stairs and instead found the rain McCreary mentioned. Bentsen said he'd dash for the car while Strand hugged the entrance door under the shallow awning. The rain pelted down, its effect deafening.

Already regretting a favor to his brother, Strand punched in Jonathan's number and it went to voicemail. Before he could make his other call, however, he could see Jonathan was calling him back.

"I hope you're calling with good news, little brother," Jonathan said with more of a demand in his voice than a hope.

"I suppose that'll depend upon your point of view, Johnnie. Nathaniel Robertson was murdered earlier this morning." Strand waited for the reaction and he got it. Even with the sound of pounding rain, he could hear Jonathan's intake of breath.

"What?" he nearly shrieked into the phone. "Are you shittin' me, little detective?"

"No. You don't deserve this favor, Johnnie, and you'll get no details from me, but I warned you to distance yourself from this creep. He was the head of a drug ring, probably in addition to being a lousy doctor. But all that is your problem, so I suggest you get your news puppets busy to put the right spin on this for you and the VP."

"You're a bastard, you know that, Fletch?"

"What? For doing you a favor? I could have kept silent and let this hit the news—at least now you have a small chance to get ahead of this. And you know what, Johnnie? I didn't make this call for you. I made it for Mom—she would have thought it was the right thing to do. And you're fucking welcome," he said and clicked off.

Next, he called Charlie Niven, and luckily found him on the second ring. "Hey, Charlie, this is Fletcher Strand," he began, and after they'd exchanged a pleasantry, he added, "you can call off the hounds on Nathaniel Robertson. He's dead. But if there's a way to go after his estate for some bucks to my brother's partner, Bob, I hope you'll check it out."

"Wow, that's a better jolt than I can get from the diner's coffee. Can you give me any details?"

"In the cone of deep silence, Charlie, here's all I'll give you. The bastard turned out to be the head of a drug ring and murdered by one of his flunkies, apparently. For all he's done to the medical profession, he got some justice—rough justice, I'd say."

Niven remained silent for a moment, then said, "You know what, Fletch, don't expect any bill from me on this whole thing. Somebody's death should never be satisfying, but God help me, this one is."

∼

As the rain slowed to a pour, Strand dashed to the waiting Vic, its exhaust coughing through the raindrops. Glad for a warm place, he saw that Bentsen had apparently finished what he had to do.

"And?" Strand asked, well aware, as partners often are, that words need not be wasted.

"And Montgomery swore for a full minute when I told him about

Robertson, but when he finally calmed down, I could almost hear a sigh of relief coming through the phone. For sure, he's been taking some heat from Harrisburg and the media about the two slow-witted detectives on this case who let four murders happen."

"Don't tell him, but I'm betting it's more than that."

"Right. And there's been no trace of Meister or his van. Like he melted away."

"Not all that hard to do when it's been raining so hard and visibility is next to nothing. He's had plenty of time to get where he's going."

"You know, Fletch, I keep wondering how Meister thought that by murdering everybody in sight, he would somehow escape being caught."

"I'm sure you've noticed over the years, Joe, that when this sort of thing starts, it's 'in for a penny, in for a pound.'"

"Yeah, I suppose so—they can't stop, and a perverse logic convinces them to take it all the way."

Strand's phone buzzing interrupted their chatter. It was a number from the mine.

"Hello?"

"Detective Strand? It's Judy Conlon, and I just found something that means nothing to me but might to you."

"Really? What did you find?"

"Well, for quite a while I couldn't make myself tidy up Mr. Masters's office, but I finally got around to it late yesterday and this morning. I can assure you there was nothing in his desk—I think you already checked that, anyway—but I noticed his desk blotter was pretty well worn, so when I went to replace it, I found a note he'd apparently written to himself. It was underneath."

"Any date on it or a signature or anything?"

"No date or signature, but I'd know his handwriting anywhere."

"So, what did it say?"

"It was on a yellow Post-It and the words were 'How could I have missed Amos?'"

"What? Can you please repeat that?"

"Sure. 'How could I have missed Amos?'"

LXVIII

"**W**HAT THE HELL does that mean?" Bentsen asked, sighing. Without waiting for Strand's response, he turned the key in the ignition. "What next, pard?"

"Let me think about that comment for a minute," he responded, staring straight ahead, "but in the meantime, let's head back to the barracks and take another look at Meister's files. I know you looked at them and I looked at them, but damn it, Joe, we both missed something."

"I guess, and while you're doing that, I need a restroom stop, and if we're really in luck, maybe our roadies and the locals might have spotted Meister's van."

"Let's hope."

As the windshield wipers swept the rain aside on the fifteen-minute ride to the barracks, Strand sat quietly, attempting to fathom Masters's meaning. Several possibilities crossed his mind. The most obvious take would be that the two of them were acquainted, but how would that be? Somehow Strand and Bentsen, separately, blew right by something—probably something obvious in hindsight.

Strand's phone buzzed again just as they approached Mercer.

"Honey," Aurora said, her voice tinged with fear, "a white van has been going by the house every ten minutes or so. I don't know if it's the one you were concerned about, but I thought you'd want to know."

"Where are the kids?"

"At school, Fletch. I called Hillcrest and the Junior High and they're both where they're supposed to be."

"Listen, hon," Strand said, "call the PD and let them know about the van—maybe they can intercept it. Then go to the schools, pick the kids up, and head to the station up the street."

"You think so?"

"Just to be sure. And when you get to the station, just tell Georgie Hallon I asked if you could wait there for an hour or so."

"Alright, Fletch, whatever you say. I'm leaving now."

~

"Jesus, Fletch, you want me to head to your house?"

"Nope. Aurora's got it in hand, and Georgie, God bless him, will take care of them. What's more, Georgie just might get the collar, if that's Meister's van she's talking about." He took a deep breath. "For now, let's just get to the barracks and see what we can find."

Standing by Gloria Moses's desk was the irrepressible Walter Montgomery, his uniform still pressed, his shoes still gleaming. Patience was not something anyone saw on his face. All that was missing was a tapping foot, but Lieutenant Montgomery was not that kind of guy. The soul of leadership and decency, his expectations were high, but he didn't have to imitate Napoleon to get the job done. He just wanted it done.

"So, you two have been running around the county looking for more dead bodies, I understand," he said.

"Nothing new to report, sir," Bentsen said, despite usually referring to him as "boss."

"How about reporting a solution to this murder spree? The media people are becoming like a pack of baying wolves, and I can't hold them off with non-answers, boys."

"Well, then, Chief," Strand said, marching to his desk, "I think we're right on top of an answer, so if you'll give us an hour, we might have it."

"What answer is that, Fletch? You know Meister did it, so what answer are you looking for?"

"You're right, Chief, but right now, we don't know why, and we don't know where he is, except that he might be driving around Foreston or going where he feels safe. And besides, unless Doc Mc-Creary and his lab magicians can tie the steel bar to one or more of the other murders, we have Meister only for Robertson."

"Because?"

"Because it's the only murder for which we have an actual eye-witness."

"I thought she confessed to it. How good a witness is she going to be for us?"

"She'll be fine, boss, just give it a little time."

"Hey, where are the files from the mine? Gloria!"

Moses poked her head in from around the corner. "What's the problem, Detective?"

"The files from the mine. Where are they?"

"You and your buddy here gave me orders to pack them up and get them back into government hands."

"They're gone?"

"Yep. On their way back to the mine two hours ago. Probably on their way to DC by now."

"Oh, Christ!" Strand swore, more in a panic than frustration.

"Joe, check your notebook. Do you have Lafferty's number in DC?"

"Hold on." Pages flipped. Epithets flew. "Here it is," Bentsen said, and handed it over to Strand.

Strand was already grabbing the phone, and with number in hand, he dialed for Washington. "Please don't let him be in one of their goddam meetings," Strand muttered as he waited for an answer.

"Mr. Lafferty, please." Minutes elapsed.

"Detective Strand, how can your uncle help you today?"

"First, I need to fill you in on a new development. Nathaniel Robertson is dead—murdered in his office this morning, but we got lucky. His aunt and receptionist caught the murderer finishing the job. He ran. It's Elgin Meister from the mine."

Lafferty remained silent for a moment. "Bittersweet. One of ours a killer, but a solution, perhaps, to all the others?"

"Not sure yet, sir, but I need your help. Please tell me you have copies of the files you let us have."

"My God, don't tell me they're lost."

"No, sir. In fact, they're all on their way back to you as I speak. For the moment, I'm interested only in Meister's. Do you have something on him there?"

"Just a moment." It was a moment that turned into more minutes.

"Not that we don't trust our friends from the Commonwealth of Pennsylvania, but we do have a copy. Now what?"

"Read it to me, sir."

"You must be kidding."

"Then get someone else—quickly. Time is of the essence now. Meister's van has been cruising by my house, but we don't know where he's going."

"His house?"

"Between Foreston PD and our own troopers, they visited and staked out all of his known places of habit. Gone. Into the wind."

"Alright then, I have it. Let's go. I'm ready."

"Let's skip all the other stuff, and go right to your security form."

"The SF86?"

"Yes, and his medical forms."

"OK," Lafferty said, and began to read through Meister's identifying information, his residences, education, employments, law enforcement and credit history, and finally, his relatives."

"Wait, did you say he is from where?"

Lafferty repeated it. "And yes, both parents deceased. No siblings," Lafferty said.

"Deceased, you say?

"Yes. Eli and Lena."

"You can stop there, sir. One last question. When a relative is listed as deceased, do your investigators check that out, or is it assumed to be correct as given?"

"Why would anyone want to check out someone who's dead?"

LXIX

"J ESUS, MARY, AND Joseph! Joe—get your coat. We've got to go now."

"Good Lord, Fletch! What's gotten into you?!"

"I know where he's going. Keep it down. If Montgomery hears us, we'll have to loop him in."

Bentsen hurried—if that was possible—to the oaken coat rack, grabbed his parka, and headed for the door even as he looked around to make sure no one had noticed them leaving, especially the boss. "Got it," he said in a lower voice.

And in a few seconds, the detectives were out the side door and in the Vic with Bentsen at the wheel, as was almost always the case.

"Going to fill me in, pard?"

"In a minute," Strand said as he fished out his cell phone and called Aurora. After several rings, she picked up. "Hon, where are you?"

"Where you said we should be," she said, almost with a giggle.

Strand checked the time. "It's been nearly an hour. I'm guessing he's gone, so if you're comfortable with it, go ahead and take the kids home, but ask Georgie to send a cruiser around during the next hour, just in case."

"Is it over?"

"Almost—in another hour or so."

"Thank God! Chief Hallon has been so nice to us. His dispatcher even rounded up some milk and cookies, but for all the world, Fletch, I feel like we've been pulled in for disorderly conduct or something." She laughed again. "Sorry to be taking this so lightly. You sure it's OK to go?"

"As sure as I can be, hon. Love ya."

Strand turned to Bentsen. "Phew! OK, point this beast toward New Wilmington. I think we'll be able to tie a bow on this one pretty quick."

Bentsen nodded, and off they went.

But oh, how wrong Strand was.

~

"I know New Wilmington's not a big place, Fletch, but are you going to be more specific about where we're going?"

"To the Mast farm, Joe."

"So, is he in Foreston or not?"

"If Georgie's and our guys haven't found the white van yet, he left. Going to ground, and we have to get there before he harms anyone else."

"Then, let's play the official music and we'll get there in no time."

With their siren shattering the air, traffic parted. Strand said, "You know, Joe, it was all there for us to see if we just had the eyes to see it."

"You sure like drama, Fletch!"

"Sorry, pard. You and I each looked at Meister's files—his Official Personnel Folder, his background investigation, and his insurance forms. When Lafferty was reading me the info on his security form, it clicked. I didn't wait for him to cross-check the other forms because I'm betting he lied on all of them."

"Lied about what?"

"On his SF86, he was required to list his immediate family

members, but he said his parents were deceased, and there were no siblings."

"But?"

"But the parents he listed are the same as Abel Masters's parents."

"Christ!"

"Right, and by listing his parents as deceased, no one would think twice about them, and neither would an investigator be concerned about any siblings if none were listed."

"So, they're brothers?! Son of a bitch! How could Elgin Meister have worked there for a few years and neither of them ever crossed paths? Abel Masters made a practice of walking around and getting to know all the employees, for God's sake!"

"Right you are, my friend, but remember, someone told us Meister never seemed to be around when Masters did his walkarounds. And Rieger's men were gone part of the time. None of them sat at a machine, so it would have been pretty easy for Meister to make himself scarce. It might also explain the note Judy Conlon found. Remember? 'How could I have missed Amos?'"

"Amos?"

"Only a guess, but a good one, I think. Amos is Elgin's real name. Robertson's wasn't the only file to cross Masters's desk. Something was going on with one of Rieger's men, we heard, but nobody knew what."

"I can see why that note makes sense."

"True. He could have written, 'How could I have missed my brother?' and that would have been nice for us, but he did what you or I would do—called him by his name."

"Somehow, Amos Meister got through the security dragnet, and that'll give Lafferty nightmares, I'm sure."

"It's not Amos Meister. It's Amos Mast, of course. He came to work here because of his brother, I'm guessing. He just used the German word for 'master.'"

"I still don't understand what was motivating Amos Mast, or whatever the hell his name is."

"We're only speculating, of course, Joe, but how's this? We never covered with Eli Mast or his wife about how many sons there were. I should have asked Lafferty to pull up Masters's SF86—I'll bet they're all listed there, including Amos!" Strand thought for a moment, as if picturing the security form in his mind. "Jesus! I know they're there—Abel Masters listed three brothers, Levi, Martin, and Amos. Dammit! I missed it."

"Keep going."

"And want to bet that when Levi told us about the accident with Hannah, he was talking about Amos? So, he left the community, or they asked him to leave, and he knew where Abel worked because of his visits in Gilliland's parking lot, right?"

"Right, so far."

"So, he gets a job, stays out of sight, and because he is who he is— the bad seed, if you will—he had no scruples about getting involved in the drug ring—maybe to stick a finger in his brother's eye."

"Yeah, I can see that."

"So, here's what I think happened. The drug thing went along for a few years without a hitch until Rieger figured out something hinky with his trunk runs. Remember, they were all concerned about their jobs ending, but it wasn't about the jobs for Meister and Manzini—it was about the drug ring—that was their way to smuggle the drugs from DC to here. If that came to an end, it would have been a problem for them. When Rieger went to see Masters, it was about drugs."

"And Stoddard was up in Masters's office about Robertson, but nobody compared notes."

"Yep. It was all coming undone in a short period of time. I'll bet Masters couldn't believe it. He couldn't have known about Robertson and the drug ring, but Robertson and the Purcell murder would have been enough to bother him."

"But why did Stoddard point Masters to Robertson about the Purcell thing?"

"To eliminate him. Stoddard had ambitions, but he outsmarted himself."

"Jesus!"

"So, here's another guess. Masters made a big mistake," Strand said. "He called his physician, Nathaniel Robertson, and told him there was a problem they needed to talk about."

"I can see it," Bentsen said. "Only Masters was thinking about the Purcell murder, but Robertson—who couldn't have known someone connected him to the Purcell murder—thought Masters tumbled to the drug thing."

"Right," Strand said. "And that's why Robertson murdered Masters—to silence him. He didn't know silencing Masters would have made no difference in the outcome of his background investigation."

"And Meister murdered his brother for what?"

"Maybe he thought murdering his brother might slow down the big change with the trunk runs—and with privatization—a threat to their drug empire, but who knows?"

"Then, last big question about this whole thing," Bentsen continued, "is why did Meister move Masters's body from the house? That made no sense to me."

"To me, either, Joe. Another guess. It was Meister's way of telling the world his high-flying brother fell to earth like everyone else, but maybe he'll tell us."

LXX

THE RAIN CAME again as they reached the gas station at the junction of Routes 18 and 208. They plowed on and made a right somewhere, and after a series of more turns and passages over rut-ridden roads on a different route than they'd taken before, they came to Mast's lane.

Bentsen steered the Vic up the long lane, but little could be seen through the sloshing rain on the windshield. Finally, they could see the barn on the left, and parked beside it, on a side away from the main house further up, was a white van with a PA plate on the rear bumper. It had the right number, from what they could see.

"Joe, tell you what. Drop me here. Call for backup. Head up to the main house. Make sure everyone is OK. Then come back for me."

"Are you nuts? The Amish are great hunters. He could take you out in a second."

"I doubt it. He's desperate now. He knows the end is coming, but he gave away his weapon of choice in Robertson's office. Now go, dammit! If he's already seen us, he'll take off. Let him see you drive up to the house."

Before Bentsen could nod in agreement, Strand was out of the passenger door, in the car's headlights, and splashing up the ramp toward the barn door. Bentsen followed the plan and skittered the car in the mud up to the house.

At the barn door, Strand eased it open as quietly as he could with his left hand. In his right was the nine-millimeter Glock he carried as his service weapon. He made sure a round was in the chamber.

He stepped inside and out of the light from the door opening. "Amos! Amos Mast! I know you're here, and you won't get away!" The rain pounded the barn's metal roof. In front of him stood the Sitrex, the same steel monster he recalled from their earlier visit. There was no response.

"Amos! We know what you did, and we're here to arrest you!"

"Sure you are. I killed five people!"

Surprised, Strand didn't reply immediately. *Five? Should I tell him he didn't kill his brother, Abel?* He moved to his right, to a place under the wooden floor of the second level. "Five? Who did we miss?" he challenged, as he moved quietly around the barn's main floor, circling the Sitrex as he did so."

"Ah, you don't know about my brother, Martin! I killed him, too. Held his head under water when we were swimming."

Strand could feel the bile rising in his throat. "You're right, Amos. We didn't know about Martin. You had us all fooled. But why did you kill Robertson?"

"Robertson would give us up. David told me so before you took him away."

"And little Hannah?"

He could hear sobbing. "I let her fall toward the Sitrex, but caught her. Too late for pretty Hannah. I didn't mean it. I couldn't help myself." The voice was coming from above him.

"Is that why you left here, Amos? Because of Martin and Hannah?"

No sobbing now. Anger. "They thought something was wrong with me. They knew. But I left to get Abel. He was always so smart. He had everything. Me? I hustled trunks. I hated him."

Strand didn't want to close in on Meister without Bentsen at his back, but he felt himself move forward. A ladder appeared to his front, and with one stealthy step at a time, he rose to the second floor, where the ambient light was markedly lower. Little came in from the outside, and in front of him were shadows.

A few steps more and he found himself facing Amos Mast, standing with a pitchfork in throwing position, and no more than eight feet away. Mast couldn't miss.

"Put it down! Now!" Strand yelled through the rain. He could see the dark form pull his arm further back. Later, he admitted that a bullet in Amos's chest would have been the smart thing to do, but there were questions to be answered, and without thinking, he lunged forward and the two of them went over the loft's edge. Face to face they flew into empty air, then down.

In the half second or so it took them to land, Strand could see what remained of the tears in Amos's eyes, but in those same eyes was the look of unrelenting anger and hate.

And then, with a loud thump, they hit the Sitrex.

Between the two of them, nearly four hundred pounds struck the metal tines with such force, Amos Mast was stunned into a death trance. Life remained, but little of it. Blood trickled from his lips, and his eyes found Strand, pleading, but in a moment, the light flickered out.

As for Strand, he only knew everything went black, but he could feel blood everywhere. In his darkness, he didn't know if it was Mast's blood or his own. And with the blood, he felt pain. Sharp and unforgiving pain.

～

Later—how much later, Strand couldn't really say—he woke up in Shadyside Hospital in Pittsburgh. Aurora was at his side, her eyes red from what was likely an endless tear storm. He felt her hand in his, at least he thought it was his hand. He thought he smiled at her.

"Don't you dare smile at me, Fletch!" she said with mock disapproval, her hand tightening in his. "You've been out for a while now—after all the surgery, I'm not surprised, but the doctors here are the best, and they say you'll be all right, but it'll take some time."

Fear crept into his chest. "Do I still have all of me, hon?"

"Yes, she said," smiling broadly. "You have all the usual parts and even the best part."

Strand tried to laugh, but the pain, though dulled by heavy meds apparently, drummed a steady beat against his nervous system. "I'll take you up on that!" he said, trying to smile back, but with little success. "And what's the damage?"

"I don't think they're telling me everything, but you should see Joe. He rode to the hospital with you, and then, in the helicopter to Pittsburgh."

"I'm in Pittsburgh?"

"Hon, what they did tell me was they almost lost you—at least twice. Father Mike gave you Last Rites."

Strand was speechless.

"Bentsen's quick thinking saved your life, someone told me."

"Hah!" he said, weakly. "He just didn't want to lose a partner for The Spot."

"What?"

"Nothing—just partner stuff."

"I know—your other marriage. I get it, but I'm not jealous, Fletch. I still have you."

"Thanks, hon, I don't know what I'd do without you, the one love of my life."

"You're sweet, but I think you're just trying to get rid of me."

This time, Strand managed a laugh which sounded like a grunt.

"Joe went to the restroom. He'll be back in a minute."

"Where else!" Serious, he added, "And when he gets here, hon, would you mind stepping out? I need to ask him some things you won't want to hear."

"Whatever you want, Fletch, but do you think you're ready for any of the cop stuff? You just woke up, for heaven's sake." Her tone wasn't scolding so much as concerned.

"Now or never, hon. I've got to know what happened."

~

Joe Bentsen lumbered into the room looking for all the world as if he was carrying a bucket of rocks in his stomach. "I'm worried about you, Joe," Strand said.

Bentsen started laughing in spite of himself. "That's rich. You worried about me!"

"I am, Joe. You know more restrooms than Charmin." He paused to catch his breath. "Hey, find the button to raise me up a bit, will you, please?"

"That better?" he asked through the hum of the bed's motor.

"God, yes! I could hardly breathe lying flat. Hey, how can I thank you for saving my life. Aurora said you're the man of the hour."

"Bullshit. You owe me nothing, except maybe a new suit Montgomery won't pay for."

"Bet he won't pay for mine either," Strand said, and they both laughed. "So, how about filling me in after the lights went out."

Bentsen cleared his throat and spoke softly. "Listen, pard, when I pulled you off of Meister's body—yeah, yeah, I know it's Mast— all the blood between the two of you created a suction—sorry to be gross—but getting you off of him and throwing a horse blanket on you was all I could think of to do. You were bleeding all over."

Strand nodded; his eyes closed.

"Good thing Meister, I mean Mast, was a well-built guy, barrel-chested, because only a few of the tines went all the way through him and into your vitals, but not deep enough to kill you."

"Then why have I been out of commission so long?"

"Blood infection—when the tines went through him and into you, you absorbed a good bit of his blood, and they had to transfuse you several times to clean out your system. At least, that's what I understood one of the nurses to say."

"So, I'm not badly wounded?"

"I didn't say that, Fletch. All in all, you've sustained more punctures than a pin cushion, and they say you'll need a good bit of recovery time."

"Christ! That's not what I wanted to hear."

"Sorry, Fletch, but the best news is your impairments

aren't enough to keep you from being my partner again—say, in mid-summer."

Strand blew out all of his air. "And Amos Mast?"

"Dead and gone—no second chances for him. A few days afterward, your friend, Lafferty, came up from DC. I brought him in to see you, but you just mumbled something about relatives, and we left."

"Did you hear any of my chatter with him before the end?"

"No—nothing."

"He confessed to killing Martin and maiming Hannah." He breathed deeply. "And the only other thing you don't know, probably, is why he killed Robertson."

"Because?"

"What we thought—Stoddard put him up to it. The son of a bitch!"

"You know, Fletch, we've had so many motives for killing so many people, I don't know how we ever explain all of this to anyone."

Strand chuckled.

"What's so funny?"

"I'm recovering, remember? You and your pal, Lieutenant Montgomery, can do all the explaining."

~

Later that evening, before he was fully awake, Strand heard the sound of whispered words, words beseeching the Almighty, and when he opened his eyes, there stood his good friend, Father Pallison, his hands folded in prayer. With the priest's eyes closed in deep concentration, Strand lay there basking in the warmth of pleas on his behalf.

Finally, he coughed and Pallison returned from the religious plane to their mere earthly one.

"Ah, a miracle," Pallison exclaimed with an Irish jollity Strand had come to enjoy. "You were dead, and have come back to us."

"For some time, Mike, I've felt lost in here. I know neither the day nor the hour."

"Sounds like a verse from Matthew. But just to satisfy your curiosity, it's March 27th, and visiting hours are almost over."

"Thanks for coming, Mike. I know it's a bit of a drive from Foreston."

"Don't mention it, this isn't my first time here with you. I have a brother in Pittsburgh, and besides, I wanted to see how you were doing."

"I've had a lot of time to let the images of what happened to me—and to Amos Mast—do their work."

"And? Is your conscience troubling you in some way, Fletch?"

"No, Father, he was ready to pin me with that pitchfork."

"From what Joe told me, you had your gun, and while this is a question a priest probably shouldn't ask, why didn't you just shoot him?"

"Like all cops in a situation like this, I had a fraction of a second to decide, and I thought by tackling him, we might get some answers from him." He stopped, staring at the ceiling. "But I was so turned around up in that loft, I didn't realize that behind him there was nothing but air—and the machine. Good God, Mike, I can't get his face out of my mind. Regret and anger at the same time. How can that be?"

"I don't have an answer for you, but perhaps there was part of him that hadn't been corrupted by evil."

"Evil. That's what I saw in his face—until I saw the tears. His sorrow may have been about Hannah, but despite what he said, I'm still not sure why he killed his brother."

"You know, Fletch, if you ask me, it's all in Genesis. The first murder—like so many millions of others in the millennia since—was about jealousy. It may have been as simple as that."

EPILOGUE

THOUGH SCARRED APLENTY from the Sitrex tines, Strand regained full use of his limbs, and suffered no permanent mobility problems. By September 1993, a month after he'd returned to work, much had happened to put the "Mine Murders" in the rearview mirror for most citizens of Mercer and Butler Counties.

The late Nathaniel Robertson's patient list produced several more dealers in the doctor's drug ring, and within a few months, every one of them was brought to justice.

It was never going to turn out well for David Stoddard, and he paid a heavy price for his lifetime of big and small crimes, all driven by his incurable insecurity. Unable to attain power in the bureaucracy that he detested, he thrived as a small-time drug dealer and big-time manipulator of his civil service bosses.

After two months of wrangling by his high-priced attorney, Reinhard Koenig, to little avail, his daddy turned off the money spigot when the options ran out. On the plus side, the feds agreed to drop all charges against him, including murder conspiracy, running a drug ring, smuggling, possession for sale and selling dangerous drugs.

He took ADA Carstairs's offer of thirty years in prison with the possibility of parole, rather than risk what the state was asking for: life imprisonment without the possibility of parole. That better prison accommodations might have been available to him had he opted for federal prosecution never occurred to him, but he seemed oblivious to one more misjudgment in his life.

Williamsport State Prison opened its doors to David Stoddard on August 1st, about the same time Strand was cleared by his physicians to return to duty. For Strand and Bentsen, the balance of the summer remained gloriously free of all but the most mundane sorts of cases, which meant regular hours and plenty of family time.

Over lunches and at cookouts, Strand and Bentsen regularly hashed over the motivations of men like Nathaniel Robertson, David Stoddard, Angelo Manzini, and Amos Mast. That good men like Abel Masters and Al Rieger, not to mention Nella Purcell and Martin and Hannah Mast, all got caught up in webs of deceit, greed, jealousy, and hate endlessly fascinated them. Whether or not Robertson's partner, Dr. Carl Joseph, had been murdered remained unresolved, but Strand harbored little doubt.

～

One quiet fall day, when Lieutenant Montgomery had little for them, Strand suggested he and Bentsen take a ride into the idyllic countryside of New Wilmington. As usual, Bentsen piloted the Vic down Route 18 toward a part of the state where the 18th century was as present as Brigadoon's fairy tale. Hay had been raked and stacked, leaves were turning, and pumpkins were piling up for sale in Amish yards at good prices.

Up the lane where the Masts lived, life went on in the neat, white frame house, and a smile greeted them when the eldest daughter opened the front door and invited them in.

"Good afternoon, Emma. Where might we find your ma and pa?" Strand asked.

Emma's face clouded over. She didn't speak, but pointed beyond the barn and sheds to a great oak tree.

Strand and Bentsen walked in that direction, perhaps a hundred yards or so, until they saw a trim and painted white wooden fence surrounding the Mast family plot, a place reserved for those who'd passed to another universe. On the far side, outside the fence, sat old Eli Mast on a weather-worn kitchen chair, and next to him, her arm on his shoulder, stood his wife, Lena.

As the detectives came closer, they could see what commanded the elder Masts' attention. They were at the foot of a burial mound circled by small stones chosen for their sameness, and at the head was a new gravestone, upon which was the simple inscription, 'Abel Mast, 1950–1993.' Fresh-cut flowers decorated the grave.

"We are sorry to intrude, Mr. and Mrs. Mast. We wanted to see how you were getting along."

The older man looked up and acknowledged their presence. "Our bishop says I must go on with life—Lena says the same. Yet I cannot comprehend the loss of three of my sons." His chest heaved a sigh. Lena bent down and whispered to him. "What have we done to merit God's displeasure?" he asked looking up at his visitors.

"May I say," Strand struggled to say, "Almighty God has given you a good wife and family, Eli. Abel may have left, but I know he has returned much to you for your well-being. He never stopped caring for you and your ways. That Martin had to give his life is another unanswered mystery, but God has also given you the strength to bear that which no other Amish family has had to bear, not in generations."

Eli Mast stared at Strand, listening hard for words to pry him from his grief. Finally, he nodded. "The Lord's message has been plain. Here lies our Abel, and there," he said pointing to another mound a dozen feet away and marked only with a wooden tablet, "there lies our Cain."

In a few moments, Emma and Hannah appeared, as did Levi, and the other two girls, whom the detectives learned were Sadie and Rachel. Levi had Hannah in his arms, but as they came closer, he put her down, and she walked on her own with a new prosthetic.

Bearing the brightest smile, Hannah said, "See! Our Abel made sure this could happen for me."

Rewarded with smiles in return, she went on. "Apples and peaches are good this year, and we have fresh pies," she said to the visitors. "Would you like some?"

Bentsen's broad smile left no doubt about his answer.

Strand couldn't help himself. "Count me in, and in fact, I know an old lady in Foreston who would love to have one of your peach pies."

ABOUT THE AUTHOR

PHILIP WARREN is a retired national security executive who reads extensively in historical, espionage, and crime fiction and various non-fiction genres, but prefers writing historical fiction as well as political and crime thrillers. He lives with his wife in western Pennsylvania's Amish country.

Email: philipwarrenwriter@gmail.com
Website: www.philipwarrenwriter.com

As John P. Warren, the author invites readers to enjoy *Turnover* and its sequel, *TurnAround,* political thrillers about national election fraud published in 2013 and 2014, respectively. What was true then about political ambition and the lengths to which someone might go to achieve the presidency remains true today. Stories like these never get old.

Made in the USA
Las Vegas, NV
18 September 2023

77763610R00203